Babies in Groups

Babies in Groups

Expanding Imaginations

Ben S. Bradley, Jane Selby, and Matthew Stapleton

Great Clarendon Street, Oxford, OX2 6DP,
United Kingdom

Oxford University Press is a department of the University of Oxford.
It furthers the University's objective of excellence in research, scholarship,
and education by publishing worldwide. Oxford is a registered trade mark of
Oxford University Press in the UK and in certain other countries

© Oxford University Press 2024

The moral rights of the authors have been asserted

First Edition published in 2024

Some rights reserved. No part of this publication may be reproduced, stored in
a retrieval system, or transmitted, in any form or by any means, for commercial purposes,
without the prior permission in writing of Oxford University Press, or as expressly
permitted by law, by licence or under terms agreed with the appropriate
reprographics rights organization.

This is an open access publication, available online and distributed under the terms of a
Creative Commons Attribution – Non Commercial – No Derivatives 4.0
International licence (CC BY-NC-ND 4.0), a copy of which is available at
http://creativecommons.org/licenses/by-nc-nd/4.0/.

Enquiries concerning reproduction outside the scope of this licence
should be sent to the Rights Department, Oxford University Press, at the address above

Published in the United States of America by Oxford University Press
198 Madison Avenue, New York, NY 10016, United States of America

British Library Cataloguing in Publication Data

Data available

Library of Congress Control Number: 2023945980

ISBN 978–0–19–285951–8

DOI: 10.1093/oso/9780192859518.001.0001

Printed and bound by
CPI Group (UK) Ltd, Croydon, CR0 4YY

Oxford University Press makes no representation, express or implied, that the
drug dosages in this book are correct. Readers must therefore always check
the product information and clinical procedures with the most up-to-date
published product information and data sheets provided by the manufacturers
and the most recent codes of conduct and safety regulations. The authors and
the publishers do not accept responsibility or legal liability for any errors in the
text or for the misuse or misapplication of material in this work. Except where
otherwise stated, drug dosages and recommendations are for the non-pregnant
adult who is not breast-feeding

Links to third party websites are provided by Oxford in good faith and
for information only. Oxford disclaims any responsibility for the materials
contained in any third party website referenced in this work.

*To Peter and Rebecca
with love and admiration
and to Tom for his support*

Preface

We celebrate babies—their creativity, generosity, and the pleasure they give us. We aim to convey the excitement of being in contact with their wonder and joy. The prism we develop forefronts groups evolving and working. Like us, babies need people. And, lifelong, they will live and learn as group members, both at home and in class, at work or at play, in their prayers, and in their imaginations, plus in all the places where we link to others in the forging and re-forging of our identities and actions, through scholarship, employment, entertainment, art, and meditation.

As we develop our ideas about the broad implications of babies' capacities for participation in groups, we find ourselves at odds with the entrenchment of conventions, in policy, practice, and thought, which idealize a one-to-one 'attachment' between baby and mother as a universal source of child and adult well-being. Exalted claims are made for this vision. And yet our research and our practice, both laboratory-based and in early education centres—not to mention ordinary observations in playgrounds and living-rooms—daily prove babies act in ways which are multiple in nature and which an attachment perspective does not countenance. Hence the need to examine the 'clan infant' to open up imaginative space for shifting ideas about ourselves and our very young. We hope our sketch of this more spacious human world will give pleasure to the reader.

Readers wishing to view videos referenced in this book—or who wish to read about new findings and discussions arising out of the work discussed in this book should visit babiesingroups.com.

Between the three of us we have decades of inspired input from those around us, academic, professional, personal. Intellectually and politically, Denise Riley's work stands as representative of one tradition to which we would like to think this book belongs. In 1978, Denise advocated the construction of what she called an adequately *socialized* biology—a biology which was not limited to research on hormones and infant-mother interaction, but also encompassed the societal roots of such research and of the experiences common to mothers in contemporary Britain.[1]

We want to express gratitude to those who have helped us in our work. In particular, we thank the babies studied, their parents for permitting their children's participation, and the educators who agreed to help us with our research. We also thank Jennifer Sumsion, who spear-headed the grant which first introduced Jane and Ben to Matt. Valerie Sinason and Joan Raphael-Leff helped seed the idea of the book by inviting Ben and Jane to present their work to the lively Zoom-group of analytic clinicians based at the Academic Faculty for Psychoanalytic Research, Anna Freud Centre, London, in October 2020. Thanks too to James Cook University, Mark Morrison of Charles Sturt University, the Australian Research Council, and the British Academy for funding. Last but not least, we thank the Tavistock Centre for providing space and support for our British Academy-funded research via the agency and participation of the much-missed Cathy Urwin.

More personally, Ben and Jane acknowledge their Cape community, the Rossato family (four generations, especially Guilio, Marisa, and Anthony), John and Karen Rennie (and Brandy the dog) and Mark Comollatti, with parents Joy and Bryan—you have all helped to create this best of work environments. Thank you.

Contents

List of Figures   *xi*
List of Tables   *xiii*

1. Changing Stories   1
2. Babies in Threes   23
3. This Is Not Happening   48
4. Making Visible Ordinary Groupness   73
5. Prisms and Multiplicities   101
6. Concluding Remarks   135

Appendix: Intersubjectivity and Attachment: Alternatives   *141*
Notes   *157*
Index   *187*

Figures

1.1 Summer on the beach at Barry Island, Wales.   1

1.2 Attachment theory has at its heart an idealized image of a Madonna-like 'natural' mother who is unceasingly devoted—available, sensitive, and appropriately responsive—to her adoring infant.   5

1.3 A cartoon outing group assumptions.   7

1.4 An images of 'the traditional family' in an advertisement from the 1950s in the USA.   9

1.5 Emperor Tamarins raise infants cooperatively.   11

1.6 Baby in a group of the Kung.   13

1.7 Data for different primate species (solid dots) and human species (open dots): average size of social groups plotted against the ratio of the volume of each species' neocortex to total brain volume. The bigger the social group a species lives in, the bigger its neocortex-to-brain ratio.   14

1.8 The 'en face' paradigm for recording infant–mother communication. The mother (her right shoulder and the side of her head is visible at left) has her image captured via a front-silvered mirror (on the right).   19

1.9 *Asymmetry*: Angela (aged 23 weeks) resisting her mother's attempt to force eye contact in an *en face* 'conversation'.   21

1.10 Diagram of our set-up for recording the behaviour of 'babies in groups' (drawn by Colwyn Trevarthen).   22

2.1 Floored: a free-form trio.   23

2.2 Our 'Babies in Groups' recording setup.   25

2.3 Anatomy of the human eye.   32

2.4 Comparison of the narrow (18°) spread of light focusable on the *macular* part of the retina in the human eye, versus the broad field (220°) of unfocused vision endowed by the *peripheral* regions of the retina.   32

2.5 All the pulses represent calls by Ann, except pulses 3 and 4 which are Joe's calls.   35

2.6 Three babies in a quartet watch a fourth clap. Note the differences in foot-tension and toe-positions.   37

2.7 Two babies in a threesome touch toes (Joe, left, and Ann, right). The third (Mona) watches them attentively.   38

2.8 Joe turns away from Ann towards Mona, leans forward, and smiles.   40

2.9 Ann makes a gesture to Mona.   41

Figures

3.1 An example of 3→1 attention with the looked-at baby addressing the baby on his right, 45 secs into the interaction.   48

3.2 Group engagement at eight months: a lot is going on in this picture.   50

3.3 'Jealousy' by Edvard Munch (1930).   51

3.4 Seating arrangement for Anna, Paul, Barbie, and Clare.   52

3.5 Seating arrangement for Ruby, Pearl, Paul, and Dawn.   53

3.6 Configuration of babies and cameras in our research on all-infant quartets.   62

3.7 Two combinations of a **mutual gaze** (B↔D) along with different kinds of **simultaneous coordinated** gaze, namely: on the left side (i) **two** babies, A + D simultaneously engaged in coordinated gaze; and on the right side (ii) **three** babies, A + C + D, simultaneously engaged in coordinated gaze (as in Figure 3.1).   64

4.1 'What can we see in the drain? Is there any water down there?'   73

4.2 Lined up for mealtime in a regional NSW centre.   77

4.3 In groups at mealtime.   78

4.4 Seating arrangements for Isla, Jack, Harper, and Henry.   83

4.5 Six images illustrating the infants' interest and discoveries around the camera.   84

4.6 Four images which show Isla demonstrating to Daniel how to drink from a bottle.   89

4.7 Collaborative play: Harper, Kaden, and James (left to right).   92

4.8 Where 'group care' means 'babies in groups'.   99

5.1 Children often picture their worlds as containing many characters and features.   101

5.2 '… A small child … may chase away a full-grown male. He is able to do so under protection of his mother or "aunt". Like the children, these females are basically inferior to the males, but they, in turn, can rely on support of other females and sometimes can appeal to dominant males for help …'—a complex multi-member dynamic to which young chimps are so well attuned that they commonly use it to their advantage.   104

5.3 The laboratory set-up for the 'Strange Situation': 'Two adjacent rooms were employed for the experimental room and the observation room, connected by two one-way-vision mirror windows'.   114

5.4 Poet and psychotherapist, Valerie Sinason.   129

6.1 Belonging from the start: The herd happily welcomes a newborn baby.   135

6.2 Baby with sibling.   137

6.3 The internet is replete with instances of the young in group formations, and of team sports.   139

Table

5.1 'Dimensions of disrupt[ive] maternal affective communication' 108

1
Changing Stories

Figure 1.1 Summer on the beach at Barry Island, Wales.
Mark Lewis / Alamy Stock Photo.

1.1 Setting the Scene

Babies, like their older relatives, are group beings (Figure 1.1). We evolved in groups, and, to this day, the world of almost all newborns is a family group surrounded by a broader network of friends and relations. At birth we may look like tiny helpless organisms, but right from day one, we respond to and act on those around us. In this chapter we flesh out the insight that humans are 'political animals' to set the scene for what it means to say babies are born clan-ready and so do best when brought up in groups—the central argument of this book.

Thinking about how to understand our very young, scientific ideas typically make their starting-point a just-so story about human evolution. A favourite just-so story has pictured our pre-human ancestors living on the savannah, under constant threat from big hungry cats. Framed like this—especially if Stone Age babies were reared solely by their mothers it is easy to imagine that babies who cried more loudly, clung more firmly, or were otherwise born better equipped to stay close to their mothers would have best avoided providing a meal for the cats. In this story, Stone Age bubs with the most effective ways of 'attaching' themselves to Mam would have been the most likely to survive to grow up and breed. Over countless generations, various such 'attachment' behaviours would slowly have been built into our basic biological makeup by natural selection. Which suggests that, to this day, we are each born pre-equipped by evolution to grow a strong one-to-one or 'dyadic' bond to our mothers—or to another familiar adult—which, once formed, will activate whenever danger threatens. How this relationship is managed then becomes the cornerstone and prototype for all our other social relationships.

However, the last thirty years of research on human evolution paints a different picture. At last science is confirming what the grandfather of evolutionary theory Charles Darwin argued: that all of the most human of our human qualities go back to the fact that our ancestors lived and evolved *in groups*, and adapted *as groups* to the dangers and opportunities in their surrounding environment.[1] Recent findings about group-care in primates, about the structure of primate brains, and about the customs and genetics of ancient clan-based tribes, all show that the environment to which our long-ago ancestors had first to adapt was not made up of grassy savannahs and fierce big cats, but above all, of a stable group of familiar human beings. The children of our pre-historic ancestors were born into long-lasting, cohesive tribes. It was as tribes that we gathered food, hunted game, and fought off predators—mothers did not mother alone. Which means, when babies were frightened, or danger threatened, they would have survived best if they had snuggled up to any one of a number of different tribe members, whoever was nearby and happy to help. In short, the drama of our psychological origins has shifted from a two-hander starring the mother to feature a stable ensemble of familiar characters working together.

Given this change of story, we are challenged to re-imagine the evolution of infant experience and what it means for humans to be social or political animals. What babies must need most in this scenario are skills for group participation. *None* of today's theories of child development consider the possibility that young babies might have evolved to be able to engage in genuine, *group-level* interaction from their earliest months onwards.[2] Nor do they provide any way to understand how, well before they can crawl, babies can interact with more than one other person at once. Such capacities are consistent with the ordinariness of how we continually perceive and respond to the myriad of events and items around us. For example, when with several others, our peripheral vision constantly picks up others' movements and actions going on simultaneously with our own. The studies which gave rise to this book show us that the same is true of babies. Which means human social life has a foundation in the multiplicity of ordinary togetherness—something to which today's favoured story about the psychology of our very young gives no clue.

The following chapters elaborate findings that show group capacities and memberships are there from the start of life. This works against the grain of seeing the newborn as 'an individual' who *subsequently* needs to be 'socialized' before they can learn how to be in groups. It also works against claims that the infant–mother relationship is the template for later social life, including group life. Instead, *individuation* becomes the crux of development, an insight which goes back to the Greek philosopher Aristotle (384–322 BC). It was Aristotle who called human beings *political* animals—which, taken literally, meant not merely *gregarious* animals, but an animal 'which can individuate itself only in the midst of society'.[3]

This chapter sketches the background and rationale for our research, which examines what happens when we put babies together in groups, without adults. We will then argue that the findings from such research open up new horizons, both for scientific understanding of the very young, and for building good policies and practices to advance the care and development of our children.

1.2 Introducing the Twentieth Century

The best-known story in today's science of babies is a heroic romance. Its plot draws on a history of childhood which culminated in the liberation movements rising out of the ashes of the Second World War. In the USA, the message of Benjamin Spock's post-war manual *The Common Sense Book of Baby and Child Care* made it a fifty million best-seller.[4] Pre-war psychologists had warned parents not to spoil babies by 'rewarding' them for crying, by picking them up and comforting them, or by feeding them: babies should be left to 'cry it out', and should be fed only once every four hours. On the contrary, said Spock's new book: babies don't need cold-hearted regulation and rigid discipline. You won't spoil your little darlings by hugging them when they cry or feeding them when they feel hungry. What they need is love and affection, recognition, and understanding. So follow your parental instincts, act on your loving feelings, and treat your children as the unique individuals they are.

In Britain, a like revolution was afoot. This rose out of a century of tension surrounding British society's inhumanity to the very young during the

Industrial Revolution. The urban poverty sustaining Britain's rise as an industrial power was targeted by a series of Victorian writers who made children their focus. Most notable was Charles Dickens (1812–1870). Dickens' famous second novel, *Oliver Twist*, featured an orphaned boy who spent his infancy and early childhood in a 'baby farm' run by the nasty Mrs Mann.[5] Baby farms were a widespread form of childcare among the Victorian poor. A Mrs Mann would be paid a small fee by a mother to take over the responsibility and care of her baby—especially if the mother were unmarried. Babies would then join a room full of little companions to spend years of neglect in foul conditions. If they were lucky. Because, should they not quickly die of disease, it was to the advantage of a real-life Mrs Mann to 'hasten the death of the child', once she had pocketed the fee from the mother.[6]

Of course, children of wealthy Victorians looked forward to a vastly different future. Yet their infancy was also farmed out. As babies, they would be breast-fed by 'wet nurses', rather than their mothers. And the bulk of their early years would be overseen by nannies and nursemaids, not parents. Girls would then be educated by governesses, and their brothers too. Until, around the age of seven, the sons of the rich would be posted off to often-abusive boarding schools, where they spent all but the summer holidays of their next ten to twelve years—as depicted in *Nicholas Nickleby*, Dickens' follow-up to *Oliver Twist*.[7]

British baby farms finally fell foul of government regulation just before the First World War; with Rhoda Willis, the last baby farmer executed for infanticide, being hanged on her fortieth birthday, on 14 August 1907 in Cardiff prison. Boarding schools have done far better than baby farms, however. To this day, they have continued to grow in number, in the numbers of children they enrol—now including girls—in influence, in international reach, and in wealth. They have largely escaped criticism and government supervision, though one old boy from Eton (a major British boarding school), Auberon Waugh, commenting on the repeated employment of known pederasts as teachers by boarding schools, remarked: 'Of course, the English are famous throughout the entire civilised world for their hatred of children'.[8]

Waugh's observation nicely sets the scene for the exploits of British child psychiatrist John Bowlby (died 1990). Born in the same year as Rhoda Willis was hanged, Bowlby was yet another boy raised in a big house by a nanny and nursemaids—excepting a one-hour visit each day to his mother 'after tea'.[9] At age seven he was dispatched to boarding school. It appears that Bowlby did not much like his school. He later complained: 'I wouldn't send a dog away to boarding school at age seven'.[10] Perhaps he did not like the remoteness of his mother either. Either way, after the Second World War, when he began to make a name for himself on BBC chat shows, at the World Health Organization, and in psychological journals, by publicizing his newly devised theory of 'infant–mother attachment', his success had a double significance.[11] On the personal side, his theoretical claim that all human babies biologically require their mothers' undivided love and attention looks like a covert attack on his own parenting, or, to be precise, his mother (Figure 1.2).[12]

Figure 1.2 Attachment theory has at its heart an idealized image of a Madonna-like 'natural' mother who is unceasingly devoted—available, sensitive, and appropriately responsive—to her adoring infant.
Artist Emma Barnet.

At the same time, but far more consequentially, Bowlby's theory was the trumpet-blast which launched a post-war cultural protest against British society's cold-hearted 'hatred of children'. From the 1950s on, his formulation of attachment became the foundation-stone for enlightened thinking about the needs of babies.

Bowlby dressed up his theory in the apparel of science. Yet it is less science than an assumed aura of humane righteousness which today fuels the promotion of attachment theory among psychologists and other professionals who deal with young children. Which creates the growing tension that this book later documents. Not only has subsequent research quietly refuted the scientific grounds for Bowlby's theory of infant–mother attachment—despite its advocates' continuing protestations of their scientific credentials.[13] Its claims to promote a humane vision of early childhood sugar-coat cultural bias and misogyny. This double jeopardy presses the need for a book which tells a different story about human beginnings—a story rooted in what today's observational studies show babies really are and can do.

1.3 Groupness

Our scientific starting-point is that young babies manifestly possess what we call groupness. In the social sciences, *groupness* refers to the fact that a social group has characteristics which go beyond those of its individual members.[14] So, to call a group a group is not just to talk about physical proximity. When the anthropologist Sarah Blaffer Hrdy notes that today's hunter-gatherers 'live in tight-knit groups', she is raising something beyond the fact they just happen to hang out together.[15] Somehow, they *act*—and think and feel—cohesively.

This kind of groupness underpins much of our everyday lives, though in unspoken ways—providing a magnet for metaphors (such as 'tight-knit'). Most humans work in teams, dwell with others, sport in groups, relax among friends. Each such group soon tacitly develops traditions, rules, or basic assumptions about how to behave, such that the members 'will be singing from the same hymn-sheet'. Taken-for-granted mores often only come to light when someone 'steps out of line'—a newcomer perhaps—and 'drops a clanger', or makes a 'faux pas'. Suddenly, 'one could cut the air with a knife' (Figure 1.3).

Unsurprisingly, a productive life requires a capacity to 'read the room', and methods of dispelling 'an awkward atmosphere'. Otherwise a work or sports team, a classroom of children, a family, a band, or a committee, may become 'dysfunctional', succumb to 'groupthink', 'split', or fall foul of 'infighting', and so

"That's an excellent suggestion, Miss Triggs. Perhaps one of the men here would like to make it."

Figure 1.3 A cartoon outing group assumptions.
Punch Cartoon Library / TopFoto.

fail to achieve what it set out to achieve. A team or committee which is 'harmonious', 'humming', or 'on song', on the other hand, will perform well.

Many of the metaphors used to capture groupness do not refer to vision. They more often draw from the world of sound, as sound is omnidirectional, open to everyone within earshot—sometimes thousands. Sound-based metaphors are apt because group dynamics are not just one-to-one (as in 'seeing eye to eye'). They simultaneously embrace all the members in the group. This requires a form of interaction that differs from the person-to-person communication found in dyads. Groupness is *supra*-dyadic. In a tight-knit group, each group-member's behaviour affects and is affected by *several people at once*.

1.4 Extended Families

One of the rarest kinds of family in human history is the kind which lives in its own dwelling, with Dad going out to work and Mum staying home-alone to look after the kids.[16] These *nuclear* families are often called 'traditional', though any such tradition has always been a minority affair. Nuclear families which centre on the idea of a single-waged male earner with a stay-at-home wife with children, had their heyday among better-off whites in countries like those of Western Europe, Australia, and the USA during the years of the post-war 'baby boom', in the 1950s and 1960s. In Britain, for example, VE-day saw women sent home *en masse* from offices and factories to make way for employment of the men being demobilized from the armed forces in their hundreds of thousands. Rather than continuing in paid work, His Majesty's government urged wives to stay home and 'have babies for Britain'.[17]

War nurseries closed down in 1945 so childcare became harder and harder to find. There were hard barriers preventing married women from participating in the workforce. In the Netherlands (until 1957) and Ireland (until 1973), for instance, wives were barred by law from working outside the home. In France (until 1965) and Spain (until 1975), once they had married, women needed their husbands' consent to work. Meanwhile, for the better-off—in place of servants and nursery-maids—TVs and a host of labour-saving domestic appliances became widely available: dishwashers, clothes-washers, vacuum cleaners, and food-mixers. In 1951, the first commercial 'infant formula' was released, largely replacing breastfeeding in some countries. And the buying-power of wages was on the rise, so that a single salary was more often sufficient to support a growing family than today, or prior to the Second World War.

Outside advertising, and government policy surrounding the post-World War II baby boom, nuclear families look like oddities (Figure 1.4). Far more commonly, across human history and around the world, *several* people have taken responsibility for looking after a baby. And nowadays, in many Westernized nations, around one-half of all infants spend some of their week in non-parental childcare—either formal or informal. When we look more broadly at other times and places, we find children come to life surrounded by *extended* families, with several kith or kin—including older siblings, fathers, 'aunts', and grandmothers—taking central roles in babies' daily upbringing. Some Aboriginal languages in Australia make no distinction between 'mother' and 'aunt'.

Contemporary comparisons between the babies of isolated sole-care mothers and those experiencing other kinds of care, as in extended families, show that babies do better with more than one caregiver. For instance, in the USA, babies born to inexperienced mothers do far better emotionally and cognitively if they have a live-in grandmother who shares caregiving duties. These good effects last into a child's teenage years. Teenagers even do significantly

Figure 1.4 An images of 'the traditional family' in an advertisement from the 1950s in the USA.
Neil Baylis / Alamy Stock Photo.

better socially and at school if, a decade or more previously, their inexperienced mother was visited at home just *once a month* by a helpful nurse during her pregnancy and over her child's first two years of life. Thus a study led by David Olds in Colorado shows that, compared to a 'control group' of children whose young first-time mothers were *not* visited by nurses, the children of nurse-visited mothers grew up to be more responsive emotionally, less scared when toddlers, quicker to learn language, and cognitively more advanced. The visited mothers were themselves slower to conceive a second child and more likely to be employed as their baby grew up than were unvisited mothers.[18]

Other cultures show similar results. In urban Sudan, a comparison of children brought up in nuclear families with those living in extended families—especially those where grandmothers are centrally involved in childcare—has shown that the children with several caregivers grow up better adjusted, socially and emotionally, than those with just a single mother-figure.[19] As Stephanie Coontz puts it: 'children do best in societies where childrearing is considered too important to be left entirely to parents', so that bringing up baby becomes a *cooperative* project.[20]

1.5 Cooperative Breeding

It is easy to assume that chimps, gorillas, and orangutans furnish the best models for understanding how our first human ancestors looked after their young. We assume these great apes are 'more like us' than any other primate. But not necessarily. Or, at least, not where bringing up babies is concerned. Great apes all show continuous 'care-and-contact' mothering, where mothers do all the childcare and often do not allow anyone else to touch their babies for several months after birth.[21] We are not like this. Nine in ten human babies are *first touched* by *someone other* than their mother.[22] We also break the cross-species rule that animals who have bigger babies relative to their mother's size leave longer intervals between births. This rule comes about because the more effort and energy babies take a mother to produce, the more time she will need to recover before reproducing again. Great apes average six years between births. Human babies are relatively larger, and human children take far longer to reach independence from their parents, than those of any other ape. Yet, worldwide and over history, human mothers have produced their offspring almost *twice* as fast as orangutans, gorillas, and chimps do. What might this mean? It suggests our ancestors' mothers needed and got significant support from other adults (sometimes called 'alloparents').

Continuous care-and-contact mothering is only one model of childcare among primates. Nearly half of the two hundred plus primate species are *cooperative* breeders. Amongst these, the primatologist Sarah Blaffer Hrdy argues that marmosets and tamarins provide good parallels for human breeding (Figure 1.5). Marmoset and tamarin species—the so-called *Callitrichidae*—mostly live in close-knit groups where mothers may suckle other mothers' babies, not just their own—as Islamic 'milk mothers' have done for thousands of years in Muslim communities. Babies get handed around between group members, the mother showing none of the jealous possessiveness that great ape mothers do. These cooperative breeders can produce their young extremely quickly, especially as some species typically produce twins or triplets. This means, when food abounds, marmosets and tamarins can swiftly spread into new territories and colonize them. Callitrichid mothers also show a more calculating attitude to maternity than do care-and-contact primates, killing their babies or leaving them to die if they sense they have insufficient social support from their group. Marmosets and tamarins prove the most altruistic and helpful of primates too, being significantly more likely to assist others of their species to get food in experiments that test their willingness to cooperate. Their helpfulness is only exceeded by humans.

Hrdy argues that all these features of cooperative breeders from the *Callitrichidae* have parallels in humans: helpfulness to others; swift rate of

Figure 1.5 Emperor Tamarins raise infants cooperatively.
Tierfotoagentur / Alamy Stock Photo.

reproduction; capacity for speedy colonization of new territory; willingness of mothers to let others hold their newborns; multiple caregivers for each infant; attitudes to infanticide; and a willingness to feed other mothers' babies. Which suggests that our first human ancestors were cooperative breeders.

1.6 Human Evolution

The make-up of human DNA suggests that, for hundreds of thousands of years, our first human ancestors lived in Central Africa, in small, isolated groups. During this period, the entire human species totalled little more than ten thousand souls. Then, around fifty thousand years ago, there was an exodus from Africa and human population numbers quickly began to grow. Some of the original population migrated to sub-Saharan Africa, where their descendants still live: San-speaking Ju/'hoansi people, also known as the Kung or 'Bushmen'.[23] Hence, there is great interest in how these desert-dwelling people rear their children.

Like most people who traditionally live by hunting and gathering, the Kung live, seek food, and rear their babies cooperatively. Given the fragility of their food supplies, Kung people maintain both the close collaborative groups within which they live, *and* strong ties *between* groups. These wider social networks ensure the sharing of valuables—tools, weapons, clothes and, particularly, of food—by groups living in different areas, making a much wider range of food sources available to each individual. It has been calculated that, as a result of being networked, the Kung are nine times more likely to survive famines than they would be if they had no network.

Like babies in many other hunter-gatherer peoples, Kung babies spend a considerable portion of their day being looked after, caressed, held, or sung to by group-members other than their mother (Figure 1.6). As Hrdy observes, from a position on the mother's hip, Kung babies have available to them the mother's 'entire social world':

> When the mother is standing, the infant's face is just at the eye-level of desperately maternal 11- to 12-year-old girls who frequently approach and initiate brief, intense, face-to-face interactions including smiling and vocalization. When not in the sling [babies] are passed from hand to hand around a fire for similar interactions with one adult or child after another. They are kissed on their faces, bellies, genitals, sung to, bounced, entertained, encouraged, even addressed at length in conversational tones long before they can understand words. Throughout the first year there is rarely any dearth of such attention and love.[24]

Figure 1.6 Baby in a group of the Kung.
agefotostock / Alamy Stock Photo.

A hunter-gatherer baby is commonly fed by several different people too.

From the evidence collected, Hrdy concludes that it was cooperative breeding which made humans the hyper-social species we are, and gave us the capacity to spread successfully, from such tiny beginnings, over the planet we now so ubiquitously inhabit. In which case, the sociability of little humans will need to encompass many more people than does the sociability of baby great apes, including 'others as well as mothers'.[25]

1.7 Social Brains

Converging with this conclusion is a line of research that comes from studying primate brains. The question at issue here is: how come we humans evolved to have such large brains relative to our body-size? What were the selection pressures? Note that the main part of the brain which varies between primates, relative to their body-size (and the rest of their brains), is the newest part, called the *neocortex*, and largely responsible in humans for 'higher' forms of agency: imagining, attending, thinking, perceiving, remembering events, decision-making, and using language.

14 Babies in Groups

The ratio of neocortex to body-size in humans (30:1) is twice that in chimps (60:1). So the question becomes, how come humans have evolved such large neocortices? Many speculations have been put forward as to the distinctive pressures which made us brainier than our apish cousins, for example: tool-use and tool-making; the large size of the territories humans inhabit in contrast to other primates; the complexity of the human diet; our long life-span; and our use of language. Only recently have the relevant data for testing these hypotheses been collected, sorted, and systematically analysed. It now looks more and more as though it is the *complexity of the social relationships* which different monkeys and apes experience that determines the relative size of their neocortices. The more complicated a primate's social life, the more brain-power it evolves.

The first test of the relevant data assumes social relationships are more complicated in apes which live in larger groups—not just as one pair of parents and their young. The data show a strong linear correlation between group size and relative neocortex size (Figure 1.7).

Similar results have been found for other measures of social complexity. The sizes of grooming cliques correlate positively and significantly with relative neocortex sizes across many primate species. And the frequency of deception

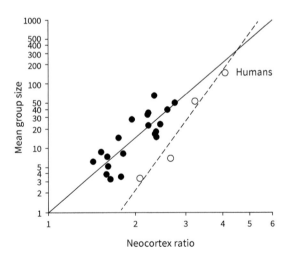

Figure 1.7 Data for different primate species (solid dots) and human species (open dots): average size of social groups plotted against the ratio of the volume of each species' neocortex to total brain volume. The bigger the social group a species lives in, the bigger its neocortex-to-brain ratio.

Used with permission of Dunbar, R.I. from "The Social Brain: Mind, Language, and Society in Evolutionary Perspective". *Annual Review of Anthropology*, 32, 2003, pp. 163–181. Permission conveyed through Copyright Clearance Center, Inc.

in different primate species also correlate positively with differences in neocortex ratio. Like results have been shown for social play—the more there is in a species, the bigger the neocortex ratio—and for the formation of coalitions.[26] All of which suggests that the distinctive features of human agency resulted from living in large social groups, where complex social relationships were maintained. This implies that human babies must be born with a 'social brain' of which the most distinctive feature must be a capacity for acting as members of social groups.

1.8 Recent Research on Babies in Groups

The key question raised by what may seem today to be a new story about the group-based, tribal context of human beginnings, is this: what adaptations would best have fitted our young to grow up as engaged and effective group members? This new story has a long history, however. One hundred and fifty years ago Charles Darwin was puzzling over the same question. His answer? 'The connection between the related members of the same tribe, exposed to all sorts of danger', he wrote, would be 'much more important, owing to the need of mutual protection and aid, than that between the mother and her child'.[27] For Darwin, babies should be born with a capacity to integrate themselves into 'the connection between the related members of the same tribe' rather than solely a capacity to form a relationship, connection, or 'attachment' to their mothers. Despite Darwin's own publications on infant behaviour, science forgot his group hypothesis for more than a century.[28] None of the themes discussed in this chapter had been investigated before contemporary research on infants in groups began in the 1990s. Which makes our own research-story relevant.

By 1995, two of this book's authors, Jane and Ben, had been recording and studying the social lives of babies for twenty years.[29] (Matt came in later; see Ch.4.) As with the majority of similar researchers, their primary focus had been on infant–adult 'dyads,' mostly baby–mother pairs. Then, in 1996, Jane began organizing a series of interdisciplinary conferences in Townsville, Australia under the banner 'Freud in North Queensland' (FINQ—tagline: 'snorkelling in the unconscious'). Speakers included international innovators, practising artists, but, in the main, Australian psychoanalysts and psychotherapists: a first day of talks being followed up by a second day of workshops. The first FINQ conference saw psychoanalytic clinicians Campbell Paul and Frances Thomson-Salo give a workshop on their therapeutic practice at the Royal

Children's Hospital, Melbourne: weekly group therapy with four or five mothers, *plus their babies*.[30]

Frances' and Campbell's videos showed excerpts from a therapeutic group that had been meeting for several months. Seven adults were seen sitting on chairs in a circle surrounding five babies disporting themselves on the floor. Frances and Campbell showed us how, over time, the group's dynamics were not just affected by the therapists' interventions and those of the mothers, but also by *baby-led* innovations. They asked us to watch a seven-month-old, Ian, who had a severely depressed mother. On his first visit to the group, Ian's mother behaved as if every time Ian looked at her, she had to smile. This led to rather wooden smiling on her part. Meanwhile, Ian's body-tone remained flaccid, he could not sit up, and he too looked depressed. Yet he could not fail to be aware almost immediately of the response of the other infants. As soon as eight-month-old Mary saw him, she reacted with pleasure, trying to reach him and touch him, but she also seemed to be aware of his lack of responsiveness and perturbed by it. Ian withdrew from Mary into holding and mouthing a toy. By the next week, however, Ian was a transformed child, he was sitting upright, and more engaged with the group leaders and Mary; he smiled, moved, and vocalized with pleasure, and more clearly communicated what he wanted.[31] Mary the therapist!

By raising the possibility that Mary's intervention had *helped* Ian, Campbell and Frances were suggesting that, even before they were old enough to begin the process of forming a solid attachment to a parent (at nine months), babies could participate in group dynamics. They backed up this assertion with several other video examples. Their claims struck us as a brand-new idea. So we decided to put it to the test.

This decision coincided with Ben and Jane's move from the shore of the Coral Sea in tropical North Queensland to the hilly vineyards of Charles Sturt University in New South Wales. Here we were soon allocated funds to set up a laboratory for studying babies. Plus, serendipitously, we were blessed by a visit from Kiwi-turned-Scot Colwyn Trevarthen, a major figure in contemporary infancy studies, on one of his dives 'down under' from Edinburgh. Colwyn helped design an appropriate observational regime to test Campbell and Frances' group hypothesis. Our plan was to put three babies of the same age together in a group and then, with cameras a-whirr, all adults would vacate the filming studio to watch from a nearby room what the babies did (via CCTV). Colwyn insisted that our films should include the babies' feet in our cameras' fields of view, as babies' feet were very expressive. How right he turned out to be! (See Chapter 2.)

1.9 Old and New

So far as we could find, besides Campbell and Frances—who had done it with therapeutic aims—no psychologists had ever put several babies together in a group and studied what happens. The nearest were two then-recent studies where babies had been recorded in trios—which included adults. In Switzerland, Elizabeth Fivaz and her colleagues had invented the 'Lausanne Trilogue Play' procedure. This was a therapeutically inspired project where a baby would be recorded in a trio made up of a baby plus his or her parents. Around the same time, Jacqueline Nadel's team was undertaking experiments on trios in Paris. These consisted of two babies and an adult 'stooge'—who had been instructed how to behave by the researchers.[32]

However interesting the results from these two projects, neither provided a satisfactory model for our research. That was because neither escaped the 'scaffolding' criticism that had dogged studies on infant sociability since the 1970s. At issue here was a conflict that stretched back to the beginning of the twentieth century in psychology—and far further in philosophy—about *how much* psychological and social competence we can attribute to babies. Are babies blank slates who are capable of almost nothing until 'written on'—trained and socialized—by the adults around them? Or do they arrive in the world ready-to-go, with lively interests and functional abilities? The early 1970s saw these two questions fought over in two distinct battles: one about infants' competence as such; the other about their social abilities.

1.10 The Competent Infant

The first battle targeted psychologists who had for decades argued that the main motor of early development is learning. New-born babies learn faster than at any later period of their lives, we were told, but they have little idea about what they need to learn: they were shaped solely by their post-birth experiences. Any stimulus associated with pain was avoided in future, and stimuli associated with pleasure were the more sought out. Even psychotherapists and psychoanalysts, professions with a focus on childhood experiences and thus perhaps more open than others to seeing the complexity of how babies viewed the world, subscribed to views like this (see Ch.5 section 5.5 'Seduction by attachment rhetoric'). For example, in 1960, the psychoanalyst Anna Freud (1895-1982), one of the pioneers of child study, wrote that humans were born in 'an undifferentiated state' without any semblance of 'complex mental life'.[33]

In the 1960s and 1970s new methods of research produced laboratory findings which persuaded many academic psychologists to dismiss such low estimates of babies' abilities. This became known as 'the competent infant' movement.[34] Its main drive focused on perceptual and reasoning powers, until then only attributed to older children by the influential Swiss psychologist, Jean Piaget (1896–1980). At the leading edge of this new movement was Tom Bower (1941–2014), an inventive experimentalist who sought to reveal in tiny babies cognitive achievements of the kind Piaget attributed only to walking, talking toddlers. Did Piaget say it took two years for a child to acquire the idea that things like feeding-bottles and apples continue to exist even when out of sight (a skill he called 'object permanence')? Bower devised an experiment to show babies could reach accurately for an object made invisible to them, before they were five months old.[35] Had Piaget concluded the capacity for intentional action only emerged at 15 months? Bower got a study into the science journal *Nature* demonstrating intention in new-born babies.[36] And so on. Yet, despite all the path-breaking claims it made about the very young infant's understanding of the *physical* world, Bower's (1974) book *Development in Infancy* said nothing about babies' *social* competence.[37]

This was because most of those pushing the timetable for Piaget's 'stages of cognitive development' onto younger and younger babies tested babies in isolation, believing that infants were born as *asocial* beings.[38] (This was also taken to be Piaget's view.) The key concept here was, once again, 'socialization': psychologists widely assuming that babies needed *socializing* before they could distinguish people from things. According to the earliest estimates, children only learnt this distinction at the end of their first year.

1.11 Born Social?

The main opposition to the idea that young babies were *not* social came from Bowlby's theory of infant–mother attachment. The starting assumption for attachment theorists was that babies are 'born social'. They pointed out that babies reliably orientate toward other people from birth onwards, by smell, when touched, or by sound or vision. Underlining this point was an experiment by Robert Fantz which showed that young babies prefer to look at a diagram of schematic face than at any other two-dimensional pattern.[39] Bowlby and his followers also reminded us that tiny babies are best comforted *by other people*. And pointed out that we are all born with ways which attract other people's attention (e.g. smiling, sucking, clinging, crying, gazing into their eyes).

However, even according to attachment theory, a baby's first social attachment only *begins* at nine months of age.[40] Regarding the eight months before that, Bowlby had nothing much to say. Furthermore, the formation of infant–adult attachments was only proposed to explain how and why older babies seek proximity to others *when they are stressed*: afraid, or hungry, or ill, or tired. What babies do with people for the first three-quarters of their first year—when they are too young to have any attachments; or what they do when they are *not* stressed; or when they are *already* in proximity to other people—did not come under the theory's consideration.

How to explore the various gaps left by attachment theory? Here the new availability of relatively cheap 'consumer' video-recorders helped—first marketed by Sony in 1971. Soon a number of researchers were setting up 'infant laboratories' for face-to-face (*en face*) recording sessions with mothers and their babies, from as young as six weeks old (see Figure 1.8). This was where Colwyn Trevarthen (b.1931) was a trailblazer. His analyses of infant–mother interactions quickly led him to conclude that, long before they might form

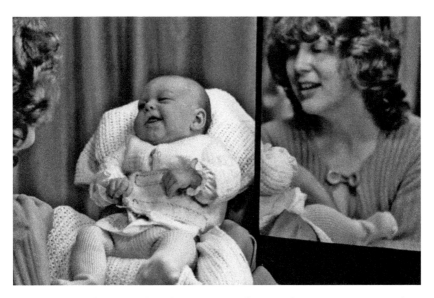

Figure 1.8 The 'en face' paradigm for recording infant–mother communication. The mother (her right shoulder and the side of her head is visible at left) has her image captured via a front-silvered mirror (on the right).
Picture kindly supplied by Colwyn Trevarthen.
From Dunbar, Robin. 2003. 'The Social Brain: Mind, Language, and Society in Evolutionary Perspective'. *Annual Review of Anthropology* 32: 163–181.

attachments, babies have an awareness specifically adapted to receiving, communicating, and sharing mental states with their companions. One of his early publications, complete with photographic stills from his films by way of illustration, featured in the *New Scientist* in 1974: 'Conversations with a two-month-old'.[41] It christened babies' capacities for interpersonal awareness *innate intersubjectivity*. Trevarthen's has proven an influential conclusion, which he and his colleagues have since elaborated into a theory which helps explain children's early communicative development, their humour, culture, and musicality, plus conditions like autism (see Appendix, A.1).

1.12 Scaffolding

Influential as it was, Trevarthen's work quickly attracted criticism. Psychologists who preferred the 'blank slate' view of babies said he was over-interpreting his data.[42] Before long, an alternative account of his research was gaining traction. Fascinating though his films of mother–baby 'conversations' might be, the *appearance* of infants engaging in symmetrical proto-conversations with their mothers, such that young babies actively and appropriately took turns in animatedly gesturing, cooing, and mouthing, at their attentive mothers and then more passively 'listening'—watching and smiling while the mother talked—was all due to the mother's *scaffolding*. Her superior skills in pacing and vocalizing allowed her to *make it seem* like her baby was a genuine conversational partner. The mother was like a ventriloquist with a dummy. Her attitude and actions allowed her to guide and mould the infant's behavioural output into the form their culture required.[43]

Adding to the criticism was the fact the analyses of video and film data which Trevarthen and his supporters held to show young babies could 'share' mental states with their mothers, or had 'mutual awareness' of mothers' 'complex and expressive communications', did not say what kinds of thing mothers and babies 'shared'. The few studies that did analyse mothers' behaviour typically showed that, during recording sessions, mothers acted in a way which *mirrored* their baby's actions and expressions. Not just what mothers said but *how* they spoke reflected the infant's vocalizations—in volume, pitch, and phrasing. Infants' facial expressions were mirrored too, right down to subtle movements of lips and eyebrows.[44] Which confirms what Donald Winnicott had observed: 'when the mother is looking at the baby ... *what she looks like is related to what she sees there*'. The mother makes herself a mirror. So when a baby looks at a mother's face, 'what the baby sees is himself or herself'.[45]

All of which suggests that much of young babies' attraction to interacting with their mothers has mainly to do with their enjoyment of having an audience, giving them a delicious sense of power from seeing what they are doing reflected 'at twice its natural size' a kind of narcissism—not with seeking to understand what the mother herself is really feeling or thinking.[46] Certainly, babies typically turn away in dismay if their power over their mothers is experimentally removed.[47]

1.13 Symmetry

From all this we concluded that the best way to ensure we were in a position to rebut claims that infants' social competence in groups resulted from adults' 'scaffolding' was to ban adults from the recording studio. After all, the only reason that critics of work like Trevarthen's could mount their arguments was because the *en face* mother-infant recording paradigm was so asymmetrical. Mothers can speak, understand instructions, act out what experimenters tell them to do, and interpret instructions in their own unique ways. They are bigger, stronger, louder, and cleverer than babies (Figure 1.9). This is what made

Figure 1.9 *Asymmetry*: Angela (aged 23 weeks) resisting her mother's attempt to force eye contact in an *en face* 'conversation'.
Source: author's picture.
See Bradley, Ben S. 1981. 'Negativity in Early Infant-Adult Exchanges and its Developmental Significance'. *European Monographs in Social Psychology* 24: 1–38.

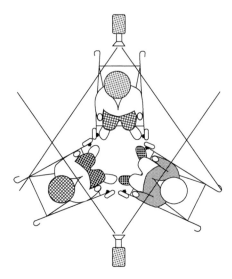

Figure 1.10 Diagram of our set-up for recording the behaviour of 'babies in groups' (drawn by Colwyn Trevarthen).

Kindly drawn for the authors by Colwyn Trevarthen.
See Selby, Jane and Ben S. Bradley. 2003. 'Infants in Groups: A Paradigm for the Study of Early Social Experience'. Human Development 46: 197–221.

it so easy for Trevarthen's critics to maintain that adults were manipulating babies or simply fitting their own behaviour around a baby's patterns of action to make them *look* conversational.[48]

So, when we came to arrange our own 'infant laboratory' for recording infants in groups, we set it up symmetrically, as an equilateral triangle, where each baby was approximately the same age, had not met before, and was equidistant from the other two babies (Figure 1.10).

The next chapter describes our first findings from this triadic set-up. Chapter 3 describes the second phase of our research, which focused on babies in fours and examines why all-infant quartets present far greater interpretive challenges than do trios. Chapters 4 and 5 focus on developing the implications for policy and practice of the group story of infancy, first in commercial childcare settings, and then in psychotherapy. Chapter 6 concludes.

2
Babies in Threes

Figure 2.1 Floored: a free-form trio.
Source: authors' photo.

Having decided to study babies in all-infant groups, we chose to focus on the smallest possible non-dyadic group: babies in threes.[1] In 1998, we recruited a few trios of babies around eight months old for a pilot study. We began by putting three similarly aged tots on a well-padded floor and set our cameras rolling. The results were undoubtedly interesting, in a comical Buster Keaton kind of way (Figure 2.1). Too often the babies' lack of postural control, and their difficulties in moving around, led them to end up out of sight of each other—one face-planting the rug, the second grumbling with her head in a corner and unable to reverse, the third tumbling down on top of the first and left staring at the ceiling.

Hence our decision to sit the babies in baby-strollers—which had their front wheels removed, so they would stay where they were put. Our recordings thus became more standardized, with the strollers always arranged for maximum symmetry in an equilateral triangle. This set-up meant the babies were *just* in touching distance of each other, and could easily see what both their companions were doing. Their feet were free too (see Figure 2.2).

As soon as we viewed the first recordings from our three-stroller set-up, we realized we needed to do more than create a new studio procedure for recording babies. We needed to find a way of *describing* what they did, because the babies seemed to be *creating* meanings as their group process went along.

2.1 The Traditional Approach

In nearly all observational studies of tiny tots to date, psychologists design their study having already adopted a hypothesis to test. They then decide, before looking, which behaviours to code and measure, and what these behaviours will mean with respect to the prediction being tested. Typically, each study codes very few infant behaviours. For example, the most widely used method of assessing a baby's emotional response to stress—the eight-step Strange Situation Procedure[2]—was devised to code just *five* behaviours, once every fifteen seconds, over 20 minutes. These comprise: *one* out of the hundreds of different facial expressions babies can make (namely, the presence or absence of 'smiling');[3] two broad categories of sound-making ('cries' 'vocalizes'); plus two categories of body movement ('orients' and 'moves' towards or away from).[4]

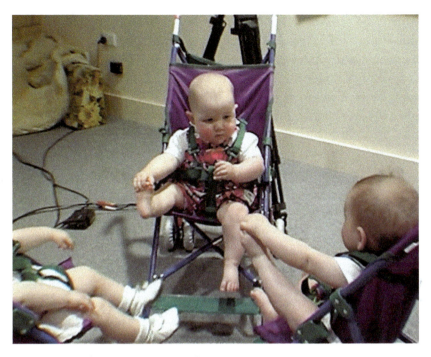

Figure 2.2 Our 'Babies in Groups' recording setup.
Source: authors' photo.

In such studies, the only behaviours recorded are those made relevant by the observers' meaning-making process—in the case of the Strange Situation Procedure, via the theoretical context of 'attachment theory'—not by *the babies' meaning-making process*. In this way, different theories give different meanings to the same behaviours—or encourage researchers to invent a situation which would elicit different focal behaviours (e.g. game-playing, gaze-following, problem-solving).

There are serious flaws in this theory-first approach to observational research, illustrated by a classic review of research on human gaze called *Gaze and Mutual Gaze*. This book reports that over *seventy* different meanings have been given to the act of one person 'looking at' another, depending on which psychologist is testing what hypothesis.[5] Different projects and researchers will assume you look at someone or something because: you hate them; or out of love; or from lust; or because you fear them; or because you seek what is useful; or because you want to hit them; or because they surprise you; or because of their comforting familiarity; or because they are interestingly novel; or because they are similar to something you know; or because they *slightly* differ from something which bores you; or because they are a puzzling stranger who greets you half-heartedly then sits down and ignores you; or because you are conflicted and need a displacement activity ... and so on. But if babies create *their own* meanings for what they and their companions are doing—and add *new* meanings over time—then what a behaviour means cannot be decided beforehand by professional observers. Meanings are created *by* babies doing what babies do. In which case, when observers describe babies, they need to think about *what babies themselves* might mean by their doings.

2.1.1 Baby meaning-making: an example

Take for example a still from a five-minute group interaction starring one of the first trios we recorded (Figure 2.2). Three baby girls—in the middle Paula[6] (eight months old), on the right Esther (seven months old), and at left Ethel (six months old)—had been brought into the recording studio by their mothers, and then each carefully strapped into three identical strollers. Unlike her companions, who seemed more interested in inspecting their surroundings, Paula had looked up and beamed a broad smile at her mother, who was bending over Paula to fasten the straps of Paula's stroller. Again, unlike Esther and Ethel, who did not seem concerned when their mothers left the room, Paula's face fell when her mother stood up and turned to depart, watching with dismay as she walked out through the studio door. As her mother left, Paula grabbed onto her right foot with her right hand. Frequent viewings of this episode and what followed suggested that Paula grabbed her foot in order to *contain anxieties* aroused by her mother's departure. We arrived at this interpretation from noting that Paula first grasped her foot *immediately following* the transition from happiness in her mother's proximity to downcast dismay as her mother left. This prima facie interpretation was supported by our observation that Paula engaged more with the other two babies in the trio when holding her foot than when not holding it—as we discuss later (see Section 2.2.2: 'The two steps').

This is not the end of the story, however. As soon as Paula grabbed her toes, Esther turned to watch. She immediately became fascinated by Paula's foot-holding and began to mirror it (left hand to left foot), making a series of 'initiations'[7]—first to Ethel, who continued to look on quite passively, apparently happy to watch what the others were doing without joining in—and then, repeatedly, back to Paula. A minute and a half into the group process, Esther's fourth initiation attracted Paula, who responded by grabbing her toe again and thus imitating Esther's foot-holding back to Esther (the moment captured in Figure 2.2). From this point on, Paula's foot-holding formed part of a playful imitation game with Esther. Over the remaining three and a half minutes of the group interaction, Paula made thirteen initiations (behaviour plus look) to Esther and none to Ethel. Eight of these initiations involved a look plus toe-holding. As a result Paula looked three times as much at Esther as at Ethel in the remainder of the group's interaction. Paula's foot-holding had thus gained a new meaning. It was no longer just Paula's way of containing anxiety. It had become a move in a two-baby game—a new meaning which *emerged from* the communicative process specific to this group.

2.1.2 False assumptions

Theory-driven approaches to observation ground what is called the 'hypothetico-deductive method'. For most researchers, defining behaviours before you observe them marks the gold-standard for any valid and objective science. Which is all well and good for sciences that deal with things that don't make up new meanings as they go along: iron filings, suspension bridges, atoms, mitochondria, and potatoes. But humans, whether young or old, customarily derail the hypothetico-deductive method.

This problem has long embarrassed behavioural scientists. Most ignore it. As a consequence, we now have what psychologists call their 'replication crisis': the majority of psychological experiments produce results which cannot be replicated in repeat-studies. Why? Because, by copying the methods of the sciences that study microbes and molecules, psychologists who conduct experiments on people are forced to assume their recruits will follow their instructions to a tee, acting exactly as told. Sadly for such experimenters, human beings rarely act like clockwork. They are meaning-makers through-and-through, who always act on their own perceptions of what is going on. Most typically, recruits try to act in a way which *they think* will help the experimenter to succeed (the 'good subject' effect).[8] Sometimes though, if they don't like the experiment or the experimenter, they act in a way they hope will derail the experiment. These processes are not confined to humans even studies of rats are affected by the *rats'* perceptions of how kindly different experimenters handle them.[9]

2.2 Method Development

Rather than plumping for an experimental method which treats people like billiard balls, we have adopted the attitude which produced what was once called 'natural history'. Observers who embrace natural history, as Charles Darwin did, recognize that the natural world has *its own* stories to tell—stories often entirely new and unexpected for the observer.[10] Which means that, though observation must usually be 'for or against some view' or theory, said Darwin, it remains 'a fatal fault' to allow that theory to influence one '*whilst observing*, though so necessary beforehand and so useful afterwards'.[11] Should an observer stick too strongly to their own theory *whilst observing*, they become blind to any unexpected events and behaviour which may occur. Hence the premium Darwin put on 'never letting exceptions pass unnoticed', which his son Francis, also a man of science, called: the 'one quality of mind which seemed to be of special and extreme advantage in leading him to make discoveries'.

The need to describe the world before trying to explain it gets little airtime in many psychologists' research training—unlike other sciences.[12] A whole branch of biology is devoted to describing and classifying the creatures which fill the world—taxonomy. And taxonomy has a history which goes back thousands of years in pretty much every known human culture, two of its Western stars being the ancient Greek philosopher Aristotle and the Swedish zoologist Carl Linnaeus (1707–1778). Taxonomy systematizes findings from natural history: the observation, and description of plants and animals. Likewise, geography starts by systematizing descriptions of the spatial organization of the terrestrial and human world—just as geology begins by describing the rocks and fossils lying under the earth. Equally, the periodic table systematizes descriptive knowledge of all known chemical elements. Most pertinent here: when minted, the new branch of anthropology called ethnography set out in the early 1800s *to describe* the many different cultural forms of living-arrangement then being discovered by Europeans as sea travel opened the door to scientific exploration of many different kinds in far-flung regions of a then-unknown human world.

2.2.1 Case studies

Ethnography makes a good model for describing infant sociability. Writers like Clifford Geertz (1926–2006), Edwin Ardener (1927–1987), and Bent Flyvbjerg (b.1952) stress that the first step in studying real human lives should comprise rich or 'thick' description.[13] When any observed act or sequence of actions may turn out to have *several* possible meanings—as earlier illustrated from research on human gaze—first attempts at describing must contain enough depth so as not prematurely to close off the range of potential meanings the act might have. Whether an 'at first look' or prima facie meaning *remains* plausible depends—as in law courts—on a second phase of analysis, that is, on the cultural experience of the observers hypothesizing meanings for the given act, on the details of that act, its circumstances and contexts, and on how the hypothesized meaning/s fare when linked up with other related observations. Hence the best approach to the observation and interpretation of infant actions is a forensic form of case analysis which has *two* steps.

Case analysis is arguably the most powerful type of scientific theory-elaboration and hypothesis- testing. For example, in the late 1500s, Galileo pointed out that Aristotle's then-popular theory of gravitation could be disproved by a single observation. Aristotle held that the acceleration of falling objects due to gravity was faster for heavier than lighter objects. Galileo argued that Aristotle's view could be overthrown by a comparison of the time taken for a heavy object and a lighter object to fall the same distance from the same place. As soon as it had *once* been shown that the two objects fell at the same speed—as proven in 1586—physicists would know that all future formulae for a body's acceleration due to gravity should exclude the weight of the falling body. Galileo's skill was to identify a critical case for observation: so as best to test the merits of two different views of gravitation. Since Galileo's time, single observations and case studies by scientists as varied as Marie Curie, Charles Darwin, Rosalind Franklin, Thomas Edington, Alexander Fleming and Shirley Strum have overturned accepted theories of the natural world.[14]

In 1998—when we started to study babies in groups—we knew that human sociability was held by most behavioural scientists to be generated by a 'dyadic programme' that imposes *monotropy* or one-to-one-ness on human social life (in parallel to what in adult sexual relationships is called *monogamy*). Dyadic developmental theories assume peer relationships can only form some time *after* the baby's first dyadic bond to an adult has become well-established, that is, some time after the baby reaches two years of age. And, even when they do form, toddlers' peer relationships are also assumed to be one-to-one, because they are generated by the same dyadic template which purportedly underlies all human sociability.

Our research was planned to test the dyadic formulation of human sociability. This is why we chose to recruit children before the age at which existing theory told us they could have started to form a strong attachment to a single adult, that is: at an age of nine months or less. Because then, if we could show even one all-infant group manifested group-level *supra*-dyadic ('polyadic') interaction, any theory claiming that human sociability is generated by a dyadic programme would be disproven.[15] Any adequate theory of human social development would henceforth have to be able to explain how even young babies could interact in a polyadic, groupy way.

2.2.2 The two steps

To illustrate how we seek to uncover the ways babies make meaning in trios—via two-step case analysis of an ethnographic type—we take as our exemplar Paula grabbing for her foot as she watches her mother exit the recording studio. As noted, step one in our method is a rich description. Each such description must focus on the particularities of infant action. Thus, what the observer makes out of Paula's act will at first depend mostly on what they can visually detect, and the amount of detail they consequently gather into their description. This, in turn, will depend upon their own interpretive resources—their capacity for insight, their theoretical reading, their personal experience, their knowledge of other babies, their cultural assumptions. They should be able to generate several potential prima facie meanings for the act: Is it random? Deliberate? An idiosyncratic habit? A reflex that all babies show? A communicative act? A form of attachment behaviour? A symptom of arousal?

Each such question and each prima facie meaning forces the observer to look further afield for what might subsequently prove relevant to the act—the richness of rich description depending on the inclusion of as many potentially relevant details as possible in an initial account of a given infant act. Which foot does Paula clasp? With which hand? Exactly when does she first move her hand towards her foot? How long does she hold it? What makes her let go? What else was going on at the same time, and just before, and just after she reached for her foot? What were the other babies doing? What did Paula's face express? Did she vocalize? How was her breathing? Where did her eyes go? What was her posture? Were there any extraneous noises? From these details, we then construct from our various prima facie understandings what we deem the best-fit account of Paula's action, so conveyed as to give a nuanced sense of her own and her companions' experiences within their group's relational dynamics. Geertz likens such constructions to making clinical inferences: having considered *every* facet of Paula's act that might prove significant, within its context, we then attempt to construct for these an intelligible frame.[16] In Paula's case, notwithstanding other possible constructions of the details of her act, we propose that she grabs her foot to *contain her anxieties*.[17] In the same way, an adult who feels a sudden sadness might light up a cigarette, or open the fridge door.

From here we proceed to our second step. Just as in a legal case, the prima facie interpretation of an event—Jill killed Jack—must be capable of continuing to yield defensible interpretations 'as new social phenomena swim into view'.[18] Did Jill *really* mourn the death of Jack? How was their relationship before he died? Did she act guilty afterwards Did she have a motive? Who hid the murder weapon? And so on. Similarly, if there were no obvious changes in Paula's actions when she was holding her toes compared to when she wasn't, or if the changes in what she did while foot-holding did not support our 'containing anxiety' interpretation, we would have to jettison it and look again. In Paula's case, our idea that her foot-holding gave her a sense of having a secure base[19] could subsequently be tested by calculating whether she looked significantly more at her peers when she was holding onto her toes than when she was not foot-holding. Why? Because this would make her toe-holding homologous to an oft-stated finding that mothers give toddlers a sense of security which gives them courage to explore their environment—a central plank of attachment theory. So, was Paula's foot-holding correlated with an increased curiosity about her surroundings.[20] It was.

2.3 Beyond One-to-One

The classic measure researchers use to chart babies' sociability, particularly babies with peers, assumes all infant social behaviour *is directed* at a single someone else. This directionality is supposedly proven by where a baby is looking when she or he smiles or waves or vocalizes or makes some other move.

The assumption that infant behaviour must be 'directed' at someone else to count as social was first formalized in 1977 by two researchers from Boston, USA, studying toddlers in playgroups.[21] In fact, they proposed that a behaviour *only* counted as social when it was combined with a look at another person. Since then, what these two researchers dubbed 'socially directed behaviours' have become the cornerstone of research on babies' social lives. Yet this measure renders genuinely groupy, polyadic interaction impossible to observe (for more on this, see Chapter 3).

Why? Because, given the design of the human eye, a human being can only focus on one person at once, especially when in close proximity to their companions. This is because the field of view of our *focal* vision is fixed by the spread of light that can be *focused* by our eyes' lenses onto the most sensitive portion of our eyes' retinas (the highly sensitive 'macular' region or 'fovea'; see the small dip in the retina below the optic nerve in Figure 2.3). The field of view converged by an eye's lens onto its macula is less than $18°$ (5%) of the $360°$ available (see Figure 2.4).

32 Babies in Groups

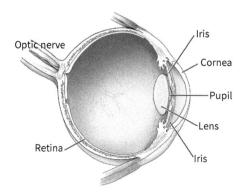

Figure 2.3 Anatomy of the human eye.
National Institutes of Health, part of the United States Department of Health and Human Services, in the public domain.

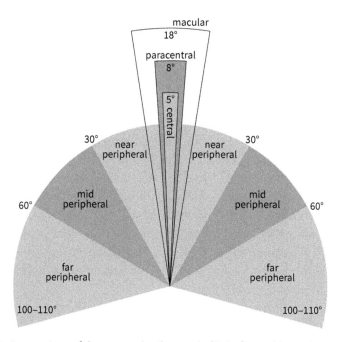

Figure 2.4 Comparison of the narrow (18°) spread of light focusable on the *macular* part of the retina in the human eye, versus the broad field (220°) of unfocused vision endowed by the *peripheral* regions of the retina.
Wikimedia/CC- BY SA-4.0.

Hence, when a baby is sitting with two peers in a tight equilateral triangle—as in previous experiments on babies in groups conducted in Paris and Lausanne, and as in our own studies (see Chapter 1, Figure 1.10)—the narrowness of his/her field of focal gaze means s/he cannot socialize with both peers at once using 'socially directed behaviours' as evidence' (because her/his two peers are separated by 60°). Ironically, then, the widespread use of a method which assumes all human social behaviour is 'directed' makes it impossible to code infant sociability as anything other than one-to-one.

On the other hand, if we drop the assumption that infant behaviour must be focally 'directed' to count as social, then numerous dimensions of infant action—or channels of communication—can sustain group-level interaction (where a baby interacts with *both* their companions *at the same time*). Moreover, once we abandon the assumption that social behaviour requires *visual* directedness, two or more different channels of communication may plausibly *combine* to enable a baby's interaction with two companions at once.

2.3.1 Peripheral vision

Humans have two mechanisms of vision: focal (or 'central' or 'macular') and peripheral (or 'ambient'). Peripheral vision coordinates the whole field of space within which we respond and into which we can act. Peripheral vision guides orientations of the head, postural changes, and locomotor displacements that alter the relationship between the body and spatial configurations of contours and surfaces, events, and objects. Compared to focal vision, peripheral visual awareness has far greater breadth (up to 220° laterally), low resolution for stationary features, low sensitivity for relative position, orientation, or line, but high sensitivity to change in any of these attributes.[22] In this sense, *peripheral vision affords simultaneous responsiveness to a wide array of events*. Focal vision, by contrast, has a very narrow field of view, being principally applied to one target area which it swiftly samples by means of swift, jerky eye movements. It thereby highlights a narrow field of identified objects, into which it may guide voluntary action. *Focal vision is thus associated with intentional action.*

Responsiveness to large-scale postural changes can be afforded by young infants' use of peripheral vision in social situations. Thus, by using the wide field of view detectable through their peripheral vision, babies would, at least theoretically, be able to respond to more than one other person at once when seated in a triangle or square (see Chapter 3 for a demonstration of this capacity). And there's more ...

2.3.2 Sound-making

Babies make sounds in an enormous variety of ways: with their voices, by sneezing or coughing, by blowing raspberries, by clapping hands, and by banging objects. Sound is perceptible to everyone within earshot, whether they be behind us or in front. You do not need to be looking at someone to communicate with or influence them by the sounds you make. The same is true of babies.

By nine months of age, babies have begun to articulate sounds, as in 'babbling'—'mamamam', 'babababab', 'dadadadad', and so on. The sounds they make vary enormously in frequency, loudness, pitch, timbre, intonation, rhythm, intervals, pattern, and combination. For example, from a few weeks onward, babies 'coo'—making sonorous high-pitched drawn-out 'oo' sounds which are often taken as signs of curiosity or appreciation. Contrastingly, a nine-month-old in our study (Ann, the girl with the hat in Figure 2.7) made a number of high-pitched vocalizations. Whilst these were pitched in the same way as coos, they were differently articulated ('ah' rather than 'oo'), being brief, frequent, staccato, rhythmical, and very copious: Ann produced one hundred and twenty-nine 'ah' calls in 4 minutes!

Sound-making is eminently sharable. In our groups, all three members of a trio would sometimes make sounds at the same time, subtly echoing, 'answering', accompanying, or challenging each other's calls. For instance, as a finale to one fifteen-minute threesome, we recorded a 'cats' chorus' of interwoven vocalizations. It started when one baby, close to crying, gave voice to an intermittent querulous wail. A second baby almost immediately copied the wail quite precisely in terms of vocal contours. The first baby, seemingly 'contained' by the second baby's 'mirroring' of him, then repeated his initial vocalization in a modulated form. During this interchange, the third baby contributed a rhythmical continuo of raspberries.[23]

2.3.3 Rhythm

A baby's solo vocalizations—or bangs on a table—are usually rhythmical. Thus the rather similar staccato utterances (Ah! Ah! Ah! etc.) made by Ann, as just mentioned, largely had the same pitch and occurred in regular rhythmical bursts of between two and eight calls. These chants were frequently repeated, with or without variations: for example, a sequence of three three-beat utterances followed by a four-beat utterance followed by six two-beat utterances.

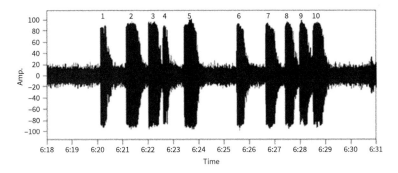

Figure 2.5 All the pulses represent calls by Ann, except pulses 3 and 4 which are Joe's calls.
Source: authors' image.

Sometimes, though, one of the other group members would echo the rhythm of a chant that Ann had just made. Depiction of the sounds' waveforms allows us visually to represent the rhythm (the timing and length) of these calls.

Figure 2.5 shows a two-beat chant by nine-month-old Ann (pulses numbered 1 and 2) which is quickly echoed (at a similar pitch) by nine-month-old Joe (pulses 3 and 4) and then capped by Ann (pulse 5). Occasionally, Ann would follow up vocalizations by the other babies, repeating or elaborating on the rhythmical structure she and her peers had just co-produced. In this example we can see how the first five-pulse rhythmical collaboration between Ann and Joe (pulses 1–5), is quickly reproduced in a solo by Ann (pulses 6–10)—the same number of pulses in the same period (4 seconds) though with a slightly varied rhythm.

Given an appropriate setting, rhythm can be simultaneously shared among a large number of sound-makers—infant or adult.

2.3.4 Facial expressions

Babies have long been assumed to be too young to have developed the necessary level of interpersonal awareness to show such 'non-basic' or 'social' emotions as shame, embarrassment, coyness, shyness, empathy, jealousy, envy, pride, contempt, gratitude, and so on.[24] According to this story, babies' faces supposedly only show a handful of 'basic' 'hard-wired' emotions: interest, disgust, joy, distress, anger, sadness, surprise, and fear. In the same simplifying vein, researchers have classically codified facial expressions like smiles and frowns in a way that assumes they have a single unvarying form and meaning—a movement is categorized either as a smile or not a smile: there are no grey areas.[25] Such an approach outlaws any idea that babies might flexibly combine different expressions at the same time, or smile in different ways with different intensities—as research now proves they can.[26]

Babies' facial expressions are generated by forty-two different muscle segments or 'action units', each of which moves the surface of the face in a different way.[27] Activation of each individual unit may vary in intensity and duration, while being severally combined in an enormous number of different ways. For example, in one detailed analysis of a nine-week-old, Sarah's en face interaction with her mother, the first seventy seconds contained seven *different* smiles by the baby.[28] The first occurred as Sarah's mother sat down in front of her in the recording studio and greeted her with a joke ('Hello darling [sitting down]. Hello! Oo-oo-oo-oo!'). This produced Sarah's broadest (combined with fewest other 'action units') and longest (6.3 seconds) smile of the seven. Ensuing smiles varied from less than one second to 3.4 seconds. Sarah's smiles also varied in intensity, being more or less open-mouthed and lopsided, whilst variously combined with tongue movements, and frowns, and head tilts, and one-handed and two-handed gestures, and foot movements.

2.3.5 Gestures

Babies point, clap, move their arms out and in, and up or down, and hold them still in significant positions, while making countless delicate finger movements. Likewise, if their feet hang free (as in our studies), they can move and hold one or both their feet in different positions, and splay or clench their toes. They may 'direct' such movements towards others, or not.[29] Either way, any gesture they make, whether with legs, feet, toes, fingers, hands, and/or arms, will potentially be visible to *all* their companions at the same time (Figure 2.6). Infants' hand gestures have been studied in detail, young infants making more frequent expressive movements with their right hands than with their left. Such movements are often synchronized with the lip and tongue movements which foreshadow speech. Left hands seem to be more expansive, often being swayed by the self-regulation of the baby's own emotions. Their right hands make more precise and detailed movements, predominating in expression to others. From three months on, babies pay particular attention to others' hands when interacting. By nine to ten months they have begun to use gestures to convey particular, idiosyncratic meanings—as is shown by the fact that deaf babies can acquire arbitrary hand-signs to encode discrete meanings by nine months. Both hearing and deaf babies have been observed to 'babble' with gestures during the last third of their first year.[30]

Babies in Threes 37

Figure 2.6 Three babies in a quartet watch a fourth clap. Note the differences in foot-tension and toe-positions.
Source: authors' photo.

2.3.6 Touch

All the babies in the trios we recorded were within touching distance of each other, both by hand and by foot. For feet to touch, the babies involved had each to stretch their feet towards the other(s). Likewise with hands. Hence, potentially, they could touch two other babies at once.

2.3.7 Orientation

Babies have very flexible bodies. How they orientate their bodies to the other members of their group may speak volumes, and carry more than one meaning at once. Thus, the torsos of toe-touchers Joe and Ann in Figure 2.7 are clearly oriented more towards each other than to the third member of their group, six-month-old Mona. Ann's left foot is particularly expressive. Prior to this photograph, she had been stretching both her feet out symmetrically while looking at Joe. Mona then reached out with her own feet so that her right foot briefly touched Ann's left foot. Ann immediately withdrew from the contact, moving her left foot as far away from Mona as she could—and

Figure 2.7 Two babies in a threesome touch toes (Joe, left, and Ann, right). The third (Mona) watches them attentively.
Source: authors' photo.

holding it there. As a result, the orientation of Ann's body in Figure 2.7 is simultaneously expressing her attraction to Joe and her rejection of Mona (see Section 2.4 'Rude signs').

2.3.8 Imitation

We have already seen how commonly babies imitate each other's actions—from holding toes (Figure 2.1) to vocalizations (Figure 2.5). Imitation is a form of communication which allows meanings to evolve, and several different babies to 'get in on the act'.

2.3.9 Combination

As we have said, all these different means of multi-directional communication are typically *combined* with each other in free-form group interaction, hence the enormous complexity of the group dynamics we describe.[31]

2.4 Rude Signs

The blending of vocalizations in the 'cats' chorus' (mentioned earlier) illustrates a relatively harmonious communication. That harmony does not always prevail is illustrated by more extended observations of the trio comprising Joe (nine months), Ann (nine months), and Mona (six months). Their session lasted 12 minutes.

The first 3 minutes of the recording featured: a great many short looks by Ann at both Mona and Joe; Mona's glue-like 'gripped' attention to both Joe and Ann (but increasingly to Joe); and Joe's smiling overtures to both Ann and Mona. By the fourth minute, both Ann and Mona were looking mainly at Joe (Mona looked for 54 seconds at Joe and 5 seconds at Ann during minute 4; Ann looked at Joe for 39 seconds and at Mona for 6 seconds during the same minute). Meanwhile, Joe looked relatively little at either of them (12 seconds at each). This pattern coloured the whole interaction, with Joe looking at the others least (total 410 seconds, or 57% of the whole interaction) but being looked at most (713 seconds).[32] Mona looked at the others most (640 seconds or 89% of the total) but was looked at least by the others (total 248 seconds); and Ann was in the middle on both counts: looking at others for 488 seconds (68% of the total interaction); and being looked at for 580 seconds.

Whilst both Ann and Mona seemed to prefer Joe to each other, this was far more the case with Ann than Mona. Thus Ann spent three times as much time looking at Joe (365 vs. 123 seconds) as she did at Mona, whereas Mona spent only slightly more time looking at Joe than at Ann (348 seconds or 54% of her total). Joe looked more at Ann than at Mona (285 seconds or 70%). Ann and Joe's interest in each other increased as their conversation progressed, largely because Ann found two ways to keep his attention: frequent vocalizing and 'playing footsie' by reaching out with her foot to touch his foot (Figure 2.7).

To begin with, looking was the main form of interaction for all three, though both Ann and particularly Joe made brief smiling overtures to both the other babies during the first minute—overtures which soon faded (Mona did not smile throughout the recording). During the fifth minute, Ann began to make frequent staccato vocalizations, predominantly whilst looking at Joe (she made 25 brief vocalizations in the fifth minute and a further 104 over the next 3 minutes; 73% while looking at Joe and only 6% while looking at Mona). The rate at which she called increased markedly after Joe made two brief vocalizations to her (cf. Figure 2.5; Ann made 2 sounds in 20 seconds prior to his vocalization, and 10 in 10 seconds after; throughout all this Mona was mute).

After watching Ann make this flurry of vocalizations, Joe then turned to Mona to make an expansive initiation, as if 'bringing her in' to the

Figure 2.8 Joe turns away from Ann towards Mona, leans forward, and smiles.
Source: authors' photo.

conversation: he reoriented his body towards her, leant towards her, waved both his arms up and down, all accompanied by an 8-second-long wide-open smile and raised eyebrows (Figure 2.8). This attracted Mona's attention, who had also been watching Ann vocalize. In contrast, as Ann saw Mona and Joe make mutual gaze, she looks down at herself, seemingly deflated; then her legs, which had at first been stretched out towards the other two, drop down.

Joe looked briefly back at Ann, still smiling and they made mutual gaze. But then he turned back to Mona, still smiling. After this, 30 seconds passed before Ann and Joe made mutual gaze again. Five seconds after Joe's big initiation to Mona, Ann turned and scowled at Mona—an expression which she never made to Joe. Ann also reached out and briefly touched Joe's left foot with her own right foot during this period of the interaction (immediately thereafter bringing her right foot to touch her own left foot). Mona watched this sequence and then rubbed her own feet together.

In the eighth minute, Ann began an intense game of footsie with Joe that lasted until the interaction broke down 4 minutes later. Twenty seconds into this game, Mona once again held her own feet out, rubbing them together, looking at Ann. After a minute she stretched her own feet out even further, now towards Ann, still rubbing them together, apparently trying to touch Ann's left foot (which was symmetrically stretched out, at the same angle as her right foot that was touching Joe's foot, and hence was close to Mona). At this point, Mona whined loudly (as if to say, 'what about me?'—Mona's first vocalization). Both Joe and Ann briefly looked at her and then back at each other. In the tenth minute, Mona finally managed to touch Ann's left foot with her own right foot. Ann looked at her, in contact through her feet with both Joe and Mona simultaneously. Ann then withdrew both her feet, clutched her right foot in her right hand and her left foot with her left hand and deliberately brought her two feet together with her hands until they touched in front of her face. She then looked at Joe and reached her right foot to make contact with his foot while tucking her left foot under her stroller, bending it as far as possible away from contact with Mona.

Whereas hitherto both Ann's feet were stretching out symmetrically, she now was sitting asymmetrically, apparently to avoid contact ('contamination'?) by Mona's attempts to touch her. During the eleventh minute she was not only looking at Joe, vocalizing frequently and playing footsie with him but also was pointing at him with both index fingers. (Both Ann and Mona pointed at Joe but never at each other.)

Finally, in the twelfth minute, Ann turned to sneer towards Mona, making a gesture with the back of her hand, index finger raised, at Mona, who was looking straight at Ann (Ann drew her foot back from Joe whilst making this gesture; Figure 2.9). Ann then turned back to Joe, stretched out her foot

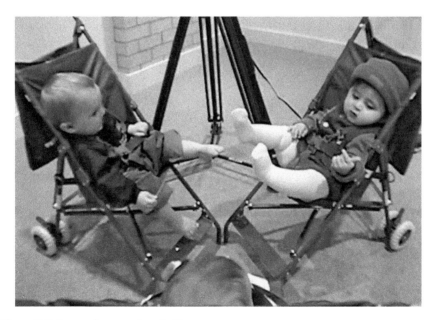

Figure 2.9 Ann makes a gesture to Mona.
Source: authors' photo.

towards him and gave him a brief smile. Joe, who had been watching Ann throughout this sequence, then turned away to Mona with big smiling initiation similar to those 6 minutes earlier—as if to comfort Mona by saying, 'Don't mind about her'. Mona turned to look at him. Ann, watching Joe 'deserting' her for mutual gaze with Mona, immediately pouted and began to cry (the first crying in the session). Her crying built up and within thirty seconds, we decided to terminate the session.[33]

2.4.1 Comment

The sense here is of powerful feelings circulating in the group, even though these babies had never met before. Joe is interested in both the other babies, smiles at both of them throughout the interaction, and also seems to have a sense of 'fair play' in that, twice, when it seems Ann gets too exclusively pro-Joe, he turns away in a friendly fashion to make compensating overtures to Mona.

Mona mainly watches, though she seems to prefer Joe (despite Ann's greater activity) and acts 'left out' when Ann engages Joe in prolonged games of footsie: making a complaining vocalization, rubbing her own feet together when Ann's and Joe's toes touch, and stretching out to 'join in' by touching Ann's foot at the same time as Ann's foot is touching Joe's. The most active is Ann, who seems increasingly pro-Joe and increasingly less interested in—if not antipathetic towards—Mona, and resentful of Joe's even-handed interest in Mona, a resentment which ultimately leads to the termination of the group.

Experimental studies of infants' jealousy typically code as jealous any reaction to social exclusion that involves negative affect (crying, distress, negative vocalizations).[34] Our description of the Ann–Joe–Mona group shows an interplay of inclusion and exclusion in the spontaneous behaviour of the three babies but is more complex than can be caught by the term 'jealousy'. Three instances of possessiveness—or protest against exclusion—occurred: twice when Ann seemed to 'deflate' after Joe had made an overture to Mona (the second time Ann burst into tears, so that we ended the interaction) and once when Mona stretched out her feet towards where Ann and Joe's feet are touching, rubbed them together (self-comforting), and whined.

But we can also see some facets of jealousy observed in this trio as parts of a larger picture. An important factor is Ann's attraction to Joe, shown by her looking at him three times as much as at Mona, making 12 times as many vocalizations to Joe as to Mona, pointing at him, smiling at him, and playing footsie with him. There is a sense of possessiveness about this attraction as Ann does not point at Mona, smiles at her only once at the start of the interaction, removes her foot from Mona once touched, tucking it under her seat, and makes three ambivalent gestures towards Mona with a scowling facial expression. Yet Ann's expressions of sensitivity to exclusion would hardly have come about had Joe not shown a very different attitude to Ann than she showed towards him.

Joe clearly enjoyed and engaged with Ann's overtures, but his actions towards Mona were inclusive rather than exclusive.[35] He made three expansive smiling initiations to Mona: once near the beginning of the interaction, once after Ann had begun to vocalize frequently and pointedly at him, and once after Ann had directed the last of her ambivalent scowling gestures towards Mona. Meanwhile, though Mona seemed to want to be included in the footsie game Ann began with Joe, she was content (like Ethel in the Paula–Esther–Ethel trio described earlier) to watch Joe and Ann's interchanges for much of the interaction, her head turning from one to the other, like a girl watching a tennis final.

2.5 Conclusions

2.5.1 The challenge of babies in threes

Our films show babies engaging in group-level interaction well before they reach nine months of age.[36] The babies we record have many ways of communicating with several others at once by: combining gestures; touch; gaze; facial expressions; sound-making; rhythm; postural orientation and imitation. The dynamics of baby trios are complicated and unique to each group. Each group can generate new meanings specific to its own dynamics.

These findings depart from the general assumptions made about babies—whether researching babies' social lives, advising parents how to look after the very young, or constructing policies and government regulations to ensure a good quality of upbringing is provided by early learning centres. The very possibility of babies interacting with more than one person at once has almost completely escaped behavioural scientists. Even the few who have tried to study babies in threes choose to describe and score early social behaviour in ways which cannot help but blind them to the fact that babies can address and respond to several people simultaneously.[37]

The nearest any well-known theory of child development has got to hypothesizing an alternative form of sociability to the kind of one-to-one interactions that obtains between a mother and her own baby is a brief aside in John Bowlby's book on *Attachment*. Bowlby proposes a secondary 'behavioural system' of childhood sociability to augment the infant–mother 'attachment behavioural system'. This he calls the 'affiliative system'. The affiliative system, he writes, is not intended to explain 'behaviour that is directed towards one or *a few particular figures*,[38] which is the hallmark of attachment behaviour'. He illustrated 'affiliative' sociability from research showing young monkeys manifest an 'infant-infant, age-mate, or peer affectional system through which infants and children interrelate … and develop persisting affection for each other'.[39] As for the springs of sociability, he suggested that a young child 'seeks a playmate when he is in good spirits and confident of the whereabouts of his attachment figure; when the playmate is found, moreover, the child wants to engage in playful interaction with him or her'.[40]

Bowlby's approach cannot handle our results. Bowlby calls playmates 'subsidiary figures', because they are only sought out once a child: (a) actually *has* 'an attachment figure' to give them a motivating 'secure base' for social adventures; and, (b) is 'confident' of the attachment figure's whereabouts. Our results relate to babies with an average age of eight months, who are thus too young to have solidified an attachment to a mother figure—something which only happens between 9 and 30 months of age according to Bowlby's timetable.[41] Furthermore, whilst in fantasy, each baby *might* feel confident he or she knows where the person who brought them into our lab is, they cannot *actually* know where their guardians are. Furthermore, Bowlby's descriptions make it clear he is conceiving of infant sociability with 'playmates' through a dyadic prism—blinding him to infants' participation in the kinds of group process described in this and the next two chapters. Unsurprisingly, Bowlby's proposal about the 'affiliative' (or 'sociable')[42] system continues to foster dyadic thinking: all too predictably, writers on children's friendships presume that early sociability with peers is either a matter of representations contained in the head of a single child or is best represented by one-to-one relationships.[43]

Why do such psychologists not countenance the possibility that babies can participate in group-level dynamics? Mainly because most have never conceived such a question. Especially those who believe that mothers—attachment figures—are so central to their babies' lives that babies plunge into a debilitating state of 'separation anxiety' whenever they doubt the whereabouts of their attachment figure.[44] The ability to conquer such doubts when with other people, such as peers, supposedly results from a toddler's development of an 'internal working model' of his or her attachment figure—something only acquired after the age of two or three years.

On this score, one of our most challenging findings must be that our experimental baby trios last for *up to twenty-five minutes* of often lively, largely undistressed interaction, with no adults present. This is despite the fact that the babies in each of the groups we film: have never met before; are aged nine months or less; are in an odd and unfamiliar place surrounded by cameras and lights; and have, at best, only a fantasized idea of where their parents are. Given all this, we have clearly discovered a form of sociability in our infant trios previously unknown to developmental science. And this kind of sociability differs completely from what Bowlby called *attachment or affiliation*.

2.5.2 Conjecture and negotiation

Descriptions of infant actions are usually identified with confidence by observers, especially if they seem to mesh with before contemporary studies of infant emotional life,[45] or with common sense (though common sense is sometimes cast as antagonistic to science by psychologists).[46] While we too write with conviction about the powerful emotions circulating within the trios we observe, we need to consider how to place such descriptions within the complex field of the ways humans come to understand each other.

In our research, the forms of agency we observe and describe cannot be attributed to adult scaffolding, because no adults are present in the interactions we record. Yet the babies we describe manifest a recognizable set of interpersonal feelings. Such recognizability remains conditional, however, in that some of our perceptions of all-infant groups may not have been picked up by researchers several decades ago. For instance, our example of the changed significance of Paula's toe-holding in the Paula–Esther–Ethel group might have escaped us before the invention, around 1950, of ideas about: the 'containment' of anxiety; 'transitional' objects; and the importance of babies' gaining a sense of security through relationships (and 'attachments') to a caregiver.[47]

Most contentious, perhaps, is how we felt compelled to interpret a gesture by Ann as flicking a 'rude sign' at Mona after a sequence of triadic interchanges including Joe. 'Giving the finger' is a culture-specific gesture which some observers might assume inappropriate to attribute to such a young girl. Yet Ann's gesture appeared as deliberate as anything else she did. So we felt justified in presuming it meant something, making us—who observed the interaction which gave rise to it—both confident and unsure at the same time.

Ann's rude sign helpfully raises larger questions about the extent to which observational descriptions such as ours accurately reflect what we see. Or do describers project meanings onto what is seen? Our view gains strength from our that Ann increasingly resented *any* involvement Mona had with Joe, and can conclude with more confidence that this trend culminated in Ann's 'rude' gesture. Yet, surely, it is unlikely that a nine-month-old had absorbed the cultural significance of 'giving the finger'—something which is typically performed coolly and knowingly. Some colleagues might hazard that Ann's gesture was somehow 'hard-wired' or 'natural' to the human antagonism implicit in jealousy. We take a more conservative view: however much such a gesture comes over time to be used as a directed insult, its meanings will always draw from current circumstances, cultural contexts, and learning—as it does here. In time, Ann will come to learn the wider significance of such gestures. Yet, even now, by constructing what she did as rude, we participate in the very processes through which she will herself come *to develop* a recognition of such cultural significance.

A more generic way of raising this sort of question would be to ask: Is what *we see* to be going on in a given infant–peer interaction what is *really* going on? Here, our method gives our answer. We have developed a forensic form of proof, which involves two phases of case analysis. First, we construct our prima facie interpretation—of which the validity and plausibility rest on the ways the richness and detail of an act's character and circumstances are entailed in our descriptions. Next, we assess the truth of this initial interpretation by projecting how the rest of the interaction should bear it out. Then we test our prediction using numerical evidence. If our prima facie conjecture passes its subsequent test, we accept it—though our acceptance remains provisional: all our descriptions (and recordings) always remain open to amendment or refutation, subject to the negotiation of alternative tests of contrasting conjectures.[48]

A slightly different line of inquiry also questions the relationship between seeing and describing a baby's acts—questions which have a long pedigree in the annals of natural history.[49] This further inquiry brings into focus the intrinsic disproportion between the constraints of worded representations of human behaviour on the one hand, and, on the other, the enormous volume of potentially significant data any verbal description of social interaction implicitly subsumes. We return to this issue of disproportion in the next chapter, where we discuss the problems of description—and the opportunities for insight—offered by research involving infants in fours. The dynamics of infant quartets prove far more complex than those of infant trios. And, unlike the cultural provision of easy-to-recognize 'scripts' applicable to the dynamics of trios—featuring inclusion, exclusion, jealousy, and possessiveness—there are few, if any, such scripts to help interpret our findings about quartets.

Finally, we ask: does 'observing and describing' infant action relate in any significant way to human development and change? On this score we note that, for decades, several research-based traditions have worked with the insight that we shape one another by how we understand each other. For example, Labelling Theory highlights processes whereby our understandings help create what is being described.[50] And the school of thought called 'symbolic interactionism' also teases out how our senses of 'self' and 'other' reproduce themselves through cultural action.[51]

Regarding the interpretations presented here, we recognize both these traditions—taking up in later chapters the question of how different descriptions of the 'fundamental nature' of babies' sociability—as generated, either by a dyadic programme, or a capacity for groupness—may justify very different policies and practices to shape and regulate the professional care of very young children in Westernized countries (Chapter 4). Then, in Chapter 5, we examine how different descriptions of what humans socially *are* (dyadic versus group-capable) influence and inflect a variety of different approaches to psychotherapy and clinical psychology.

3
This Is Not Happening

Figure 3.1 An example of 3→1 attention with the looked-at baby addressing the baby on his right, 45 secs into the interaction.
Source: authors' photo.
Images of babies in quartets are illustrative only. The textual detail does not address the particularity of the photos.

Typically, the babies appear curious, the atmosphere light-hearted—with smiling and laughter, especially during the first half of the recording. In the first few seconds, the babies look about at their surroundings, then find each other and 'latch on'. Thereafter their attention is on each other virtually the whole time, through looking at each other, touching feet, homing in on the resonance of body movement, and through listening and vocalizing. We see a rhythm grow in the group as, for several seconds at once, three babies are all looking at the fourth baby who then 'holds the floor', actively appearing to command the group's attention, occupying 'centre stage', before this position is taken or handed over to another baby (Figure 3.1).

Unless we have been taught to expect that infants left by their mothers will be racked with 'separation anxiety' or 'stranger fear'[1]—in which case what we are looking at will come as a profound shock—this scene is easy to absorb. No one familiar with babies will find it hard to imagine that healthy eight-month-olds show interest in each other, or feel puzzled by how this group acts. Yet the more we look, the more there is to see. And the more researchers are likely to feel surprised.

3.1 Hello Complexity

3.1.1 The binocular view

When we look at babies in threes, description comes relatively easily because we have ready-made themes that help us imagine what happens when three people socialize: attraction and pairing; inclusion and exclusion; preference; rejection; and jealousy (Figure 3.3). About fours, our culture is quieter. In what ways is it possible to pen a verbal description of groups larger than three which accurately conveys what is happening *at group-level*? Even making sense of gaze is hard enough—there is more than one new baby-to-baby look every second in our quartets, many gazes being very short (19% were less than half a second long). Add to this all the babies' other continuous movements—some gross, many delicate—of faces, bodies, arms, legs, fingers, and toes, plus their vocalizations and their touching, plus the complex interrelations between what several babies are doing at Time A and what they do at Time B ... and it is easy to become overwhelmed by the quantity of data (Figure 3.2). Babies can apparently handle it, at least for much of the time. But can we? And, if so, how? Here it behooves us to recall Karl Popper's words:

> If we wish to study a thing, we are bound to select certain aspects of it. It is not possible for us to observe or describe a whole piece of the world, or a whole piece of nature; in fact, not even the smallest whole piece may be so described, since all description is necessarily selective.[2]

One advantage we have over Popper, writing in 1957, is the use of film and video—which allows us to explore different ideas about our data by taking repeated passes through our recordings to pursue different lines of inquiry.

50 Babies in Groups

Figure 3.2 Group engagement at eight months: a lot is going on in this picture.
Source: authors' photo.

Nevertheless, infant quartets prove an order of magnitude more difficult to describe than trios.

And to what extent can such descriptions include or exclude the individual perspective of each group member? In the animal world—for example with flocking birds, or bees and ants in their colonies—and perhaps in studies of crowds, we might provide descriptions of group activity of some complexity without recourse to the experience or behaviour of the individual. But here we must adopt what group psychoanalyst Wilfred Bion (1897–1979) called a *binocular* view, in which describing a baby quartet *both* as a group *and* as four individuals is taken to invoke 'different facets of the same phenomenon', not least because these two kinds of account cannot help but draw upon each other.[3] For Bion, combining the two traditional perspectives of 'the individual' and 'the crowd' means prioritizing *the dynamics of the group* which generates or conditions both individual and crowd behaviour.

For a group to exist, group members must be aware of and affected by *relationships* between *other* group members, as in a status hierarchy or the complexities of jealousy. Group-minded babies must be able to 'act into' *a group* of people, all of whom are already positioned with regard to each other, as in a family or in a day-care room. For example, a jealous person does not usually suffer in silence. They *act into* a threesome in a jealous way, whether they

Figure 3.3 'Jealousy' by Edvard Munch (1930).
Edvard Munch lithograph 'Jealousy' IV, 1930 in the public domain.

mean to or not, often disrupting the relationship which they feel excludes them—as is to be observed in the interactions described in the last chapter between Mona, Ann, and Joe, as well as in experiments on infants, and in toddlers' interactions with their siblings.[4] But equally, as we saw with Joe, a generous impulse may lead an infant to intervene to help someone they feel is being excluded by others from a group.[5]

Below we describe what we see in groups of 6- to 9-month-olds. Settled into their quartet of strollers (as in Figures 3.1 and 3.2), the cameras roll. And, when we show these and other films to professionals—clinicians, educators, and researchers—excited discussion ensues. Even while picking up different aspects or disagreeing on a role played by a quartet member, no showing has prompted a view that nothing of significance is happening for the infants. This is consistent with our argument in Chapter 2 (see e.g. Chapter 2.5.2): we see the diverse responses our films provoke as contributions to a larger cultural project required for the interpretive process of documenting babies' groupness. The following sections refer to how, in discussion with others, we came to see in baby quartets some of the group dynamics more usually understood to occur in older children and adults. We thus convey the complexity and challenge of description.

After the following descriptions, we turn to a more formal appraisal of groupness in infants (Section 3.2).

3.1.2 Group conversation

Babies in fours prove to have a simultaneous awareness of what all their fellow group members are doing, presumably through ambient vision, touch, and hearing (Chapter 2.3). Thus we see quick shifts of interest within baby quartets, much as we would when four adult friends converse while seated at a table. For example Figure 3.4:

> PASSAGE 1: *Clare is centre stage, holding the focus of the group. She looks and smiles at Anna opposite her and Barbie on her right and does a quick look to Paul on her left, smiles, then vocalizes, and claps, looking at Anna, then back to Paul, with a grin. Paul now grins himself and becomes centre stage. All babies look and smile at Paul who is arm-waving and vocalizing in a chatty way. After six seconds, Paul coughs. Barbie, facing him, laughs. Paul coughs again; Barbie chortles, then vocalizes, and chortles again. Paul and Clare look at Barbie now, Anna remains watching Paul until Barbie waves her arms; now Barbie holds centre stage.*

At first pass, much of our recordings of babies in fours look like this. However, there is more going on in an infant-group 'conversation' than at first appears.

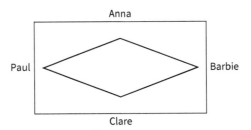

Figure 3.4 Seating arrangement for Anna, Paul, Barbie, and Clare.
Source: authors' image.

This Is Not Happening   53

3.1.3 Routines

Let us now take a different quartet of three girls and a boy (see Figure 3.5): Pearl, Dawn, Ruby, and Paul (the only one of these babies who also figured in the previously discussed quartet). Group members ranged in age from 6 months 21 days to 9 months 16 days. The group lasted 6 minutes and 18 seconds. Here is some of what we saw (in this and the next section, underlining indicates what we call a *routine*—a term we explain shortly):

> PASSAGE 2: <u>Dawn uses her feet in initial connections with Pearl</u> on her left and Paul on her right. <u>Dawn flips both Paul's and Pearl's feet</u>, to which they both respond, sometimes by just holding their feet in contact with Dawn's feet, albeit with some pressure. At the same time members of the group are using other means to connect: gaze; sporadic vocalizations, and, in the case of Pearl, <u>stretching out her hand towards Dawn</u>. At one point, <u>Ruby</u>, whose expression had been somewhat grim, looks to Pearl and <u>makes a 'hoooh' call at her, then looks to the door, then back at Pearl with another 'hoooh' sound</u>.

Amongst much else that's going on in the group, this interaction contains elements in a combination which is repeated and which we identify as a 'routine': for example, Dawn's links to Pearl through her feet in a game of footsie. And Ruby's orientations to Pearl, often vocalizing and glancing at the door—something which occurs (with variations) seven times during the whole interaction and seems a robust routine—perhaps giving Ruby a platform for more complex emotional responses (see Passage 7). Other such routines are underway, sometimes overlapping each other and sometimes disrupted. For example, a little later in the group's interaction:

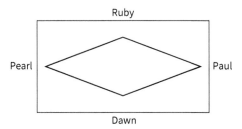

Figure 3.5 Seating arrangement for Ruby, Pearl, Paul, and Dawn.
Source: authors' image.

PASSAGE 3: <u>Paul is continuing to look at Ruby who is looking at him</u>. Ruby then shifts her gaze to Dawn. Dawn lowers her eyelids, whereupon <u>Ruby looks back at Paul</u>. Pearl, who has also lowered her gaze, again <u>extends her arm out towards Dawn's hand</u>. Perhaps seeing Pearl's movement, Paul briefly takes his eyes off Ruby to glance at Pearl, then looks back to Ruby. <u>Ruby and Paul continue to look at each other</u>, bringing each other into relationship. <u>Dawn then looks across to Pearl with her outstretched arm and looks up at her face. Pearl raises her eyes</u> to meet Dawn's gaze, and when this occurs, Ruby does a slight bounce back in her stroller and orients towards Pearl. Ruby vocalizes 'errrhhhhh' to Pearl and then focuses her look on Pearl. Ruby's bounce-and-call now manages to attract Pearl's attention, Pearl switching away from Dawn to look at Ruby. Paul follows Ruby's gaze and looks at Pearl, while <u>Dawn, who continues to look at Pearl, moves her foot</u> as Pearl moves her gaze from Dawn to Ruby.

Given that Pearl and Ruby already had a connected history by this point in the group process—see Ruby's 'Pearl-door-Pearl-hoooh!' looking routine described in Passage 2—it now seemed Pearl was attempting to strengthen a link to Dawn. Pearl already had some routines developing with Dawn, including footsie (see underlined observations in Passage 2). At the same time, it seemed that Ruby, glimpsing Pearl's overture to Dawn, even while looking at Paul, took exception to it and interrupted her involvement with Paul, challenging Pearl's approach to Dawn by gaining Pearl's attention in what we refer to below as a possible 'attack on linking' (see Section 3.1.5).

Passage 3 amounted to only nine seconds of group process, yet we already see the emotional complexity of unfolding relational dynamics within this group of four previously unacquainted babies. Aspects of this complexity have already been described: responses to being excluded as a result of others connecting together; being involved with more than one other at the same time; and responding to group activity. What is added here raises the bar on acknowledging infants' experiences. For, simultaneously, an infant (Ruby) is involved with one peer in mutual gaze (Paul), and yet, at the same time, responds to a link forming between the third and fourth group members (Pearl and Dawn: see Passage 3). That is, while Ruby is engaged in a looking 'routine' with Paul, she clocks an interchange between Pearl and Dawn and responds to that. As mentioned, Ruby and Pearl had already built a routine during the course of the group interactions. Thus we have Ruby's two routines at odds, her gazing with Paul and her interactions with Pearl. In interrupting her gaze routine with Paul to interrupt Pearl's growing routine with Dawn, we are struck by Ruby registering and acting out overlapping emotional complexities, which are being evoked by her participation in the group.

To describe different routines established within the group is to flesh out observations made earlier, by illustrating how infants can interact with more than one other at the same time. We thus demonstrate the relative autonomy of routines of behaviours: the interactions of playing 'footsie' with one group member may seem independent of eye contact and attention with another, and/or the twisting or bending of the torso towards a third. This raises questions about the relationship between different social routines, their possible integration, and how, if incompletely, awareness of them may develop.

3.1.4 History

The presence of routines in infant-peer quartets invites a further layer of complexity into the interpretation of baby groups: the importance of history.[6] This is clearly true for adult observers, in that we use observations of earlier events to make sense of later events in a group interaction. But is history also important for infants?

Certainly, research shows infants *are capable* of remembering recent events like the previous episodes in a group interaction.[7] But what about the influence of babies' pre-visit experiences—their experiences at home? Take Paul for example in Passage 1. Paul sometimes worked one-to-one in a group, if he could attract a partner to participate. So when Clare made several inclusive gestures to Barbie *and* Paul, he reacted positively, in that he tried several times to reach over to Clare and touch her. But in all cases she curled away from him. Paul's response appeared intense, expressing a need for one-to-one intimacy incompatible with Clare's lighter-hearted overtures, which had the air of an invitation to group play.

At other times, Paul engaged in cycles of gross trunk movements and loud sound-making—calling out, coughing, clapping hands—as though to entertain and thus, perhaps, gain what he apparently sought or needed from those around him. Such gambits would typically be followed by what seemed like a somewhat anxious withdrawal, if, as usual in this setting, the habitual gambit fell flat—as on this occasion:

> PASSAGE 4. *Near the start of the group, Paul tries what becomes a repeated overture:* He provides the group with loud, not unpleasant, but sustained repeated vocalizations accompanied by vigorous trunk and arm movements and a smiling face. *All turn and look at Paul, passively, but alert to what he is doing. He coughs twice and vocalizes. Barbie, opposite him, seems to find him very funny and produces a rollicking laugh. Despite this Paul does not seem to have got the kind of response that he is*

looking for, since he pushes back into his seat, looking around him at the others. Then he tries the same again – <u>leaning forward, making sustained vocalizations, big trunk and limb movements, and giving a wide general smile into the group</u>, though without eye contact or direction to any individual companion. This time there are responses. Clare, to his right orients towards him. His vocalization as he turns to her seems like a sigh of relief and pleasure as he reaches to touch her outstretched arm. But at his touch, Clare quickly withdraws her arm. Barbie, opposite, makes a high-pitched pleased noise which Clare continues while disengaging from Paul. Paul responds ecstatically to Clare's sound-making—embarking on a spate of long drawn-out vocalizations, trunk, and limb movements. Perhaps he now feels engaged with the group, who come to watch him again, though without otherwise responding. As <u>Paul goes on with his cycles of routinized display</u>, the others watch his antics with increasing passivity. <u>He eventually withdraws more permanently</u>, fingers to mouth.

In this sequence we can see cycles of a kind which repeat throughout the group's time together. While focusing on Paul, we are also required to see the group dynamics he acts within. Each baby brings his or her own reactions, personality, and prior states of mind to the group process. Strikingly Paul strives to connect with the others through a generalized flourish which is perhaps too overblown a display to build into sustained interpersonal interchanges—a pattern which may reflect routines learnt at home. Clare, in contrast, is demonstrably able to interact through some personalized responses. Tellingly, Paul does not adjust his response in line with her initiatives. Instead, he repeats the same gambit many times. Thus, later in the group interaction:

> PASSAGE 5. *Paul's noises, although similar to his previous ones, have a more plaintive quality. Clare, remaining responsive, perhaps reflecting his more subdued affect, sighs, and holds out her strap that she is playing with towards him with a nice, inviting vocalization. Paul continues regardless.*

Focusing on Paul in this way, and speculating on what he has brought to the group from the rest of his life, illustrates the need for a binocular vision of the group's dynamics. Because Paul (unlike any other baby we studied) figured in two different quartets—and his routines were similar in both (see next Passage 6)—we may feel further encouraged to broker an historical (or individualistic) explanation for these. Yet, in both groups, we can only describe Paul's 'individual' characteristics by detailing the ways they gain sense from how his actions intersect with the actions of *other* group members. Nor should Paul's history be conceived as *individual* if, as seems likely, his routines of attention-getting, and noise-making have carried over from previous social interactions at home—where perhaps they had proved successful in entertaining others, probably older relatives—as these, in all likelihood, will also have been *group* interactions.

3.1.5 Linking, attacks on linking, and time out

To give a further sense of the complexity of infants' group process, we now give descriptions from a longer forty-second episode in the recording of the quartet Ruby, Paul, Dawn, and Pearl described earlier (see Figure 3.5):

> PASSAGE 6. *Dawn looks down at Pearl's hand and tentatively touches it. Dawn clasps Pearl's fingers and they gaze into each other's faces. Pearl lowers her eyes and looks at Dawn's hand holding her fingers. It is all very gentle. Pearl looks up at Dawn and slowly moves her hand up and away. Dawn continues to look into Pearl's face. Ruby, who has been watching Pearl and Dawn, turns to Paul and vocalizes. Paul turns to look at Ruby. However, Ruby immediately turns back to look and talk to Pearl. She makes a gentle, soft vocalization, but this has the effect of jarring Pearl into the action of turning to look from Dawn to Ruby. Pearl's arm slowly drops away from Dawn as she listens to Ruby. Dawn is listening too, and turns her eyes to Ruby. Ruby, now the focus of both Pearl and Dawn, becomes more heightened in her affect. She vocalizes more loudly saying 'fva, fva, fva . . . ,' bounces in her stroller, and swings her legs up and down. Ruby looks towards the door. She then reaches across to Pearl with her arm outstretched. Pearl sits back in her seat a little. She is still focused on Ruby, but she looks a little taken aback. Dawn who has been looking at Ruby, turns her gaze to Pearl and then back to Ruby. Ruby continues to vocalize towards Pearl.*
>
> *Now Paul, who has been looking at Ruby vocalizing to Pearl, interrupts. He does this by saying 'ah' loudly and then, with a gross trunk movement, looking down and out of the group. After he does this both Ruby and Pearl turn to look at Paul. Ruby looks down at Paul's foot rubbing against hers. Paul makes a few gurgling sounds and his arm reaches out, almost as if reaching out to make contact with Ruby. Dawn who has been looking at Ruby turns her head back to look at Pearl. Pearl and Ruby turn back to look at each other. Paul also looks up to Pearl. Ruby has her arm outstretched to Pearl and Pearl says to her 'der, der, dow'. Pearl then looks across to Paul. Her look to Paul is brief, as Ruby, who briefly glances at the door and then back to Pearl says to Pearl 'oh bub' while clapping her hands together. Ruby then stills herself and listens to Pearl who says to her 'da girr'. Pearl then looks briefly at Paul, who wriggles around in his stroller to turn and look out of the group. She then looks down towards Dawn's feet while saying 'err err her'. Pearl's arm is slightly outstretched towards Dawn. Ruby,*

who looked briefly at Paul while he turned out of the group, looks back to Pearl while she is speaking. Throughout all of this Dawn has been watching Pearl.

The intensity of interchanges continues unabated:

> PASSAGE 7. Now Pearl attends to one of Paul's attempts to engage the attention of the others through a large movement while smiling and vocalizing. But as Paul stops, or gives up, Pearl resumes interaction with Ruby while also engaging in her footsie routine with Dawn. Dawn is looking at Pearl, interested, and seemingly happy enough with the footsie game. Now it seems Pearl is interacting with all three members of the group at the same time. She seems to be calmly managing her presence to all, perhaps having the group linked as 'a group' in her experience.
>
> But it's not enough for Paul, who starts up again after retiring back into his shell. He begins with an element of frustration in his vocalizations, seemingly determined to make a go of it. Pearl looks at his display and Ruby follows her gaze to Paul too. Pearl focuses, pauses then claps her hands once and says 'Da daa?' in a questioning tone. She seems to be calling the group together, aware of the disparate systems developing, using a manner which integrates or represents her involvement with all.
>
> A second later, Paul tries yet again. All three are drawn to his activity, but none are getting involved—indicating some element of resistance, since all are clearly capable of engaging and interacting. Pearl, for example, turns to Ruby and asks 'do door?,' with some implication of puzzlement in her intonation. Perhaps the reliable 'routine' she has developed with Ruby might offer her some resolution to her puzzlement about Paul.
>
> Again, Paul vocalizes, his feet jerking forwards touching Dawn's, and claps his hands. This time Ruby, who is on the verge of developing a continuing interaction with Pearl, and is open to involvement and attentive, hears Paul's clap, and, as if she can't help herself, repeats the clap, and thus is drawn away from Pearl. But Ruby's response is not sustained and fades.

Possibly Ruby is now at some sort of loss to know or understand what is happening, especially outside the comfort zone she has set up with Pearl. If this is true, Ruby's routine with Pearl has firmed up as an interactive sanctuary or secure base which allows her to develop new experiences, including openness to exploration with Paul, rather than a disinterested gaze as seen earlier in the group process.

Throughout this long sequence, we see repetitions of routines that function and develop in different ways. For example: Pearl linking with Dawn; Ruby's linking of Pearl with the door then vocalizing; and Paul's repeated attempts at gaining the attention he seems to need. True to form, Paul repeatedly tries to draw attention to himself by making loud sounds as by clapping and/or large movements such as dramatically turning away from the group. We gain a sense that these 'interruptions' are prompted by Paul seeing growing links between others in the group, whether as twos or threes. In this regard, his interruptions have some of the features described in the psychoanalysis of groups as 'attacks on linking'.[8]

> PASSAGE 8. *Paul is continuing, and they all now watch him. But something's not working for Pearl and she throws herself backwards with a peremptory vocalization. All turn to her—is she thinking the group is getting out of hand, too fragmented, too much altogether?*

The infants are engaged in complex multi-faceted interchanges which have emotional, relational, and durational aspects. They may be seen as a group in an unsurprising way as they connect, express needs, develop routines, and attempt involvement with others. But if we dwell on Pearl here, we must consider that aspect of group life in which someone is able to be engaged in the group for a while, and then 'step back', perhaps aware of the group *as* a group, not just as a set of routines building up.

As the group process develops over time, and the relational complexities owing to its history grow, it would be unsurprising if, from time to time, members tried to escape by turning away, and or, as we sometimes observed, engaging in self-soothing behaviours. Perhaps Paul's twists away from looking 'into' the group may partly result from a sense of being overwhelmed. Alternatively, in Pearl, we have some indication of her as coping with the overload of information consequent upon her seeing the group-as-a-whole. Professional clinicians, asked to comment on the video of this group, quickly characterized Pearl as a 'leader', 'therapist', or 'teacher'—again illustrating the binocularity discussed earlier: Pearl's positioning as a particular *kind* of 'individual' character could only be perceived as such because of the part she played in forwarding the dynamics of the group-as-a-whole.

Further, we suggest Pearl's brief 'stepping back' from the hurly-burly of the group process enabled her to place herself in a new position in relation to her immediate world, potentially a crucial step towards identity or self-formation.[9] In a less obvious way, the group's routines may also function to convert the uncertainty of managing 'too much' information into a form of reliability which can serve as a platform for taking on new meanings. Such an interpretation of this quartet coheres both with traditions stressing the human need *to select* when dealing with 'too much information' in order to be able to act, and with the idea of group members' 'individuating' through their participation in an ongoing group.[10]

These possibilities sharpen our awareness of the poverty of contemporary theorizing of infant social development. The above vignettes point to the need for expanding our imaginations about what it is possible to see in infancy, a task which has a direct bearing both on how we raise our young (Chapter 4) and on how we understand our own humanity.

3.1.6 Work

Infants engage with each other almost continuously when in groups, processing a deluge of social, perceptual, and interactional information, developing significant complexity through their combined actions, all in such a manner as to maintain infant groups *as groups* for many minutes (as mentioned in Chapter 2, the longest-lasting we have observed being twenty-five minutes for an all-infant trio). Normally, babies appear to respond intelligently and constructively to each other's actions. Most notably, one of our studies has shown that babies almost always respond sympathetically to distress expressed by a group member, not only by turning to look at the distressed baby, but by facial expressions (smile or frown), vocalizing, reaching towards, and sometimes touching their upset peer. Furthermore, distressed babies were often comforted by their peers' responses to their distress—they were significantly more likely than chance would predict to regain their equanimity after other group members' interventions.[11]

We often see other kinds of 'inclusive' behaviour in our groups. In Chapter 2 we documented the repeated inclusive overtures from Joe to Mona—of a kind also reported with surprise by Jacqueline Nadel and her colleagues in Paris. For example, in the first quartet discussed above, Clare repeatedly leant towards Paul, then towards Barbie, with her arms wide, and mouth open, linking the other babies in her exploration and enjoyment.

All of this implies that babies *actively work* to maintain the groups of which they form part. Chapter 4 will use observations from within a childcare centre to draw out the implications of the idea that babies in groups 'work'.

3.2 How Numbers Reveal the Groupness of Infant-peer Quartets

While the behaviour we have so far discussed invites multiple interpretations (see Chapter 2.5.2, 'Conjecture and Negotiation'), this is intentional: our descriptions aim at a richness sufficient to convey the complexity and the depth of the significance of what occurs amongst grouped babies. In just a few seconds of careful observation, we find ourselves engaging with a multitude of events and emotions in our very young. But now we step back to provide another avenue into exploring how babies act in groups.

Group processes depend upon forms of engagement that are not just one-to-one but *supra*-dyadic. When social scientists deal with adults, they call the fact that a group has characteristics which go beyond those of its individual members' *groupness* (see Chapter 1.3). We have shown how evidence that babies manifest groupness can be drawn from rich verbal descriptions of infant-peer groups. But can groupness *also* be demonstrated with numerical data?

Several psychologists have begun to argue that it can. Most notably, Elizabeth Fivaz and her colleagues in Lausanne have marshalled evidence which they claim to show infants from birth are endowed with a capacity for 'multi-person intersubjective communication', which develops in parallel with 'dyadic communication'. Yet, when we look at their evidence, it is actually dyadic—because, as discussed in Chapter 2 (Chapter 2.3, 'Beyond one-to-one'), the Fivaz team only count behaviour as 'social' when a baby is looking *directly* at someone else (using foveal gaze). And babies can only look directly at one other person at once, given the triangular set-up used in all recordings of infants in threes. Which raises a puzzle, because three into two won't go. This puzzle is only intensified by the Fivaz team's more recent claim that, using dyadic data, they have shown infants have 'the capacity to *simultaneously* communicate with *two* partners'.

How can babies communicate *with two people at once* when they can only look at one person at once? Fivaz and her colleagues' answer—like other psychologists who make similar claims—is to redefine 'simultaneous' to mean (what seems to us to be) the opposite of simultaneous, that is: as the *successive* production of several behaviours which are aimed *alternately* at two *different* people *over a given time period*. The time period equated with simultaneity ranges from 3 to 30 seconds in different studies.[12]

Data of this kind cannot prove groupness. The idea that simultaneous means 'switching between looking-targets over several seconds' makes no sense. Furthermore, babies look so quickly from one thing to another when they are in an interesting environment that the kind of back-and-forth looking which Fivaz and others call 'simultaneous' might well happen by chance.[13] Hence, we needed to devise a different numerical test of infant groupness.

We set off by borrowing three well-established criteria from adult psychology, wherein groupness is said to be constituted by *proximity*, *similarity*, and *common fate*.[14] Of these, the key element is *common fate*, something defined as the *co-variability in time* of group members' behaviour. 'Common fate' means a group can be shown to exist wherever observers can show that the behaviour of at least three individuals over time varies in such a way that *the contemporaneous behaviour of two or more members can be used to predict the <u>later</u> behaviour of another group member.*

On these grounds, a good test for infantine groupness would be to measure whether, in a group where *similarity* and *proximity* were maximized, the behaviour of two or more members could be used to predict the later behaviour of another infant in the group.[15] The need to maximize *similarity* implies that the best test of groupness would record behaviour in *all-infant* groups—rather than in groups which mix infants and adults—and where babies were approximately the same age. *Proximity* would be ensured by a square seating arrangement where each baby was in touching-distance of its two neighbours (see Figure 3.6).

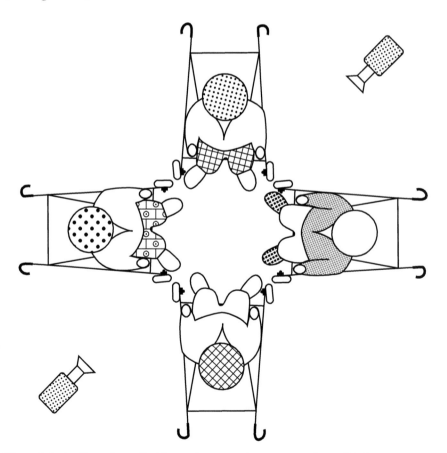

Figure 3.6 Configuration of babies and cameras in our research on all-infant quartets.
Kindly drawn and supplied to the authors by Colwyn Trevarthen.

For our test, we chose to examine gaze behaviour, but to exploit babies' peripheral vision rather than their focal vision (see Chapter 2.3, 'Beyond one-to-one'). Gaze is central to most human social interaction at all ages. The capacity to read others' gaze direction is found in several primate species but is most highly developed in humans.[16] Coding gaze is particularly popular in the study of infant sociability because it provides the simplest way to establish the directionality of an infant's (social) acts, as we have seen.[17] Looking is also one of the first behaviours to come under intentional control. Furthermore, as we noted, gaze-changes are frequent, lending themselves to statistical analysis. However, as discussed, a study which solely considers focal or foveal gaze is tied to a dyadic conception of infant sociability, hence the need to consider babies' peripheral vision.

Before ten months of age, babies' *focal* vision is not fully developed. For example, nine-month-olds in gaze-following tasks can follow someone's head movements, but not their eye movements.[18] Following head movements and other larger-scale postural changes, rather than minute adjustments of the eyeball, shows that young infants predominantly use *peripheral* vision in social situations. By using the wide field of view detectable through their peripheral vision, babies should, at least theoretically, be able to respond to more than one other person at once when seated in a triangle or square. Which gives legs to our research question: can the social behaviour of an infant at Time Q be shown to be influenced by what two or more other group members were previously doing at Time P?

To strengthen our analysis, we used our recordings of groups of four babies, not with trios. Quartets have the advantage of ensuring that mutual gaze between two members does not necessarily entail the exclusion or isolation of the residual member(s), as would be the case in a trio. Quartets also provide a stronger test than trios of the hypothesis that infant sociability is fundamentally dyadic, or, in Bowlby's words, generated by a 'dyadic programme'.[19] Bowlby's dyadic hypothesis would predict that the most frequent forms of sociability in a quartet would involve 'parallel' mutual gaze: whenever two babies link up (focus on each other), the other two—if feeling sociable—should link up with each other in parallel. If infants have a capacity for groupness, on the other hand, we would expect relatively little 'parallel' mutual gaze as compared to coordinated gaze—where two ('two-gaze') or three ('three-gaze') infants look at the fourth group member.

Our results went beyond our expectations. First, we found contrary to the dyadic hypothesis, that there was a high correlation between mutual gaze and coordinated gaze. Secondly, there was a great deal of simultaneous switching (in the same frame, that is, the same 1/25th of a second) between mutual and coordinated gaze. Yet there were *zero* frames where mutual gaze started and coordinated gaze finished or vice versa—a result which has less than one chance in ten thousand of happening by accident. This result suggested that when a baby B returns another baby D's gaze to start a period of mutual gaze— or looks away to end such a period—a third baby A (and often a fourth baby C) is already looking at either B or D (making a 'coordinated' pattern of gaze; see Figure 3.7).

Further analysis showed that coordinated gaze predicted mutual gaze up to a lag of eleven frames (.44 seconds), something which had less than a one in twenty likelihood of occurring by chance. This means that, when two, or three babies are looking at a fourth baby, that baby is likely to look back at one of them. With equal reliability, mutual gaze predicted coordinated gaze for a much longer period, thirty-nine frames (1.56 seconds). This means that when two babies (B and D) look at each other, their mutual interest is likely to attract the attention of one or both the other group members *rather than encouraging the two other members (A and C) to pair off in parallel mutual gaze*. In fact, in the two all-infant quartets we studied for this analysis there was less than half a second of parallel mutual gaze, as against more than three minutes—more than 570 times as much—of mutual gaze plus coordinated gaze (for example, Figures 3.1 and 3.4). Which disproves Bowlby's dyadic hypothesis: that infant social behaviour is generated by a 'dyadic programme' (see Appendix A.2). Conversely, the close ties between mutual gaze and coordinated gaze prove that the social behaviour of eight-month-old babies in all-baby quartets *does* manifest 'groupness' (common fate): what two or more group members are doing at time P strongly predicts what other group members will do at a later Time Q—despite the fact that the babies in our study were free to look anywhere at any time, or to stick with looking at the same thing throughout.

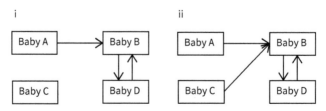

Figure 3.7 Two combinations of a **mutual gaze** (B←→D) **along with** different kinds of **simultaneous coordinated** gaze, namely: on the left side (i) **two** babies, A + D simultaneously engaged in coordinated gaze; and on the right side (ii) **three** babies, A + C + D, simultaneously engaged in coordinated gaze (as in Figure 3.1).
Source: authors' diagram.

3.3 Giving Primacy to Groups

There is a long tradition of research and theorizing by psychologists about sociability in our very young. This includes understandings which work to hamper consideration of the possibility opened up by analyses of infant groups such as this book describes, namely, the possibility that group participation is the starting point for human development. We now briefly discuss three kinds of traditional blinker.

3.3.1 The cognition-first approach

Child psychologists have often taken a cognition-first route to explaining sociability in the first year of life. This means that what each individual baby needs in order to relate to others is to have time to develop some special kind of 'internal', 'in-the-head' representation of other people. For example, the reason that Bowlby held a baby's first attachment only begins to form at around nine months of age was that any kind of *social* relationship first requires that, as he put it, 'a child's cognitive apparatus has matured to a condition in which he [or she] can begin to conceive of absent objects [including people] and search for them'. Bowlby built on this view by proposing that a child can only develop a fully formed attachment to a caring adult by constructing his or her own 'internal working model' of their relationship over the first thirty months of life. Once formed, this cognitive model would underpin the child's social behaviour ever after:

> Towards the end of his first year, a child is busy constructing working models of how the physical world may be expected to behave, how his mother, and other significant persons may be expected to behave, how he himself may be expected to behave, and how each interacts with all the others. Within the framework of these working models he evaluates his situation and makes his plans. And within the framework of the working models of his mother and himself he evaluates special aspects of his situation and makes his attachment plans.[20]

Bowlby's initial proposal was that humans' socio-emotional health depended on babies' inborn drive to develop a self-correcting thermostat-like 'attachment behavioural system'—which has 'proximity to mother' as its set goal. But this has proven unworkable. The aboves claim that the toddler's development of an 'internal working model' of the infant–mother dyad constitute 'primary attachments' now dominates attachment theory, even though evidence for the existence of such invisible constructs remains speculative. In fact, as Ross Thompson observes, the relationship of 'internal working models' to observable child behaviour is typically 'so vaguely defined that it can accommodate nearly any empirical findings'.[21] Nevertheless, attachment researchers continue to see a toddler's construction of a dyadic 'internal working model' of his or her mother-figure as the source of 'peer competence', and indeed all his or her subsequent social relations up into adulthood, including the formation of more or less long-term couples.[22]

A like need for small children to develop their own conceptual apparatus before successfully dealing with other people *as* people is assumed by those who believe that successful social development depends on the child's acquisition of a 'theory of mind'—something first found in three- or four-year-olds. In this theory, to possess a *theory of mind* a child must be keen to, and capable of, working out from another person's behaviour how that person mentally represents reality, including the child themselves. Only then does genuine sociability and communication become possible.[23]

Cognition-first views of infant sociability actually deny young babies are social. Rather, they assume babies are miniature scientists—all human social behaviour being reality-oriented, and getting progressively more so as we mature. They offer no place for the roles played by fantasy, passion, misunderstanding, and self-deception in adult behaviour, including *scientific* behaviour (see Chapter 5). It tallies even less with what we know about young children[24]—a point we will take up shortly.

3.3.2 The 'direct understanding' view

The leading alternative to cognition-first accounts of early social life, like Bowlby's, does not highlight groups. Like Bowlby, it celebrates dyads: Unlike Bowlby, the solo baby is not thought to need to acquire representations of people before socialising with them: the dyadic baby is imagined to be engaged in social life from the start, best evidenced when face to face with an attentive adult. Under these circumstances, babies, we are told, demonstrate that they have an inborn capacity 'directly'—that is, correctly—to apprehend and recognize an adult's 'psychological qualities' and 'personal meanings'.[25] According to this vision, no cognitive models, or internal representations are required when a baby socializes. Rather, any two-person infant–adult interaction will entail that *both* participants immediately grasp the psychological qualities of the other person.[26] In short, babies are born with the ability 'to share and participate in another person's feelings and thoughts'.[27]

There are several problems with this view. Most confronting is the widespread existence of human misunderstanding, even between people well-disposed to each other—because, once admitted, the possibility of misunderstanding must haunt analysis of any conversation. Unfortunately, we need not seek far to find evidence for miscommunication, whether in politics or everyday life, in literature, or in psychotherapy. Just the reverse. One well-known philosophy of language questions whether *any* utterance can ever be transparent—to the speaker, let alone anyone else—a position also familiar to anyone who has delved into the writings of psychoanalysts.[28] Just as any postcard may miscarry, so any meaning is at risk of 'failing to arrive' intact, always requiring interpretation, and hence being open to misconstrual, overdetermination, and indeterminacy.[29] (We have already touched on the provisional quality of interpretation; see Chapter 2.5.2).

Another way of stating the problem of assuming that, when engaged in conversation-like behaviour, infants are 'understanding' their mothers is that, like the cognition-first approach, it ignores the complexity of babies' engagements with others. We only have to allow babies a fantasy life, or the possibility of motivations other than gaining a grasp of '*the* personal significance' of what their counterpart is doing—as if there were always only *one* such significance—and the very idea of a baby *directly* understanding another person falls apart. As it turns out, all the evidence used to support the 'direct understanding' view of infant–adult sociability turns out to fit better with the view that babies' attraction to interacting with people like their mothers results from them enjoying a sense of empowerment and control from seeing their actions reflected back 'at twice their natural size' by the m/other—as we discuss in this book's Appendix (A.1; see also Chapter 1.11).

3.3.3 Starting from groups

Various social psychologies of adulthood give primacy to groups over individuals. Freud's origin story for the Oedipus complex was based on the view that 'the oldest human psychology is group psychology'.[30] He found this view in *The Descent of Man* by Charles Darwin, whose approach to human psychology was built out from his observation that humans are among the most social of animals. Darwin explained all our most human attributes—culture, rationality, language, conscience, moral action, aesthetic taste, racial feeling—as consequences of the fact that human beings' primary evolutionary environment has not been a physical environment but a social environment: our ancestors first and foremost had to adapt to a social life organized by the expectations and customs of the relatively small and cohesive home-group, clan, or tribe of conspecifics into which each was born. Hence, we get Darwin's telling suggestion that, for the ancestral human child, group belonging would trump the importance of dyadic baby-mother bonds (see Chapter 1.8).[31]

Twentieth-century psychology spawned several more whole-of-group treatments of adult social behaviour, amongst the better-known being: Kurt Lewin's (1936) 'field theory' and Siegmund Foulkes' (1946) 'group analysis' (both drawing on so-called Gestalt psychology); Bion's (1961) analysis of experiences in psychotherapy groups; and Bruce Tuckman's (1965) four-step sequence for how small-scale problem-solving groups typically develop (forming, storming, norming, performing). Of these, the first two largely take the group as *an environment for individuals* (and their perceptions), individuals remaining the chief focus (as in Gestalt psychology).[32] And Tuckman's model, while not refuted, has been significantly qualified by four decades of subsequent research which have shown the great complexity of group dynamics as compared to the four-step Tuckman model.[33] In contrast, Bion's approach treats humans primarily as 'group animals', and capable of 'supra-individual' engagement.[34] Hence, his model provides a possible starting-point for our discussion of babies in groups.

Of course, there already are infant psychologies which claim to be supra-individual: most notably attachment theory, intersubjectivity theory, and Vasu Reddy's second-person approach (see Appendix).[35] But none of these countenance the possibility that humans are what Bion calls 'group animals' from babyhood on. All begin dyadically. And when, from time to time, psychologists call for scientific thinking about infants to move 'beyond the dyad', they do not reference the fact that babies can participate in groups, but the fact that babies' social lives demonstrably involve people other than mothers: siblings, fathers, grandparents, peers, and caregivers.[36] This blindness to groupness means critics of *existing* dyadic formulations *remain dyadic*, typically proposing that a baby must have 'multiple' dyadic attachments if the baby has several significant others in his or her life.[37] Even Michael Lewis' treatments of babies' participation in what he calls 'social networks'—something comprising a baby's dealings with all its significant others: parents, grandparents, educators, siblings, etc.—remain dyadic.[38] Lewis does ponder the need to theorize what he calls the 'indirect effects' of 'direct' (dyadic) interactions, namely, 'those effects that occur in the presence of the child, but that do not focus on the child'. Yet his examples of *indirect effects* are *themselves* dyadic: 'identification, observational, vicarious and incidental learning, imitation, or modelling'.[39] Lewis never countenances the possibility that babies—when 'in the presence' of several others—might interact *directly* with several of those 'others' at the same time.

3.4 Discussion

Favouring a broad range of methods, theories, cultural belief systems, and ideologies, researchers converge from many directions on the need to understand how infants engage with their companions. Yet, despite many contentions, and contrasting conclusions, a widely held belief amongst English-speaking psychologists, clinicians, allied health professionals, and educationalists, is that humans start out as dyadic creatures. On this basis, it is often said that throughout life, mental health and well-being rests, above all, on the quality of each infant's first one-to-one attachment relationship, formed with a mother figure, in the first years of life. While a comprehensive review of the relevant research shows that this belief lacks a scientific foundation (see Appendix A.2), its popularity and persistence, *despite* that lack, attest all the more to the power of the cultural movement or 'structure of feeling' it epitomizes (see Chapter 5.3 and 5.5).[40]

Listen for a moment to the eminent attachment advocate, historian, and psychotherapist Brett Kahr, consultant editor to the journal *Attachment*:

> In a career which spanned over six decades, John Bowlby succeeded in demonstrating, beyond all doubt,[41] that mental health—our greatest prize—derives from consistent, reliable, and tender attachment relationships between infants and their caregivers, and that mental illness—our greatest tragedy—stems not necessarily from our genetic, biochemical, or neurophysiological endowments, but rather, from parental attacks, abandonments, and impingements. Bowlby's paradigm, now known as attachment theory, deserves a place in the history of medicine, in the history of psychology, in the history of science, and in the history of humanity, as one of the greatest achievements, on a par, I wish to suggest, with the art of Leonardo da Vinci, the music of Wolfgang Amadeus Mozart, and the nonviolent militarism of Mohandas Gandhi. For, in Bowlby's work, we find that the roots of depression and anxiety, neurosis and delinquency, alcoholism, and anorexia, can all be traced to deficiencies and ruptures in the security of the earliest bond between a vulnerable infant and his or her primary caretakers.[42]

While Kahr's tribute may sound to some overblown, there are strong cultural and sentimental imperatives for the continued celebration of Bowlby's transformation of scientific thinking about babies and young children as being creatures who have *their own* emotional needs—an insight strenuously contested by some academic and clinical psych-professionals up through the 1950s.

Amplifying the cultural success of attachment theory are several more strands of professional practice which extend 'dyadism' far beyond issues of babies' innate need for protection against 'risk of danger' with which attachment theory was first designed to deal.[43] For example, as seen earlier in this chapter, dyadism continues to shape the methods of recording, the selection of evidence, and the theory underpinning the current science of early infant communication and sociability. We have seen too how even such trailblazers of research on babies in groups as Jacqueline Nadel and Elizabeth Fivaz picked *dyadic* gaze-based measures to analyse their data.[44] One might conclude, therefore, that bewitchment by the Madonna-like image of the infant–mother bond has such cultural and affective power that scientists never think to raise the question whether babies have a capacity for supra-dyadic group interaction.

This conclusion chimes with our own experience: scientists' adherence to a dyadic view of human beginnings expresses strong emotional investments. Thus, in this chapter, we have tried to solve what might seem at first to be a descriptive or logical problem: the overwhelming complexity implied by our sense of *seeing too much* going on within baby fours. In discussing this sense, we have noted that, unlike the dynamics of trios, the dynamics of foursomes do not dovetail with familiar cultural scripts. This is a telling cultural blindness, given the extent to which modern humans work, live, and play in groups larger than three. And surely, for anyone who has several similar-age grandchildren, or spends time in the babies' room at a childcare centre, babies interacting in groups of four or more make a familiar scene. Yet, despite this, psychologists still prove unable to construct theories which can predict or explain how infants and very young children interact with each other and participate in groups in meaningful ways.[45]

Such unthinkability sprang to life for us at a conference in Leipzig in 2011. We were billed to give a talk in which we had undertaken to show an audience of group psychoanalysts excerpts from our films of infant-peer quartets. The films were at first watched with what seemed to us an encouragingly rapt attention. However, as our discussion of the baby quartet progressed, mutterings and murmurs rose to exclamations of shock and incomprehension, capped by one group therapist's dramatic blurt: 'This is not happening!' On another occasion, a leading Australian psychiatrist warned us that our recordings of all-infant groups were 'unethical', because we were 'separating' the babies from their mothers—a form of ethics which would presumably also preclude toilet breaks for any mother home alone with her bub.

These uncomprehending responses highlight the almost-visceral challenges many researchers and clinicians must overcome when watching infants with others before they can seriously and explicitly *conceptualize* the fact that there are group phenomena at play. Parents and grandparents would hardly be surprised to see several babies interacting together, or a baby actively participating in the melee of a family at mealtime.[46] Casual asides in the professional literature likewise confirm the obviousness of infant groupness, albeit without seeking backup from published research and without prompting any theoretical accommodation. For instance, as early as 1984, David Perry and Kay Bussey's book, *Social Development*, was noting that 'children's interest in their peers begins at a few months of age', going on:

> When babies are allowed to interact with each other in a relaxed situation (with mothers present), they in fact show more interest in each other than in their mothers. Their interactions tend to be positive and reciprocal rather than characterised by strife.

Even here, the parenthetical 'with mothers present' implies a nod to the primacy of dyadic attachment—though, had they checked, Perry and Bussey would have found evidence that the presence of mothers often *impedes* interactions between infants and their peers.[47]

The profound cultural momentum behind the dyadic view of infants' social capacities has had a powerful flow-on effect in moulding national regulations for childcare around the world, and in shaping clinical practice. These are both large topics, for which the discovery of groupness in infancy has far-reaching implications—as we go on to show in Chapter 4 on childcare, and in Chapter 5 on clinical practice. But our findings also cast light on assumptions made in the social psychology of groups.

For example, it is widely assumed that small groups of adults form to achieve shared goals: to design a new product; cut down a tree; raise children; enjoy a holiday; get drunk; commit a crime; or solve a problem. On these grounds, Bion defined a 'work group' as the form of interpersonal and emotional organization that leads to the achievement of the 'specific task' that a group has come together to solve. Work-group activity, adds Bion, typically uses verbal means and takes 'a rational or scientific approach' to the solution of problems. At the same time Bion's work shows how the task-oriented activity of a small group may be impeded, undermined, or sometimes aided by another kind of activity—which he variously calls 'primitive', 'emotional', partly or wholly 'unconscious'—and which typically employs non-verbal methods of communication.[48] A similar division of group activities has been proposed in social psychology. Some group activities lead towards the completion of 'instrumental' goals. Others lead towards group integration and cohesion, that is 'socio-emotional' or 'expressive' goals.[49]

From the observations discussed in this chapter, we conclude that groups made up of babies, aged nine months and younger, clearly demonstrate the kind of activities which are aimed at achieving socio-emotional goals relating to group cohesion. Babies in our infant trios and quartets cannot easily be described as having 'instrumental' goals or as displaying work-group activities.[50] Their lack of obvious *instrumental* work achievements may partly result from the situation we designed to collect the data discussed in this chapter, which meant the babies could not move around, and had no toys. For this reason, we will reserve discussion of infants' 'instrumental' work-group activities for Chapter 4, which builds on observations and films of babies' group activities in a far richer environment—a high-quality childcare centre.

3.5 Conclusion

This chapter used detailed descriptions of interactions between eight-month-old babies to open a window onto the complexity which constitutes preverbal infants' social lives once they are given the opportunity to form groups. This complexity goes considerably beyond one-to-one interaction—as we have shown both through narrative and numerical analysis. It likewise goes beyond existing explanations for infant sociability: our analyses of recordings of all-infant quartets prove babies have a capacity for group interaction that cannot be reduced to talk of cognitive representations, or attachment, or dyadic conversations, or jealousy, or inclusion and exclusion. How babies' capacity for groupness may manifest itself in their everyday lives—outside the laboratories in which we made the films discussed so far—is the question we take up next, in Chapter 4.

4
Making Visible Ordinary Groupness

Figure 4.1 'What can we see in the drain? Is there any water down there?'
Source: authors' photo.

Just as early childhood and education policies from around the world instruct educators to feed infants one-to-one in fossilized tribute to a century of struggles over hygiene, attachment discourse can throw a dated and dysfunctional shadow over the lives of babies enrolled in group education and care. By way of contrast, this chapter illustrates what happens as group-based practices are introduced into the education of our very young in two early childhood education services located in inland Australia—owned and managed by one of this book's authors, Matthew Stapleton. Matt has carefully documented the introduction of a group-based regime into his centres over the past two years (e.g. Figure 4.1). His initiative has revealed forms of group-based enjoyment, learning, comfort and creativity in infants and educators which had hitherto been side-lined by the policy-driven imperative to cultivate *one-to-one* infant-educator relationships. In particular, Matt's centres highlight how different practices of teaching and care can facilitate or curtail *infants' work*. Which introduces a framework for understanding the collective agency of babies that has previously been reserved for language-users. Once we give them the opportunity, groups of pre-verbal infants or toddlers will, unprompted, undertake the creative work of forging and maintaining group cohesion, as well as applying themselves to tasks they find amusing or important.

From such evidence, we conclude that organizing childcare and early education through groups can lead to happier children and better atmospheres at centres, plus reduced and more rewarding workloads for educators. All of which presents tantalizing challenges to current conventions and to policy-makers, as well as raising new questions about how children develop, and new themes for future research.

4.1 Introduction to a Successful Early Childhood Education Centre

Since 2008 Matt has been CEO of Centre Support, a business which provides resources and professional development to the early childhood sector across Australia.[1] In 2013 he was invited by researchers in early education from Charles Sturt University to be the industry partner in the application for an Australian Research Council 'linkage' grant—designed to bring academics and industry together to solve real-world problems. Academic members of the research group included Professors Sumsion and Harrison, who are lead authors of the Australian government's

'Belonging, Being and Becoming: The Early Years Learning Framework', which, in 2012, became Australia's first national framework for early childhood education.[2] The grant itself was awarded after a competitive process requiring that university researchers integrate the practical knowledge and evidence held by a non-university industry into a research project, as well as provide practical research outcomes of use to the industry partner. And that is what happened.[3]

The successful project, 'Babies and Belonging in Early Childhood Settings', included university partners from a range of intellectual traditions within education and psychology. Matt was particularly confronted by having to consider the new ways of thinking about infant development advocated by university researcher Ben Bradley, whose research included the work with Jane Selby described in previous chapters. Ben and Jane's emphasis on groups felt challenging because Matt had become inured to policy-drenched interpretations of what *should* happen to infants in group care, when seen as primarily revolving around the formation of two-way infant–adult bonds. Matt recognized an irony here, because early education centres, like schools, function through *group* organization. Matt saw that ideas about the group-basis of development would require him to extend the range of processes that needed covering in the training of educators to ready them to embrace practices promoting groupness when working in group-settings with groups of the very young.

While his work with Centre Support evolved, Matt came to own two Early Childhood Education and Care (ECEC) centres located in a large regional town (population 43,500), a six-hour drive from the state's capital, Sydney. The 2021 census data shows slightly more than half (51.9%) of the town's residents are female. The median age, at 36 years, is slightly younger than the national average of thirty-eight. People aged 0–14 constitute 21.2% of the population (compared to 18.7% nationally). And a far higher proportion of the town's citizens are Aboriginal or Torres Strait Islander (14.6%) than is the case nationally (3.3%). The median age of Aboriginal and Torres Strait Islander residents is 21 years.

The longer-running of Matt's two services is relatively large, providing 100 places in six rooms. Two infant rooms hold twelve babies each, each room requiring three educators to meet the government's ratio-regulations of one educator to four babies. There are two toddler rooms holding, on average, thirty-six children aged between two and three years. The educator-ratio required for toddlers is one educator for five children. As the ages rise the ratios change. One educator for ten children suffices for the three-to-five-year groups. So in each of these two rooms, of twenty older children, there are two educators. To maintain these ratios, educators are employed to cover lunch breaks and programming times. In all Matt employs thirty-six educators at his older service, mostly on a full-time basis.

Like most other long day care services there are many new young staff, most of whom are working towards qualifications ('Certificate III') in Early Childhood Education and Care. Certificate III is the minimum requirement to gain employment in an approved childhood setting and is regulated through the Australian Qualification Framework. Every three years, Matt's centres are, like all Australian centres, required to participate in the Australian National Quality Standards (NQS) rating system, last being rated in 2022—when, as with 87% of Australian services, his service was reaccredited without demur.[4]

4.2 Managing Infants at Mealtimes

Matt's interest in groups has led him to devise new practices for his centres. Matt summarizes his early thinking:

> Ordinarily, there are occasional moments of difficulties and stress when working with young children, especially at mealtimes. In 2020 I decided to work in a particular room of 7- to 15-month-olds, to investigate what might be improved. The current practice in my centre was to have the children sitting in highchairs in a horseshoe shape with the children facing in.
> Other centres either use this format or use a line of seats.

Whichever setup is traditionally used, highchairs are spaced far enough apart to ensure children do not share food (Figure 4.2). This is to maintain hygiene standards set by Australia's NQS. These *Standards* require educators to assist each infant to eat, usually by the educator spooning each child's food into each child's mouth from each child's individual bowl with each child's individual spoon. This is often difficult to achieve, so a juggling act ensues, with educators attempting to meet the demands of several hungry infants at once, swapping bowls and spoons, while also trying to take the time to encourage a less enthusiastic infant to try what is offered. The NQS formally require educators to be vigilant, which means sitting closely and being attentive *to each* individual infant. During this time another educator, is in the kitchenette preparing bottles of formulated milk for settling the infants for sleep after the mealtime has finished.

This is a demanding process, made more difficult by the fact that once a child has finished eating, they often quickly become disgruntled or start

Figure 4.2 Lined up for mealtime in a regional NSW centre.
Source: authors' photo.

crying and need to be removed from the highchairs. The length of time children spend in the chairs lasts anything from three minutes to ten, but never any longer than it takes for the child to finish eating.

Matt continues:

> I was reminded of Ben and Jane's research into infants, and their method of seating them in a circle to interact independently of adults. I said, 'let's push the children together in groups of threes and fours in the highchairs at mealtimes'. I proceeded to show the educators Ben and Jane's research, including the images of three infants in strollers we discussed in Chapter 2. I briefly described what discoveries had been made, but basically finished the conversation with the request just to try out grouping the highchairs, while observing what happens, and then to 'take some notes of what you find interesting'. In that way the educators could think through for themselves the logic of the suggestion—inviting the educators to do some informal research.

4.2.1 Observations by educators after changing infant mealtime organization

Matt continues his account:

> Sophie and Roxie, the diploma-qualified room leaders, took up my suggestion by placing the infants together in groups of four or five (Figure 4.3).

Figure 4.3 In groups at mealtime.
Source: authors' photo.

Sophie: *When placed in groups in the highchairs, the babies take the time to look at each other and I've noticed they are using a lot of nonverbal language, they giggle at each other. While waiting for the meal, one child Charlotte would bang her drink bottle and all the children in the group of four would bang their drink bottles too, but then Charlotte would look over to the other group of children in their own group of 3–4 and encourage them to bang their bottles. When food is introduced, more interesting things occur. Leo is a good example; he doesn't eat many things at home, but in the group, he eats everything. Jack picks his food up out of his bowl and makes 'mmmm' sounds and says it to his friends. Amelia likes talking to her friends; she holds her food in front to show the other children what she has. We introduced bowls for the children to eat from, then once they were used to the bowls, we introduced spoons; some children were curious to watch others how to use the spoon. For example, Mia rotated the bowl to remove the food, then Leo copied her actions. That was interesting, it was like Mia was showing Leo how to use the spoon and bowl. But most of all, we now have time to do other things in the room, as they sit in the group for up to thirty minutes with very few interactions with adults. It's definitely making our jobs easier.*

> *The sandwich story*—the first time I saw this I was shocked. Today's lunch was sandwiches with different toppings, some vegemite[5] and others ham and cheese. When the children were given the sandwiches, they looked at one another and opened the bread to show each other what was inside the sandwich; when one child had something different to the others they looked visibly shocked.

Roxie, room leader and educator:

> There are more interactions when they are in the groups. There is usually one that is first to do something, hit their hands on the highchair table like a drum, it's like they are the head or leader then the others follow. We place the children in different groups, so they are getting different views from the different angles they are placed in. We deliberately put children together in different ways to make sure they form other friendships than the children they normally like to play with. In the smaller groups, there is a lot more talking, or really babbling. (If they are in too big a circle then there is just more screaming.) In the mornings we might have a child who is upset when they first come in, and if we are having morning tea, we place the upset child with the group in the highchairs. The upset child calms downs, mostly straight away.[6]

The following is an example of what is written by Sophie and then shared with the families of the children in the room (through a digital social media platform). Such writings are formal requirements for the documentation of 'learning and assessment' under the Early Years Learning Framework—the national framework for early child education and care as approved by the Australian government. They are known as Learning Outcomes, and are thus marked with 'LO' below.

> *Following on from our group experiences during mealtimes, Sophie, Lucy, and Macey grouped the children together as per our updated daily routine and noticed all kinds of interactions between the children as they were enjoying their meals.*
>
> *Patrick, Jack, and Leo sat together, happily looking and smiling at one another before Lucy and Macey offered a serving of lunch. Together the boys dug in with hungry tummies while they looked up at each other in between bites.*
>
> *Isla, Lucas, and Jack (aged up to thirteen months) were grouped together before they were offered a bowl of food. Lucas expressed some distress when he was initially placed in the highchair, though as soon as Isla and Jack were placed into the highchair beside him, he calmed down, before taking a deep breath in, and then out—as he reached for his drink bottle to take a sip.*

Once served their lunch, Isla and Jack scooped their hands into their bowls finding sausages and vegetables. Isla took a sausage in her hand, holding it up to show Lucas and Jack before placing it into her mouth. 'Is that yummy Isla, do you have sausages at home?' Sophie asked. 'Have a taste, Jack,' Sophie explained as she pointed to his bowl.

As Sophie began to walk away, Lucas began to cry in an attempt to communicate his need for comfort and assistance. Sophie approached Lucas, acknowledging and responding sensitively to children's cues and signals (LO: 1.1). She picked Lucas up, letting him know that he was okay while giving him a reassuring cuddle. Sophie then offered Lucas a bottle before his lunch, hoping to offer him a chance to re-calm his emotions before placing him back into his highchair for some lunch.

Meanwhile, Mia, Grace, and Amelia were placed together into a group of three to enjoy their lunch. Together the girls shared their lunch in a quiet, calm, and relaxing manner. The three girls must have been hungry. Mia had a certain technique of scooping the food from one side of her bowl, before spinning it around and loosening the food inside to allow for herself to pick it up easier. Grace watched as Mia did this and was able to follow her lead, doing the same thing. This showed Grace's ability to mirror, repeat, and practice the actions of others, either immediately or later. (LO: 4.3)

Throughout our lunchtime groups, and the experiences—or rather the interactions—that unfold, the children are engaging in learning relationships (LO: 4.4) as they learn from one another just by looking at each other's actions and following them on as they use the processes of play, reflection, and investigation to solve problems (LO 4.4). This is an evident outcome, especially from the children learning from watching each other using their utensils and picking this skill up just from observation or simply from Mia showing Grace her bowl technique today.

Placing these children in groups is working so well to keep mealtimes interesting, new, and fun, as the children learn new things from others.

4.3 Filming Mealtimes

After a few months of the children being placed in a group at every mealtime, Matt began to document the infants more closely. By all accounts mealtimes were working well in their new group formations, so he then added cameras to capture the new setup. Four GoPro cameras were put on tripods and the tripods placed directly behind the highchair of each of the infants in a group of four. The camera lens was positioned facing down to capture the child directly opposite. The cameras carried wide-angle lenses so could capture the children sitting at the sides of the target child, as will be seen later (Figure 4.4).

The filming started just before or while children were placed in the highchairs. The person setting up the cameras left the room so as to leave just the children and regular educators together.

The filming continued until the last child was removed from their highchair. The videos were loaded into a video editing software program (Adobe Premier Rush) and edited to ensure all four lots of footage started at the same time. This process made it easier to identify a time-point, on one camera, which related to the time-point footage that was taken from a different angle to help see what was occurring. This process was valuable in identifying the expressions and reactions of other children taken from another angle to assist with analysis.

4.3.1 Better use of educators' time

Matt continues: We now look in more detail at one unexpected gain from the grouping of babies in highchairs at mealtimes: that educators spend far less time having to control and feed several children one-to-one and so can get on with other tasks while still facilitating the babies as required. (Refer to video-excerpts at babiesingroups.com.)

Sophie had noted earlier that educators are not always needed when young children are in groups at mealtime. Thus in the accompanying video link (see Endnote 7), we can see the children are in a mealtime group for 18 minutes and 20 seconds. Once the four children (ages 12 to 15 months) are placed in the highchairs, the educator Sophie interacts with them for a total time of 2 minutes and 36 seconds. After 6:35 seconds of filming, Sophie brings out the bibs and bowls of fruit and yoghurt. The bibs are placed on each child, then the bowl of food is placed on the highchair tray in front of each infant. Sophie rotates each bowl and positions the spoon for the child. Sophie returns to the kitchenette to retrieve the next bowls and repeats the process until all have their food. During this time Sophie's verbal communication with the children includes:

> 'Are we ready?', 'Good job using your spoon, Jack', 'Good job, Henry'.

The process of doing this for all four children takes 1 minute and 51 seconds. Sophie then returns to the kitchenette. Sophie later comes back from the kitchen with a banana; she brings it to the children, peels it, and breaks a piece off and places it on the bowl of the children while saying:

'Banana.'

This process of serving food to the children and interacting has taken a total of 2 minutes 15 seconds. Sophie continues to walk past the children from time to time. She looks at the children and each pass takes between 3–4 seconds. There's no verbal communication. Meanwhile, she is involved in doing various forms of practical work, such as re-positioning furniture or arranging and sorting paperwork.

Later Sophie gives the children a biscuit each, again no talking, and the process takes 11 seconds from leaving the kitchenette to returning to the kitchenette. Then a cough from Jack alerts Sophie and she moves towards the children and asks, 'Okay?' while she moves out of the kitchenette. She adds, 'few more bites'. Jack holds his biscuit towards Sophie and Sophie responds with words, but due to Covid-19 workplace requirements Sophie is wearing a mask and the words are inaudible. Sophie then moves away from the group. Sophie does make eye contact with the children when walking by.

The infants have successfully eaten their food.

Meanwhile, as Sophie earlier remarked, the educators 'have time to do other things in the room' as the infants sit happily in their group 'for up to thirty minutes with very little adult interaction'.

4.3.2 What are the children doing?

Now we will examine a group mealtime in more detail (as depicted in the linked video clips). At first, we see that the four children are clapping and smiling at each other, banging the surface of the highchair trays, and sharing an interest in the new cameras' positions behind each child, with children pointing and attempting to draw the others' attention to the cameras (see Figure 4.4 for seating arrangements). There is eating and a lot of staring at each other while eating the food. Their feet are active most of the time. There is friendly interchange and teasing using food, with lots of reciprocal laughter. The children take turns at making large body movements such as twisting, clapping, and rocking in the chair towards each other while laughing. At the same time, they each have their own ways of managing the food as it arrived. Jack likes to use his spoon—the gestures are there—spoon into bowl then to mouth, but not always arriving with food. Harper immediately emptied the contents of her bowl onto her tray. After some time, including holding the bowl to her face as though the food might be drunk in or magically enter her mouth, she eventually turns the bowl right side up again, puts food back in and starts again, this time, taking the food out of

Making Visible Ordinary Groupness   83

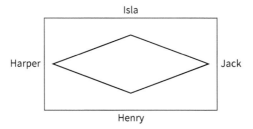

Figure 4.4 Seating arrangements for Isla, Jack, Harper, and Henry.
Source: authors' image.

the bowl to eat. When bowls are emptied, they are pushed off the highchair onto the floor and food is often thrown onto the floor which creates looking down towards the floor by the child who has pushed the bowl off or thrown the food and, interestingly, the other children will look towards the floor appearing to look for the item.

The typical mealtime is replete with incidents and interchanges, some of which may challenge how we think about infants, as we shall see.

Prior to the food being served, as we have mentioned, the cameras created a lot of interest for the children. We carefully examined their exploration of these new objects. They often looked directly at the camera opposite themselves. When viewing the footage, we found that one camera may show that a child is looking *towards* the camera to the side, and then, when we looked at the footage from the camera that is being gazed at, we saw the child was looking directly into that camera, not just looking loosely 'in the direction of' the camera.

In sequence—from which the six images in Figure 4.5 are taken—Henry is the first child placed in the highchair, Jack is the second child and it is he who (at 1.33) notices the cameras and tripods, looking at each of the three most easily visible to him. When Sophie places Isla into her chair, Jack is looking at Henry's (at 2.36) camera. He focuses intently several times at the alternate cameras, then (at 2.44), he looks away from Henry's, sighs once, and then looks back again at the fascinating objects above Henry, and behind Harper's empty chair (2.48). At the same time, he is monitoring Sophie's movement, one time vocalizing while directly looking into her face as she seats Isla. There are two themes going on here: the new cameras, and Sophie's actions in preparation for mealtime.

Sophie moved away to collect the fourth child. Isla looks with interest at Harper's camera on her right, also expressing her agitation while waiting for food—making body movements, banging her tray, and kicking her legs up and down vigorously while making excited screechy noises. She watches Sophie in the distance, seeing her as she returns with Harper. Isla is quietened now and

Image 1: Isla (sitting directly ahead) looks at the camera above Jack (right of image).

Image 2: Isla (directly ahead) looks at the camera above Harper (left of image).

Image 3: Isla (directly ahead) looks at the camera above Henry (foreground of image).

Image 4: Isla (directly ahead) looks at the camera sitting above her (midround of image).

Image 5: Isla (sitting directly in front of the camera) gains the attention of the group and points to the camera above Jack (right of image).
Source: authors' photos.

Image 6: Harper (sitting left of image) points to the camera above Jack (right of image).
Figure 4.5 Six images illustrating the infants' interest and discoveries around the camera.

knows what should happen. She points (at 3.13) to Harper's chair. Henry also is attentive and points at Sophie and Harper (at 3.08) as they walk towards the group. Earlier, Henry had also been interested in examining the cameras.

Each second seems to provide an event, shared or otherwise. At this stage, we can identify themes in the group. There appears to be a shared awareness of the cameras. In addition to the joint interest in the cameras, there's also an awareness of Sophie, and the process of placement of the fourth infant prior to eating. While commenting on the themes enacted or experienced in the same time frame, we also noticed that the interest in the cameras held yet more complexity.

Thus, at 2.57 minutes into filming, Isla looked at the camera above the chair which would be Harper's, before Harper was placed there. Then, at 2.63, Isla looks at Jack's camera, then immediately at Harper's (now present) camera. Sophie is walking past Isla back to the kitchenette after seating Harper, and claps as she passes Isla. Isla notices this, claps herself, and turns around and looks carefully at the camera behind her (3.49). Harper and Henry also join in to form a clapping game and then a banging game with vocalizations. Turning back to the group, Isla joins in the banging tray game. But she stops to look again at Henry's camera, and although Henry is right into the clapping/vocalization game, Isla takes no notice of this and remains quiet. She is not joining in, instead, looking contemplatively, she turns again and points up at her own camera at 4.09. At 4.20 there are further quiet moments for Isla and this seems to quieten the group for a few seconds, then at 4.26, Harper starts banging and vocalizing. At the same moment, Jack points at Isla's camera. At 4.40, Harper, who has been moving around in her chair, catches sight of her own camera. She looks at it briefly, then continues with the banging/vocalization game. Isla is joining in again, making banging and 'dah, dah, dah' noises with the others. At 4.43 she stops to point at Jack's camera while looking at Harper, who also then looks and points at it (4.47), quietening. They study it. Then Harper gets back to the game, Isla remaining thoughtful, pointing at Harper's camera and vocalizing (5.02). At 5.05 she vocalizes again and points at Henry's camera, then at Jack's again. At 5.08 she is distracted by Harper looking down at the floor between them. She remains thoughtful until, at 5.18, she waves at her sister, who is looking in at her and her group through the large window nearby. For a short time, the cameras are no longer of interest and all four children have turned to acknowledge Isla's older sister in the window.

By 5.32 Isla is back to pointing at the cameras.

4.3.3 Understanding what we are seeing

When the children are first placed in the highchairs the novelty of the cameras interests them. Each child looks at the camera above the child in front, then to the left and right of them, sometimes followed by looking behind themselves to see a camera. These sequences lend themselves to an interpretation of the kind: '*You* have a camera, *you* have a camera, *you* have a camera ... Do *I* have a camera?'

There is significant complexity in this short interchange between the children. We consider that being in a group context allowed or afforded the cognitive and relational capacities demonstrated, capacities touching on self-representation, analogical thinking, and communication skills.[7] We may have here a methodological paradigm to add to early childhood research traditions. The action of Isla re-alerts others to their cameras after she sees her own camera, demonstrating that she knows that they are the same as her and that 'we all have a camera'. These actions demonstrate a form of self-awareness—and a form of group awareness—both of which would be thought to be occurring several years 'too early' by many child psychologists, as these children range from 12 months to 15 months of age.[8] These grouped babies also demonstrate a group kind of 'other-awareness' (you are all like me) which is new to the psychology of babies.

4.4 Complexity

What we have described looks like a process of group formation, facilitated by the capacity of 'knowing together' based on a common ground of shared intentionality, cooperation, and meaning-making. An indicative example is when someone gains the group's attention by banging the top of their tray and pointing. In the sequence described above, there are multiple systems of collective significance. There seem to be layers of meaning to the groupness on display here. We have, for example, the 'conversations' about the cameras, teasing about food, joint banging, and vocalizing, as well as the waving sequence embedded in the joint history of knowing about the window and its familiar visitors. Indeed, the themes are less sequential than interwoven. It is *in the midst* of building the significance and joint enjoyment of the cameras, that the babies illustrate their commonplace acknowledgement of both, recognizing the toddler on the other side of a nearby window while playing outdoors—a familiar view of a familiar companion—and, of Hadley preparing their meals. We have an overlapping of themes and stories warranting multiple viewings. There is no single narrative to capture all that we can see (e.g. see Chapter 3.3.1).

In appreciating a multiplicity of group themes, we remember how individual infants, as shown in Chapter 3, easily interact with more than one other group-member at the same time, illustrating the multiplicity of 'routines' simultaneously at play. Which raises questions about how integration occurs—within the group and within the individual babies—how linkages are made, and about how 'containment' can be understood. For the infants, as individuals and as a group, prove able to manage disparate themes at the same time. The cameras are not forgotten during the waving theme, and the familiarity with the activities outside do not preoccupy them while investigating the cameras. Indeed, other themes are in evidence—around eating, around relating to Sophie, and involving the vocalizations and banging and synchronizing which are at play.

In ethnographic terms, it becomes relatively easy to witness instances of both the group dynamics and the individual management of complexity. Again, there are many stories to emerge from careful observation. For example, how Harper teases Henry with a biscuit, offering it and withdrawing it, delighted with the game (17.14–17.47). And how a child seems to be teaching another how to drink from a bottle. The educators had already noted, above, that infants teach each other, or at least, *try* to teach—as in this instance. In the foursome pictured in Image 1 of Figure 4.6, the baby on the right is Isla, and to her left is baby Daniel. Isla is an experienced bottle drinker and she watches as Sophie gives a drink bottle to Daniel, placing it in his mouth to encourage him. Sophie again presents the bottle in front of Daniel's face and moves it a little to gain his attention. She pauses, but then leaves him with the bottle. Isla, sitting to the child's right, looks at the young baby, holds a drink bottle in front of him with her right hand, and makes 'blah-blah' sounds. After hitting the drink bottle on her highchair tray, she continues to make sounds 'laa loo wha-wha'. Then she picks up her bottle to drink and turns her head to look back at the baby to see if he is watching. When Isla sees that she's being watched, she continues to drink with her head turned, looking to her left at him, head tilted up so he can see the correct use of a drink bottle.

4.5 Calculating the Odds

Our sensitivities to and ideas about the nature of groups need developing when dealing with the very young, partly because most theories of groups like Bion's, assume an ability to talk is needed to define a group's goal. We consider that group formation and group agency are evident in the infant rooms at Matt's centre and in the laboratory studies reported in previous chapters. Without such a sensitivity to group phenomena, adults, and even educators, may impede and disturb ongoing activities of value to infant autonomy and development.[9]

On the attached video-link on this book's website,[10] we can watch a lunchtime when the room's experienced lead educator, Sophie, had started her own

Making Visible Ordinary Groupness 89

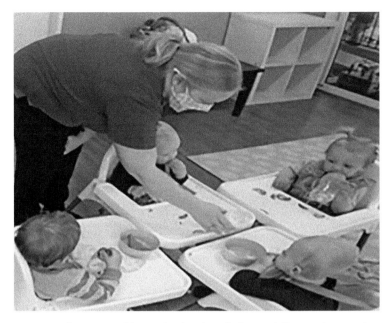

Image 1: Educator Sophie putting bottle to baby Daniel's mouth a couple of times trying to draw attention to the bottle.

Image 2: Meanwhile Isla watches Daniel carefully, twice opening her mouth widely in his direction between continuous drinking.

Image 3: Isla talking to Daniel while banging her bottle on her tray.

Image 4: Isla looking at Daniel, checking he is watching.

Figure 4.6 Four images which show Isla demonstrating to Daniel how to drink from a bottle.

Source: authors' photos.

lunchbreak, which left less experienced educators to deal with the children's meal. These younger educators appear to be less concerned with the evolving group and its social aspects, and more driven by the pragmatic aim of the routine, that is, getting children fed and then moved on as quickly as possible to the next care-phase (which is naptime).

The events we see in this clip illustrate both complex thinking by the young, and how educators may miss what is actually happening from the children's point of view. 12:50 minutes into the recording, twelve-month-old Henry is becoming disgruntled and so is removed from the circle of highchairs and lowered onto the floor of an adjacent play area. At 13:15 he makes his way over to friends on the low meal-chairs against the wall behind the circle of highchairs in order to pick up the dropped bottle of his friend, Jack. He gives it back to Jack and then just hangs out with him for over a minute. At 14:25, educator Rachel removes him from where he is standing, next to his chum, and replaces him in the area designated for after-meal activity. Soon after, at 15:42, Henry starts to make his way back to Jack. But as he crawls towards his friend, he pauses, monitors Rachel's movements, waits for her to walk into the kitchenette, then makes a dash to Jack's table. But he is foiled again when Rachel picks him up and moves him back over to the carpeted area and away from baby Jack.

Calculation, friendship, and a motivation to help Jack do the work of feeding himself: this kind of short vignette cries out for a conceptual overhaul of ideas that make an infant–adult 'safety regulating system' policy's guiding star. Given a safe, rich, and free social environment, infants step into a range of stories as agents, curious and responsive.

4.6 Out of the Highchairs into the Room

Sophie illustrates group learning in one of her 'learning stories'. The writing down of learning stories for communication to parents by educators is a requirement of Australia's Early Years Learning Framework (EYLF). Prior to her account, during the previous week, educators Rachel and Gina had discovered a big drum full of farm animals tucked away in the centre's storeroom. Tumbled in among the farm animals were some sea animals and some African wild animals.

On that day, Rachel and Gina placed the drum on the room's floor, removed the lid and several children (8–15 months) crawled towards it, and upon arrival pulled themselves up onto the side of the drum to access the animals. Interestingly, it was the farm animals which were most targeted by the children, rather than the other, perhaps less familiar, animals.

Sophie was present that day. She recognized the children's interest in the farm animals and set about singing 'Old MacDonald Had a Farm'. It was customary that, while singing this song, educators would pick up each different animal as it featured in the verses of the song. In between each verse of the song, the educator would point out the features of the animal in their hand. For example, if Old McDonald had a pig, the educator would describe and point to the pig's snout, or its curly tail, or make a loud grunt.

Figure 4.7 Collaborative play: Harper, Kaden, and James (left to right).
Source: authors' photo.

Then a week later:

> *Sophie's story (Wednesday 15th September 2021)*
> *This morning Sophie set up an activity to encourage the children to engage in collaborative play by setting up a square of artificial grass, a tub of (mainly) farm animals, and a log to create a farm landscape. Sophie planned this, knowing the children really enjoy the farm animals, and singing songs about the animals* (Figure 4.7).
>
> *Sophie invited the children to join her in exploring the area while she began singing 'Old Macdonald'. James (eight months) showed his enthusiasm and determination for the activity by crawling three metres to join. His eyes beamed with excitement when he arrived, and Sophie assisted him to sit up so he could engage with the activity. Kaden and Harper approached the space a short moment after James, expressing interest as they each reached for an animal.*
>
> *Sophie thought carefully about how the children were now grouped for play, and considered the possibilities for peer scaffolding, pointing out which animals each child was holding. 'Oh, what did you find Kaden?' asked Sophie 'You've got a horse and Harper has a sheep', 'And look, James has a sheep too', explained Sophie while pointing to each of their animals. 'Do you know the noises they make ... What colour is the fur? Oh, I wonder what their fur feels like', Sophie went on.*
>
> *The children continued to play with the animals, manoeuvring them across the play space as they mirrored Sophie's actions. James placed his sheep in his mouth.*

Kaden then tapped his horse on the wooden log. Harper then started to tap her sheep on the log while looking and smiling at Kaden. Harper and Kaden looked at James, looked at each other and continued to tap their animals on the log. James looked at Harper, then Kaden and started to tap his animal on the log. Kaden and Harper responded with a smile and laughter before clapping their hands together. The children continued tapping their animals on the log in front of them, as they happily engaged in a learning relationship.

Sophie thought this experience demonstrated these two Learning Outcomes from the EYLF.

Learning outcome: 4.1 Children develop dispositions for learning such as curiosity, cooperation, confidence, creativity, commitment, enthusiasm, persistence, imagination, and reflexivity.

Learning outcome: 4.4 Children resource their own learning through connecting with people, place, technologies, and natural and processed materials.

Sophie brought this learning experience to Matt as she thought it was significant to demonstrate children operating as a group. Sophie thought both Harper and Kaden were communicating a very clear message to James and that message was: 'C'mon, Mr Sucky! Get the sheep out of your mouth and start tapping with it on the block of wood like us!' Sophie said she has started to notice the looks between the children as a form of communication. Her sensitivity to this came about after placing the children in the highchairs and pushing them together in groups of three and four, facing each other, and then watching what they do without an adult assisting them during their mealtimes.

4.7 When It Goes Wrong

Matt's Monday observations (Monday 13th December 2021)
Monday was an unusual day, the room leader Jackie was absent at home as she was attending to her own sick child, and a new educator had started her first day working with children in Matt's centre. The other usual educators, Ben and Bianca, were there. However eleven children were booked in to attend that day, and five children had recently started at the centre in the past two weeks, all under the age of twelve months. Technically we would be meeting the regulation requirements with educator numbers and children that sit at a 1:4 ratio, but the experience and skill level of the educators meant they were not likely to be capable of dealing effectively with so many children. The Nominated

Supervisor made the decision to move three of the older children to the next room for the day, leaving eight children and three educators.

I walked into the room at 9:30 am to find eight crying babies and three stressed educators. The educators were trying to settle the crying children by physically holding them and then trying to soothe them. Bianca and Renee were holding a child each, but with all of them crying, it was an impossible task to comfort each one individually.

Ben was diligently doing his job which was the nappy change round, a routine event that occurs like clockwork four times a day. Watching him collect each child, he had a look of relief that he didn't need to deal with the cacophonous group of wailing babies. The way he conducted the process of changing the nappy of each child looked mechanical, seeming to allow him to ignore what was occurring in the room.

After quickly evaluating the situation, I could see what was required which was to get the children to work. My assumption, at this point in time, was that the children wanted to do the real work they came here for, which was to learn. But the educators' actions, which appeared to be influenced by an attachment approach, were not allowing this.[11]

The first thing I did was to get the 'Poems and Songs' folder from the shelf. This folder contains laminated pages of poems and songs which the educators had been collecting over the year. With the book I sat down next to the new educator, Renee, who had a child on her lap crying and I selected a song and started to sing it. Within seconds all the children had stopped crying, I told Renee to sing, which she did, and Bianca, the other educator, soon joined in. The feeling of stress in the room dropped immediately as all the children were now actively engaged. The child on Renee's lap, nine months of age—who was previously crying—leaned forward and started to touch the pages of the folder. He moved his hand towards the images, and then started to turn the pages, which I assisted while continuing to sing. I passed the folder to Renee and told her to continue turning and describing the pictures on the pages. Other children crawled over and began to join in.

As we continued singing, I started to move away from Renee and her newly formed group until I was within reaching distance of an activity, which was a bucket with a lid that had holes punched in it. In the bucket were coloured paddle pop sticks which I removed. Three children quickly came over to join in with an activity they recognized—knowing exactly what to do with the sticks. One at a time, I handed each child a coloured paddle pop stick and said, 'A blue stick for Henry'. Then Henry proceeded to place the blue stick in a hole in the bucket. Then I went around the group handing them a stick, describing the colour, and encouraging each infant to get the stick into a hole of the bucket *lid. There were now four children in this group. Each waited and watched as the selected child placed their stick into the bucket.*

By 9:45 am there were now two groups of children, each with an educator in the room, actively participating as groups. Bianca was able to get the room ready for morning tea, and Ben was able to complete the nappy change round. The room was calm.

The two inexperienced educators were new employees, untrained, and not parents. What stood out was their approach to attempting to calm crying children. They held a baby each and tried to soothe him or her while leaving all the other children to cry. What needs further investigation is to see why they thought this approach would be best to use, and—where did they learn this from?

An educational approach is 'distract and engage' to get children to stop crying. This process does work, but if we now add the explanatory layers of groupness and the proven value of developing a work-group mentality in babies, we have a better way to describe the process of how and why this distraction technique works.

4.8 An Opportunity for New Policies

The dominance of the dyad in theorizing and research about our very young has carried over into practice, and thereby significantly narrows the creative opportunities for infants and the educators who live and work in early child education centres. Policies about the numbers of staff required to look after babies, and the ways educators should behave, are today almost always drafted from an attachment perspective.[12] So Penelope Leach, arguably the most influential childcare guru in the UK,[13] asserts the work of early child educators 'really matters' because, in group care, no infant can have 'their own' adult: so the worker must find ways of providing 'attention and talk, laps and arms' to several. 'The fewer children per adult the better, as the more children each adult has to take care of the less close and positive the relationships she'll have with each of them and the more detached—even punitive—she's likely to be.'[14] This vision is consistent with trends for each infant in a centre to have her or his own 'key worker'.

National policies on the care and education of young children shadow attachment claims slavishly. For example, Bowlby's claim that only infant–adult attachments can provide babies with a 'secure base' from which to explore their worlds is reproduced almost verbatim in Australia's NQS and Learning Framework for early education. Educators are *required* to 'interact with babies and children to build attachment'.[15] Why? Because it is these 'responsive, warm, trusting, and respectful relationships with children that promote their wellbeing, self-esteem, sense of security and belonging'. Such relationships are basic to the child's entire education, for it is 'relationships of this kind [which] encourage children to explore the environment and engage in play and learning'.[16]

According to this vision, infants have no intrinsic curiosity *unless* they have an adult in their vicinity to whom they are attached, and from whom they can venture forth into their immediate world. This assumes a very low level of confidence and intrinsic curiosity in the child, a very constrained form of sociability, and a very low level of practical competence. So incompetent are infants and toddlers deemed to be that educators are warned to attend to children, 'at all times when they are eating or drinking', and to attend *closely* 'when they are in situations that present a higher risk of injury—[as] for example ... in a highchair'. Highchairs pose such grave risks to babies that educators should be 'minimizing time children spend in highchairs'.[17]

This insistence on infant–adult relationships in national protocols completely forecloses any opportunity to discuss the role of groups in infants' learning and enjoyment. As in attachment theory, the foundation for everything good in infancy, and in early development, is dyadic and adult-based. So Australia's *National Quality Framework* repeatedly underlines that:

> Positive and responsive one-on-one interactions, especially with children under three years old, are important to children's wellbeing and their future development. Secure relationships with educators encourage children under three years to thrive, and provides them with a secure base for exploration and learning. As children grow and develop they continue to rely on secure, trusting, and respectful relationships with the adults in their lives.[18]

We underline the stark contrast between the content of these national standards and the illustrations in this chapter. The attachment perspective such standards embody put educators in an impossible position: they are required simultaneously to act as *one-to-one* mother figures to *many* different children every week—a requirement which, as Leach observes, they can never meet. Hence they are always inferior, always 'failed' mother figures, who are consequently positioned as 'to blame' for any difficulty an infant in their care may have.

The new way of working pioneered at Matt's centres opens up new grounds upon which to build policies for the care and education of very young children. Rather than prescribing a substitute-mother role for educators, at which they must fail, we have suggested a new kind of role—one that is *complementary* to the role of parents at home. Babies flourish in groups. All early education centres are replete with groups of same-age children—unlike the vast majority of parental homes. Hence the need to construct a role for educators which will enable them to exploit the unique opportunities their group-setting offers. We have shown how the take-up of such opportunities proves to be, not only more rewarding and more creative, but less onerous and less freighted with impossibility, than the one-to-one roles that are currently enforced by national legislation. Such roles also allow and create more active and enriching experiences and social worlds for very young children.

4.8.1 The industrial context

A reshaping of the policies and laws regulating early childcare and education is not just timely theoretically and practically. It is timely in another way. Across the European Union, the United States of America and Australia, unemployment is at a record low. Which means there is a shortage of workers, particularly in small businesses and the 'feminized' caring professions (teaching, nursing, social care). This shortage is widely being addressed by expanding childcare facilities—with the aim of recruiting more mothers into the workforce. In Australia, the demand for childcare has long been increasing. In 2021, one-quarter of all Australian infants and toddlers spent time in formal educational settings and, by the age of 3, over half of Australian children were attending early childhood education centres.[19] Meanwhile, governments continue to push for greater access to early childcare facilities.[20]

As a consequence of these changes, developers build larger and larger centres. Australian state governments have now removed the caps on the number of children that can attend a service.[21] The new 'no cap' regulation has led to reducing costs by providing fewer rooms, but rooms which are larger in size. For example, in at least one Sydney service visited by Matt in 2021, one hundred children attend per day with just three rooms. The babies' room catered for children from six weeks to twenty-four months and had twenty children. This is permissible, but required five educators in the room all the time to meet ratio requirements. The 24-months to 36-month toddler room had forty children, requiring eight educators. The rooms were large and educators appeared to struggle with such large numbers of children in the rooms. In addition, having large numbers of educators in a room proved difficult to coordinate over the course of the day.

Partly as a consequence of the stresses of dealing with large groups of infants in a one-to-one way, staff turnover has dramatically increased across the sector.[22] It is now estimated that more than one-third of qualified staff have less than four years' experience in the children's education and care sector, with two-thirds having less than four years' tenure at their current service.[23]

We suggest that the inherent strains of using a scientifically-questionable group-blind attachment ideal of one-to-one infant–mother relationship in modelling best practice in the provision of education and care for very young children render current policy untenable. The increasing group size in early child education services renders a group-based model of care far more practicable than today's anachronistic attachment model.

Matt's experiences of developing new group-based practices in his own Early Education Childcare centres were partly inspired by the positive responses of educators to his earlier provision (through Centre Support) of nationwide training programmes promoting group-based care for early childhood educators. Yet, developing his ideas in his own centres meant working against some of the current national standards for registration. Indeed, the fact that Matt's practice is not in line with these requirements posed a risk of sanctions when one of his centres was assessed in mid-2022. But Matt felt confident. He knew that watching his videos of the children at his group-based centre does not cause alarm for viewers: the children are not at risk; nor are they distressed, as we have seen. And though, according to current regulations, babies' time in highchairs is supposed to be 'minimized', he knew that there was no *rational* need to stop the energetic 'conversations' that take place between babies when they are grouped together at mealtimes, facing inwards, interacting with animation and no signs of wanting to be removed from their companions. Thus, when Matt's centre finally went through its formal assessment, he was happy to show the assessor his innovations, including video-footage of groups of four or five babies eating in circled highchairs. The assessor looked on wide-eyed, exclaiming: 'Wow! We don't *need* educators!'

Figure 4.8 Where 'group care' means 'babies in groups'.
Source: authors' photos.

4.9 Conclusion

The care and education of our young is an emotive topic. We may assume that the policies which regulate how young children are raised outside the home are drawn from the best information with the best of intentions. This chapter has shown that, however good the intentions are, the information can be limiting. The way early childhood is regulated is misdirected insofar as it makes infant–adult relationships the foundation and model of best practice—and not just because of the scientific shortcomings of those foundations. There is an essential dimension of infancy that such regulations entirely miss: babies' capacity for group relations and group work (Figure 4.8). Open our eyes to *this* dimension when designing best practice, and we have seen how the work of babies and educators in centres of early education is radically changed and enriched.[24]

The next chapter examines the potential for enrichment as a consequence of opening our eyes to a group-based approach in another area of practice, namely, psychotherapy.

5
Prisms and Multiplicities

Figure 5.1 Children often picture their worlds as containing many characters and features.
Source: authors.

5.1 Introduction

Any story of beginnings built on the discovery that young babies flourish in groups queries the felt naturalness of visions which make the mother–infant pair the crux of human development and well-being. This is where *Babies in Groups* sets out: whatever our context, even prior to birth, infants and children create and are created, develop and are developed as a consequence of their participation in groups and wider social relations (see Figure 5.1).[1] But, the vision of infant–mother attachment still reigns in many psychological clinics, just as it still shapes the practices and policies which structure centres of early education, discussed in the last chapter. This chapter examines how dyadic ideals in psychotherapy look when viewed through the prism of groupness.

5.1.1 Pairs and groups in therapy

Both pairs and groups have long figured in psychotherapy. Psychoanalysis was born in the consulting rooms of the Viennese doctors Sigmund Freud (1856–1939) and Josef Breuer (1842–1925) during the 1890s. Their discovery of what they called *transference-love*—the revealing, symptom-rich passions which can build up in a patient for an attentive but undemonstrative therapist, when engaged in months of intensive, five-days-a-week, professional consultations—emerged directly from the exclusiveness of their repeated, confidential, one-to-one doctor–patient encounters.[2]

However, theorizing of the psyche as revealed in these early therapeutic encounters went well beyond the visible two-way-ness of the relationship between analyst and patient. Even though this set-up may prompt appeals to a dyadic basis for emotional life, Freud's theory assumed that a complex, three-cornered dynamic created the human psyche.[3] He pictured the background for all human socio-emotional development as a prototypical Western family, in which great tensions existed for tiny children between their feelings for their mother and for their father. These tensions were complicated by the child's fantasized understanding of the third-party relationship *between* his or her parents, the so-called primal scene.[4]

Ideas about group therapy may be traced to even more elaborate ideas about infants: that the infant imagination is at first structured around a capacity to defend itself against the primitive anxiety of annihilation (see Appendix A.1.3.1). This leads to the baby experiencing his or her family as comprising many contrasting *parts*—some malignly neglectful or poisonous, others benignly nurturing (see Section 5.5). From this starting point, the key developmental achievement is to recognize that some of these parts comprise a whole, for example, a whole mother.

Both Freudian and later psychoanalytic approaches to groups agree that the most distinctive thing about people in groups is their irrationality, their collective capacity for instantaneous panic or zombie-like conformity, mass hysteria, mindless violence, or abject terror. And they agree that this collective irrationality stems from a simultaneous reversion or regression in each group-member to some primitive, undeveloped form of reality-denying infantile functioning.[5]

Such views make collective, reality-based agency in groups—and the widespread evidence that members of human groups can effectively cooperate, work as teams, and solve problems—only possible for people who have gained sufficient maturity to communicate verbally and think rationally, through 'years of training and a capacity for experience that has permitted them to develop mentally'.[6] In short, while humans may primarily be what pioneer of group therapy, Wilfred Bion, called 'group animals', young children were in his view only capable of instantaneous forms of shared emotional contagion when in groups—because they had not yet developed a sufficiently rational grasp of reality to collaborate or sufficient verbal skill to communicate and plan together.

Neither Freud nor Bion devoted serious time to studying babies, or animals, whether as individuals or in groups. It is hardly surprising, then, that as the observations described in this book and elsewhere prove, both men got their ideas about babies in groups back to front. Not only do we now have copious evidence that young babies show a good grasp of reality and solve problems. But also, when infants are put together in groups, they understand and respond to the people and events around them in a timely and realistic way: whether comforting a distressed group member;[7] or commenting on novel events like what is in their sandwiches, the appearance of four GoPro cameras around their highchairs, or a wave from a passing friend (Chapter 4). Even ape babies are perfectly aware of *real* group structure, like dominance hierarchies, and exploit them when they can (Figure 5.2).[8]

Despite the poor understanding of infants shown by Freud and Bion, their theories do have one helpful feature. They underline the fact that one-to-one therapy forms a *subdivision of group behaviour*. Both Freud and Bion believed the human psyche to be first and foremost a group product. Hence the dynamics Freud and his followers describe as transference feelings—complemented by the so-called *countertransference* feelings the therapist experiences during a session—are *group* products. As Bion puts it: no individual—and certainly no pair of individuals—'however isolated in time and space, should be regarded as outside a group or lacking in active manifestations of group psychology'.[9]

5.2 Narrowing Our Imagination

While some branches of psychotherapy hold true to the group-based understanding of clinical work advanced by writers like Freud and Bion, the resurgence of dyadic thinking in clinical work—associated with attachment

Figure 5.2 '… A small child … may chase away a full-grown male. He is able to do so under protection of his mother or "aunt". Like the children, these females are basically inferior to the males, but they, in turn, can rely on support of other females and sometimes can appeal to dominant males for help … '—a complex multi-member dynamic to which young chimps are so well attuned that they commonly use it to their advantage.

From: De Waal, Frans. 1998. *Chimpanzee Politics: Power and Sex among Apes*. Baltimore, MD: Johns Hopkins (p. 178).

Courtesy of Dr. Frans De Waal.

theory—strips away complexity and context from psychological understanding. How best then to extend such clinical work to re-incorporate the complexity of group abilities and needs that we have shown to exist in our very young?

We start by noting several ways in which dyadic thinking removes groups from the reality psychologists and clinicians think about and discuss. We then move on to consider the various forms of blindness which infect the kind of 'scientific' looking upon which attachment theory today claims to be grounded.[10]

Dyadic thinking promotes several forms of reality-denial in clinical work involving babies. We describe four: first, disavowal by therapists of their own place as significant others in their treatment of troubled mothers, both in fact and in theory; second, mislaying the central importance of family dynamics to the genesis of mental illness; thirdly, failure to acknowledge or theorize the role of groups in promoting healthy infant–mother relationships; and fourthly, the denial of subjective complexity in mothers and babies.

5.2.1 Mother-blaming in dyadic therapy

There is now a robust tradition of providing *group* therapy for struggling mothers. Campbell Paul's ground-breaking team in Melbourne, Australia, arranged for such groups to include their infants, as described in Chapter 1.[11] In other traditions one-to-one therapy is used to help mothers who have difficulty caring for their babies. While one-to-one therapy may help, we use it here to illustrate how it may narrow assessment and intervention—as reflected in therapists' limited descriptions of mothers' and babies' realities. We take our illustration from a case study which supports an influential paper by Karlen Lyons-Ruth and Eda Spielman.[12] Mary Sue Moore has claimed this paper proves the role of dysfunctional infant–mother attachment in the genesis of dissociative illness (see Section 5.3.5).[13]

The case in question introduces a first-time mother of a nine-month-old, Brad. Janie, Brad's mother, 'was working very hard at being a good mother, albeit with a palpable sense of anxiety and an increasing sense of defeat and withdrawal', say Lyons-Ruth and Spielman. We note immediately that this description gives us no clue as to whether Janie had had any opportunity to interact with other people, supportive or unsupportive, or how many, or who, or when, or whether singly or in groups, during the early months of her child's life, nor indeed, during her pregnancy. Lyons-Ruth and Spielman thus tacitly assume that their readers will expect one woman alone to satisfy all her young infant's needs—that it is normal for her to be isolated at home all day, without needing companionship for herself and her baby (contrary to what research shows, see Ch.1.4). Lyons-Ruth and Spielman continue:

> In holding fast to her rigid view of good parenting, Janie also was initially closed to any discussion and integration of her own needs into the relationship with Brad. To think about her need for adequate sleep threatened her equation of selflessness with closeness to her baby. She was suffering, yet she could not allow herself to consider alternatives that involved a more self-assertive parental stance on her part, or any frustration for her baby. Instead, she would frequently collapse into a sense of resigned helplessness.[14]

The image we get is of a hermetically sealed dyad, where a solitary adult gets cast as deficient because—it is implied—she has been unable to invent her own ways of making sure the needs of both she and her baby are met. Yet, fortunately for this dyad—though ignored and untheorized by Lyons-Ruth and Spielman—Janie *did* find initiative enough to recruit herself into a year-long relationship with a third person, *namely, the clinician Eda Spielman*. It was precisely *this third-party relationship* which led to changes between Janie and her baby son, such that she could 'begin to respond to his distress states with more differentiated and active behaviour, balancing nurturing and limits'.[15]

While Lyons-Ruth and Spielman's paper clearly and sensitively communicates with their readers in describing clinical work which appears successful, their description and analysis reflect two confronting blindnesses. What Spielman misses out from her analysis of this case is her own presence, and its significance for Janie. This means Lyons-Ruth and Spielman never ask how come *a third person* could have helped this troubled mother–baby dyad. Any acknowledgement of such a question would have led Lyons-Ruth and Spielman to confront a second silence in their account: about the nature of their culture's mother-isolating childrearing practices, entrenched both in theory and in case work. Clinicians who work like Spielman commonly never raise how traditions of childrearing affecting their clients could *themselves* be a crucial part of what needs to be reassessed and changed in helping mothers like Janie.

Elaborating on this highly restricted group-denying vision of babies and infant care, Lyons-Ruth and Spielman adopt a model of explanation which funnels clinical thinking about infancy towards a decontextualized dyad in which perceived problems are blamed on the mother's deficiencies. Thus, as we read on, we find that their paper pushes theoretical attention onto what they evocatively call 'the developmental dynamics of fear'.[16] Which allows them to channel clinicians' attention onto 'parental' (i.e. maternal) behaviour as the potential cause of Brad's potential difficulties. This follows the logic of attachment theory, which has increasingly moved away from being a biological theory of infant sociability to becoming an environmental theory which makes child development the consequence of better or worse maternal caregiving (see Appendix A.2.3).

The explanatory consummation of this mother-blaming logic is found in Lyons-Ruth and Spielman's detailed table of deficient *maternal* behaviours.[17] Here, 'Dimensions of Disrupted Maternal Affective Communication' are itemized so as to examine a purported distinction between the development of 'hostile/self-referential' and 'helpless-fearful' attachment styles in the infant (see Table 5.1). Its authors aim to collapse this purported distinction into a newly 'discovered' a 'single hostile-helpless internal working model of attachment relationships' which supposedly structures the infant's internal working model. Yet this 'internal working model' is not only unconfirmed and unobservable, but its status as a hypothetical *intrapsychic* structure *in the baby* is supposedly created through the child's 'internalization' of representations of various different types of disturbing behaviour found *in the mother*, a process which remains undocumented and mysterious (see Section 5.2.4).

In short, the mother is to blame. Here we should probably pause a moment to echo the gentle words of family therapist Salvador Minuchin:

> The entire family—not just the mother or primary caretaker—including father, siblings, grandparents, often cousins, aunts and uncles, are extremely significant in the experience of the child … And yet, when I hear attachment theorists talk, I don't hear anything about these other important figures in a child's life.[18]

5.2.2 Disappearing the family

Valerie Sinason and Renée Marks introduce their anthology, *Treating Children with Dissociative Disorders: Attachment, Trauma, Theory and Practice* by highlighting the need for clinicians to acknowledge that dissociative disorders *do occur* in childhood. This important point ushers in a central thrust of their book, which is to link *the origins* of trauma-based conditions like Dissociative Identity Disorder (DID) to mother–infant dyadic dysfunction, construed through the prism of attachment theory (see Section 5.5). Given the enthusiastic uptake of attachment theory, it is no surprise that many serious forms of psychopathology are now being examined or explained via newly invented

Table 5.1 'Dimensions of disrupt[ive] maternal affective communication'*

Dimensions of Dysfunctional Maternal Communication	Constituent Maternal Behaviour		
1. Affective Communication Errors	a. Contradictory cues, e.g. invites approach verbally then distances	b. Non-response or inappropriate or mismatched responses, e.g. does not offer comfort to distressed infant; mother smiling while infant angry or distressed	
2. Disorientation	a. Confused or frightened by infant, e.g. exhibits frightened expression; quavering voice or high, tense voice	b. Disorganized or disoriented, e.g. sudden loss of affect unrelated to environment; trancelike states	
3. Negative-Intrusive Behaviour	a. Verbal negative-intrusive behaviour, e.g. mocks or teases infant	b. Physical negative-intrusive behaviour, e.g. pulls infant by the wrist; bared teeth; looming into infant's face; attack-like posture	
4. Role Confusion	a. Role reversal, e.g. elicits reassurance from infant	b. Sexualization, e.g. speaks in hushed, intimate tones to infant	c. Self-referential statements, e.g. 'Did you miss me?' 'Okay, he doesn't want to see me'.
5. Withdrawal	a. Creates physical distance, e.g. holds infant away from body with stiff arms	b. Creates verbal distance e.g. does not greet infant after separation	

Adapted from Lyons-Ruth, Karlen and Eda Spielman. 2004. 'Disorganized Infant Attachment Strategies and Helpless-Fearful Profiles of Parenting: Integrating Attachment Research with Clinical Intervention.' Infant Mental Health Journal 25: 318–335 (p.322), © 2023 Michigan Association for Infant Mental Health.

categories of attachment classification, with a concomitant downplay of family life.

Within this context, we focus on Brett Kahr's proposal that schizophrenia is linked to a category of attachment which he labels 'infanticidal'.[19] His evidence for the existence of 'infanticidal attachments' comes from meetings *with adults* who are, or are associated with, *adult* schizophrenics. When we read his work, we find a slippage in his prose from him hearing what adult schizophrenics *say to him* about events in *their* infancy to *Kahr himself experiencing these events as real*—whether or not they actually happened. Such is his commitment to the lens of dyadic attachment. A tortuous thought process results:

> ... patients have reported the presence of parental death threats or parental death wishes in a clear and undisguised manner. *In my experience, these events create a toxic style of insecure, disorganized attachment* which, when combined with other traumata, may, in certain instances, serve as the necessary precondition for the development of the schizophrenic psychoses.[20]

Of note, Kahr illustrates this claim with case material selected so as to pit his desocialized, dyadic, attachment-style explanation of schizophrenia *against* a group-based understanding. He targets in particular a discussion published by a pioneer of family therapy, Theodore Lidz (1910–2001).

Lidz's approach to schizophrenia was based on studies of the families of adults who had been hospitalized for schizophrenia, as compared to families of patients hospitalized for non-schizophrenic psychopathologies. He supplemented these studies with cross-cultural investigations of schizophrenia—or more precisely, the lack of schizophrenia—in the Pacific Islands of Fiji, New Guinea, and Guadalcanal. On these two empirical grounds he argued that schizophrenia is induced by experiences in profoundly troubled families, being 'a type of reaction to a sick organization'—by which he meant us to understand that 'sick' familial dynamics were typically expressions of and compounded by community and culture-wide structures. For example, he noted that the incidence of schizophrenia in North America paralleled that of broken homes, both conditions being particularly prevalent in the poorer, more disadvantaged sector of this particular society. Having noted the association of his target illness with serious disturbances in American family life, he went on to highlight the place of group-level family dynamics in the aetiology of schizophrenia. Likewise, for treatment, he advocated a group-based 'socializing' form of therapy; saying that effective hospital care needed to provide a place where patients can learn to deal with peer groups, work out problems, learn various aspects of socialization, sometimes stay while going back to school at the start, and these depend very heavily on the patients helping one another and also in governing the activities of the hospital.[21]

Kahr tries to demonstrate that a group-dynamic understanding of schizophrenia is deficient—when compared to an attachment-based view—by taking up the tragic case of a schizophrenic college student who Lidz had treated and discussed in his writings.[22] Kahr notes that the mother of this young woman had idealized Virginia Woolf, once telling Lidz that she hoped her talented daughter might 'follow in Woolf's footsteps'. When Lidz remarked that Woolf's footsteps ultimately led her to drown herself in the river Ouse after the outbreak of the Second World War, he recorded that, Ouse the mother retorted, it 'would be worth it'. Ignoring the possibility that the mother might view Woolf's fate as the best her daughter could hope for, given that the alternatives available in a patriarchal setting would be worse than death - Kahr reframes her retort as 'a profound instance of the role of both conscious and unconscious parental death wishes in the aetiology of the schizophrenic illness', stressing that this of-institutionalized student *did* later kill herself.[23]

In considering Kahr's purported insight into Lidz's patient, we may ask whether and how Lidz could have usefully applied Kahr's retrospective speculation. Suppose Lidz *had* diagnosed 'infanticidal attachment', could he then have instigated a different treatment plan and 'saved' the woman? To what extent should Kahr's speculative diagnosis have changed the importance Lidz placed on dysfunction in this patient's family, a crucial component of Lidz's case material, which Kahr's account drops without comment? Lidz's research had shown that such dysfunction is generally found in the families of schizophrenics, referring to their 'skewed' relationships, which, in this patient's family, was instanced by the father pre-eminently seeking emotional gratification *from his daughter*.[24]

If able to question Kahr, Lidz would surely have asked how Kahr's account explains how 'infanticidal' thoughts in this patient's *parents* were relayed to her infant self—in the absence of any consideration of family dynamics, or the father's perversions, as these play no part in Kahr's formulation—such that it was *the infant's* attachment which became 'infanticidal'?[25] And should we not follow Lidz's example—Kahr does not—and broaden our attention to consider culture-wide research into the ordinary lived experience of women who take sole responsibility for looking after babies in North America?

If Kahr had broadened his gaze. he would soon have found research which shows most if not all mothers have thoughts of harm befalling their babies during the first three months of the baby's life. Indeed, in one study almost half (49.5%) of mothers had thoughts of *intentionally* harming their own babies before they reach twelve weeks of age.[26] Such findings underline the insight of Winnicott—paediatrician, psychoanalyst, and doyen of clinical work with the young—who deemed hateful feelings by parents towards their children entirely normal, though typically unacknowledged due to psychologists' idealization of infancy.[27] The ubiquity of parental hate torpedoes Kahr's speculations about infanticidal attachment—a notion which nevertheless goes from strength to strength in clinical literature—because, if there is nothing peculiar about being brought up by a mother who sometimes wants to harm you (or worse), such maternal wishes cannot be the cause of what is an extremely rare condition: schizophrenia.[28] Nonetheless, with the ideology of attachment theory at their backs, clinicians like Kahr strike a pose of authoritative certainty about an arena of human life which cries out for a genuinely open-minded, complexity-aware, evidence-based analysis.

The most we might draw from Kahr's intervention is an echo of the common-sense observation that a caregiver's mistreatment of a baby may have long-term effects. If his proposal of 'infanticidal attachment' is to be of any specific use in assessing the aetiology of pathological dissociation, we need to be sure both, that such attachments can really be observed *in infants*, and that evidence for their existence adds something new to the detailing of a family history or to a treatment plan. By narrowing our focus solely to the search for often-speculative early attachment types, there is a danger of ignoring the central parts played by familial and societal dynamics in people's lives. It was an appreciation of just such complexity which gave birth to family and group psychotherapies in the first place.

5.2.3 Blindness to the benefits of group membership

The Circle of Security was instigated in 2002 by Robert Marvin and colleagues. It is a 20-week long, *group-based*, parent-education, and psychotherapy intervention, designed to shift patterns of attachment–caregiving interaction in high-risk caregiver–child dyads to a more appropriate developmental pathway. The intervention involves *groups* of six parents meeting together every week, for an hour and a quarter, with a psychotherapist:

> In the context of the group, each parent reviews edited video-vignettes of herself or himself interacting with her or his child. These video feedback vignettes, and the related psycho-educational and therapeutic discussions, are individualized to each dyad's specific attachment–caregiving pattern using *a priori*, individualized treatment goals based on videotaped interactions recorded during a pre-intervention assessment.[29]

The Circle of Security is one of many clinical innovations which is said to bring *infants* into focus in their own right. However, the Circle of Security directs nearly all its theoretical and clinical attention to what it initially calls the infant's *caregiver*—though by this it appears to mean mothers: in Marvin et al.'s introduction to the Circle of Security, fathers are mentioned once, mothers thirty-three times.[30]

> ... in designing the protocol, we have decided to capitalize on the fact that the caregiver, as an adult, has more 'degrees of freedom' in changing patterns of attachment–caregiving interactions than does the child. This focus specifically does not imply that the problematic pattern is 'caused' by the caregiver. Rather, the implication is that even for a pre-schooler or an older child, a most effective intervention for problematic attachment–caregiving patterns may be to focus directly on the caregiver, and work toward shifting the caregiver's patterns of behaviour and/or *her* IWMs [Internal Working Models] of attachment–caregiving interactions with this particular child.[31]

Whether or not one takes seriously such pleas to overlook the intrinsic mother-blaming of attachment discourse,[32] *in fact* the Circle of Security places the responsibility for change squarely on mothers—because it construes infant social life as purely dyadic: biology will ensure in most Western, Educated, Industrialized, Rich, and Democratic (WEIRD) households that the baby's primary environment *is* the mother. Nothing is made theoretically of the wider context of the mother's social life and needs. Which makes it puzzling, therefore, that one goal of the Circle of Security programme explicitly acknowledges the ameliorative role of this wider context, that is, of groups: Goal 4 is 'develop a process of reflective dialogue *in the group*—a skill that the parent can then use internally; this process is viewed as the central dynamic for change'.[33] Thus, while the theoretical focus of the procedure is on the mental life (IWM) of the solitary mother as change agent, *the process of change* requires that the mother belongs to a group. Needless to say, Marvin and his colleagues offer no way to theorize the processes whereby groups could manage to help the mother reshape her internal world or 'working model'.

The Circle of Security thus illustrates a wider tension in attachment-based training and clinical programmes—however effective in practice—between the single isolated mother as the *theoretical* fulcrum for 'infant intervention', and the practical reality of mothering, which always reflects the social support a society makes available to the mother and the ways she draws on such support to be the kind of caregiver she is.[34]

5.2.4 Attempts to deny subjective complexity

Attachment theory drew strength from a shift which took place during the 1950s in Britain, especially in hospitals: a shift from treating infants as only needing food and warmth, to recognizing that babies need human contact, relationships, and quality time with others.[35] This recognition was, as it were, biologically cemented into babies by Bowlby's uptake of then-fashionable, if simple-minded, ideas about forms of behaviour being 'hard-wired' into the human nervous system as a consequence of our species' evolutionary history.[36] Once such needs were brought centre stage, so too was the infant's mother—as required to supply the naturally complementary, uncomplicated, care which had *also* purportedly been programmed into women by evolution.

In the Appendix (A.2, e.g. A.2.5) we elaborate on the scientific status of attachment theory. Here we touch on how the theory blinkers us against seeing the complexity of human subjectivity. Attachment theory started by asserting—against psychoanalysis—the importance of focusing on the *observable behaviour* of babies, especially behaviours like smiling, crying, sucking, and grasping. The responsiveness of mothers was also supposed to be something observers could *see*, or 'directly observe'. Within the wider context of the discipline of psychology, this move to counting easily defined behaviours was welcomed by those who disliked theories of humanity which forced them to 'recognize and engage with the complexity of individual subjectivity'.[37]

An early adopter of Bowlby's attachment theory, Mary Ainsworth (and colleagues) attempted to provide standardized evidence supporting it by devising ways of observing babies when put under twin stresses, fear of strangers and separation anxiety—both of which Bowlby predicted to trigger proximity-promoting attachment behaviours. To this end, they designed the laboratory-based Strange Situation Procedure (SSP; see Figure 5.3).

However, babies did not behave as Bowlby and Ainsworth predicted in the Strange Situation.[38] Neither stranger fear nor separation anxiety were 'as ubiquitous as anticipated': 'Separation protest ... [is] by no means invariably activated by the baby's realization of the mother's departure', nor does 'separation

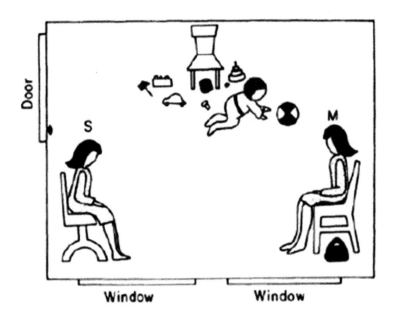

Figure 5.3 The laboratory set-up for the 'Strange Situation': 'Two adjacent rooms were employed for the experimental room and the observation room, connected by two one-way-vision mirror windows'. (S = stranger; M = mother).

From: *Patterns of Attachment: Psychological Study of the Strange Situation*, Ainsworth, Mary, Mary Blehar, Everett Waters and Sally Wall, p. 33, © 2015, Routledge, New York.

Reproduced by permission of Taylor & Francis Group.

from the mother ... significantly lower the total number of smiles, nor those directed to the stranger'.[39] Hence Ainsworth's group were forced to conclude that baby-based attachments were not directly observable after all. In order not to jettison the theory, these results necessitated a major about-face. Rather than attachments being *observable*, they proposed attachments were *invisible* 'internal structures' which existed 'inside' the baby, independently from observable 'attachment behaviours'.[40]

Over the years, contradictory pushes from attachment theory and attachment research have increasingly fudged the nature of dyadic visions of infancy. On the one hand is the push to count well-defined and objective *observable* behaviours without reference to any hidden subjective complexity. On the other hand is a push for researchers to accept the need to hypothesize increasingly complex 'internal structures' to explain the complexity and variability of infant behaviour that observers observe.

As a result we now have a host of appeals to what are called a baby's 'internal working model'[41] of his or her social world. But there is no consensus about what 'internal working model' actually means, nor about how such models may affect behaviour. As Ross Thompson observes:

> There is currently no consensus among attachment researchers on how internal working models develop and function ... This poses a problem not only for those who are trying to understand the central claims of contemporary attachment theory, but also for the coherence of the theory itself. After all, it is easy to interpret almost any research results in terms of the functioning of internal working models if the construct is so vaguely defined that it can accommodate nearly any empirical findings.[42]

Things become yet vaguer and yet more speculative when the *inner world* of a parent is purported to shape the 'internal working model' of their child.[43] Ultimately, when clinicians develop speculations which blame, say, nasty *parental* thoughts for producing a dysfunctional kind of attachment *in babies*, they invoke the kind of occult thought transfer which attachment theory's reputed scientific ambitions once led it to deny.[44] Thus, we find Kahr can only conjure up his Gothic fantasy world of 'infanticidal attachments' by proposing a process whereby 'mothers and fathers transmit death-related messages to their children, sometimes consciously, but often unconsciously'.[45]

So much for the denial of subjective complexity in attachment theory.

5.3 Group Dynamics and the Psychology of Science

As we have seen, there is a plethora of sites using attachment theory as a pillar, whether as a clinical background narrative or as a repository of taken-as-true scientific facts or both. Viewing this kaleidoscope of attachment claims through the prism of groups, we propose a marriage. Groups, group dynamics, and their creative or destructive consequences alert us to ways in which attachment theorists may themselves be thought to form a group whose activities we can examine from a group-process perspective. In this way, we illustrate how a group-based vision can help understand why it may be difficult to 'see' the groupness of the very young.

John Bowlby and Mary Ainsworth liked to refer to their dyadic attachment vision of babyhood as a new *paradigm* for research into social development, as do their followers today.[46] The word 'paradigm' was brought into science in 1962 to describe how a favoured model of reality may dominate scientific thinking for decades or even centuries, *whether or not* it continues to be supported by good evidence.[47] Some talk of the 'paradigm of phrenology', for example—phrenology being a supposedly scientific way of determining a person's character by mapping bumps on their skull, which was popular in the early 1800s.[48] Likewise, today, we not only hear of 'Newtonian' physics, 'Mendelian' genetics, or 'Freudian' psychoanalysis, *but also* of 'post-Newtonian', 'post-Mendelian', and 'post-Freudian' approaches. Paradigms occupy periods in history. Which means, paradigms end.

Every paradigm has two faces. One face is the facts and ideas it repeatedly highlights. The other face usually operates insensibly for people under the paradigm's sway. Accordingly, Ainsworth and her colleagues describe *the attachment paradigm* as doing two things.[49] It promotes 'a new way of understanding the infant's tie to primary caregivers': namely as the product of an empirically verifiable 'attachment behaviour system' innate to every human baby. But it *also* refers to a community of theorists and researchers who are bound together, both by their common belief in the importance of particular studies and ideas which they deem crucial to the science of human development, and by their common rejection of other findings and ideas challenging their views, including what Ainsworth et al. call 'psychoanalytic and learning theory perspectives'. This is nothing unusual, because:

> for well-integrated members of a particular discipline, [a] paradigm is so convincing that it normally renders even the possibility of alternatives unconvincing and counter-intuitive. Such a paradigm is *opaque*, appearing to be a direct view of the bedrock of reality itself, and obscuring the possibility that there might be other, alternative imageries hidden behind it. The conviction that the current paradigm *is* reality tends to disqualify evidence that might undermine the paradigm itself; this in turn leads to a build-up of unreconciled anomalies.[50]

Looked at from outside—or after its fall—a paradigm is thus a surreptitious form of group fantasy sustaining a collective blindness to facts which would, if acknowledged, topple its most-cherished ideas and claims.[51]

The group dynamics sustaining a paradigm like that of attachment take the form of various defences, including: gatekeeping and initiation rites; an idealization of the in-group; a 'yes man' disavowal of criticism; an ostracism of heretics; and fabrication of supporting data—all amplified by tribute from a growing entourage of fellow-travellers who label their work as 'attachment-based' as a flag of convenience. We will briefly examine these dynamics as they apply to the attachment perspective, after first sketching the context which has made the purportedly 'scientific' standing of that perspective attractive to clinicians and researchers.

5.3.1 Physics envy

By the outbreak of the First World War, psychology had begun to undertake what has now become a full-scale repudiation of its nineteenth-century roots. It renounced 'natural history': a practice involving the highly developed skills which allowed naturalists like Charles Darwin to gain scientific insight from copious, painstaking, and time-consuming descriptions, whether of babies and adult human beings and their doings, or of animals and plants,—all *while living their lives in their natural habitats*.[52] Rather than undertaking the onerous task of observing and describing all the things human beings around the world get up to, the 'New Psychology' which was launched in the early 1900s undertook to follow modern biology into the laboratory, championing experimentation and mathematical computation just like physics and chemistry.

Twentieth-century psychologists' wish to be seen as conducting a proper natural science—sometimes called 'physics envy'[53]—led to prioritization of maths-based analyses. Measurements which differed 'enough' from a conventional standard could be called a 'finding' because they had 'significance' in a new *statistical* sense, based on the likelihood that a sum of measurements of a particular, repeatable, psychologist-defined behaviour or characteristic *exceeded* a calculable cut-off point.[54] This cut-off was to be justified deductively—partly by a model of population structure, partly by a concept of probability or 'chance'. All of which means that significant findings in this kind of psychological research depend on assumptions about and calculations involving abstract features of population distribution including 'means', 'variance', and 'standard deviation', and on decisions about 'confidence levels'.[55]

By the 1950s, scientists from disciplines on the borders of psychology were concluding that the New Psychology had yielded little of scientific value. As an antidote, Nobel Prize winner Niko Tinbergen (1907–1988) argued that behavioural scientists needed to get out of the laboratory and 'return to nature' if they really wanted to understand human action:

> ... in its haste to step into the twentieth century and become a respectable science, Psychology skipped the preliminary descriptive stage that other natural sciences had gone through, and so was soon losing touch with the natural phenomena.[56]

Tinbergen advocated a science called 'ethology' which sought to build its discoveries on the descriptive foundation of natural history, just as Darwin had. Ethology's first step is to ensure the observation and description of the full range of actions of members of any studied animal species, an approach Tinbergen and his colleagues extended to the study of young children.[57] Central to Tinbergen's approach was the need to understand what each of an organism's actions meant *ecologically*, that is, to describe how every living action was interwoven with the lives and structures making up a creature's surroundings: climate and terrain, plus the other animals—both of the same and of different species—and the plants which filled its world.

Whilst no great observer himself,[58] Bowlby claimed to have based attachment theory on ethology rather than experimental psychology. This claim soon proved hollow, however. Most telling was Ainsworth and her colleagues' demonstration that attachments were incapable of direct observation in the SSP (see Section 5.2.4). Indeed, Ainsworth's very idea of assessing an 'attachment' using this laboratory procedure[59] ran directly counter to the grounding principles of ethology.[60] Conversely, Ainsworth's invention of this procedure was welcome to behavioural scientists, because it did all the things Tinbergen's critique of psychology had denounced. Rather than painstakingly observing the full gamut of infant behaviour in a wide range of everyday conditions, it based its generalizations about human nature on 'measurements' of a brief and pre-defined list of infant 'behaviours' counted over three-minute periods in an artificially standardized laboratory setting.[61]

With the 'Strange Situation' paving the way, attachment theory is now the very reverse of observational or descriptive. See for example the frequent references to ill-defined, hypothetical, infant 'internal' understandings of social reality such as, 'internal working models', 'proto-narrative envelopes', 'themes of organization', and 'relational scripts'.[62] Or, see the burgeoning industry producing non-observational measures of 'adult attachment', entailing interview schedules or self-report questionnaires.[63]

Given the failure to provide an observational basis for attachment theory, we suggest that various forms of groupthink and gatekeeping are required to maintain its high profile amongst those of its advocates who claim their approach is scientific.

5.3.2 Gatekeeping

A long-standing criticism of attachment theory's claim that all human babies are born biologically built to form a long-term life-shaping one-to-one relationship with an all-important Someone is cross-cultural: babies Western or WEIRD people have been taken as the best model for all human beings.[64] Yet only 5% of the world's children are brought up in the conditions attachment theory takes to be humanly universal.[65] So what does attachment theory have to say about the remaining 95%?

This is such an obvious criticism that attachment advocates have had to adopt special measures to defeat it. Thus, as early as 1954, the anthropologist Margaret Mead's awareness of cross-cultural evidence led her to reject what she called Bowlby's 'exaggerated and poorly supported claims of the importance of the mother as a single figure in the infant's life'. On the contrary, she said, knowledge of non-Western cultures led to the conclusion that '*adjustment is most facilitated if the child is cared for by many warm, friendly people*'.[66] Sixty years later, an impressive number of ethnographic studies has strengthened Mead's critique. Studies of childcare in peoples from all the world's inhabited continents insistently underline the cultural peculiarity of the kind of desert-islanded mothering attachment theory assumes to be universal.[67]

Nevertheless, the 2016 *Handbook of Attachment* bewails 'the current cross-cultural database' as

> *almost absurdly small* compared to the domain that should be covered. Data on attachment in a populous country such as India and most Islamic countries are still lacking, and large parts of Africa, Asia, and Latin America are uncharted territories with respect to the development of attachment.[68]

How can this be? On the one hand we have sixty-plus years of cumulative evidence presented in refereed articles, monographs, and, recently, several weighty anthologies of ethnographic study, all demonstrating the multiplicity of ways humans rear children around the world. And, on the other, we have the latest edition of the definitive *Handbook of Attachment*, stating not only that there are 'absurdly' few cross-cultural studies of attachment to review; but that, nevertheless:

> ... the *available* cross-cultural studies have not refuted the bold conjectures of attachment theory about the universality of attachment, the normativity of secure attachment, the link between sensitive caregiving and attachment security, and the competent child outcomes of secure attachment. In fact, taken as a whole, the studies are remarkably consistent with the theory. Until further notice, *attachment theory may therefore claim cross-cultural validity*.[69]

The answer is that attachment theorists have found ways to deny the validity of most ethnographic research. First, they discount studies which do not use methods developed by attachment researchers themselves, like the SSP or the Attachment Q-Sort.[70] And secondly, even cross-cultural research which *does* use these 'approved' methods may be dismissed if its authors have not been 'properly trained'.

Commenting on an Indian study which *did* use the SSP but reported findings which contradicted what 'insider' attachment researchers claim to be the 'normal' ratio of secure to insecure toddlers, a colleague wrote: 'Hmm … I'd want to know if [the study's authors] did the full training and qualification as SSP scorers and would only include this paper if I was convinced they had'.[71] This second way of dismissing findings about cross-cultural differences in infant social life is common. As the current *Handbook of Attachment* puts it: 'in many cases the coding [in cross-cultural attachment research] is done by researchers who have not been formally trained by experts, which makes the quality of the classifications unclear'.[72]

Perversely, this implies that attachments can only be 'seen' through a prism that is created, administered, marketed, and, in a word, *overseen* by attachment researchers themselves. Unlike other forms of mental testing—which can be learnt from any qualified clinical psychologist—the assessment of attachments must be inculcated by a coterie of insiders. Only insiders can count as 'experts'. Furthermore, a 'full training and qualification' in the approved methods of assessing attachments take a minimum of several weeks, is typically taught by prominent attachment personalities, costs thousands of dollars, and is only available in a few Western strongholds. The implicit function of such 'formal training' evokes that of an initiation rite or a laying-on of hands—as in the ordination of ministers to the Christian church, or the 'auditing' of those wishing to join the Church of Scientology. The uninitiated have no entrée to the attachment fold, which means their research findings are rejected or ignored.

Peer-reviewed journals exercise a related kind of gatekeeping.[73] An example: in 2003 Chris Fraley and Sue Spieker submitted a manuscript to *Child Development* reporting a careful reanalysis of data about infant behaviour in the SSP. Their article questioned whether SSP data were better described as reflecting three naturally different *kinds* of infant attachment (secure, avoidant, and resistant)—as claimed by Bowlby and Ainsworth—or as representing behavioural variations along two continuous *dimensions* of individual difference: security⇆resistance and security⇆avoidance. Their results supported a two-dimensional view. Their paper 'was rejected flat out by *Child Development* as too heretical', though no one could fault the findings it contained.[74]

When this paper was later published in a different journal, *Developmental Psychology,* it reported the same study and the same results. However, Fraley and Spieker had revised their manuscript. They had removed any implication that their work was 'evaluating' research based on the three-category assumption, or that such research was 'faulty'. They likewise explicitly denied that they were 'challenging or calling into question the significance of attachment theory and research'. On the contrary: their revised paper's final paragraph now exalts 'the ground-breaking contributions of Ainsworth and her colleagues to the scientific study of attachment processes'. And its last words clearly affirm Fraley and Spieker's loyalty to the attachment creed: 'we believe that the study of attachment will continue to thrive in the years to come'.[75]

5.3.3 Idealization of the in-group

Attachment buoys itself up by fulsome celebration of its luminaries and their work. Witness Fraley and Spieker's revised last paragraph in their *Developmental Psychology* paper, lauding the 'ground-breaking' work of Ainsworth and her colleagues. We have already seen Brett Kahr bracketing John Bowlby's contributions to science and to humanity with the work of those other great men of Mozart, Gandhi, and Michelangelo (Ch.3.4). Bowlby's findings are now 'beyond all doubt', crows Kahr.[76] Peter Fonagy and his team refer complacently to 'the complex and meticulous observational work of Mary Ainsworth', and, when introducing Bowlby's concept of 'internal working model', tell us that it has been elaborated by 'some of the greatest minds in the attachment field'.[77] Valerie Sinason refers to 'the brilliant research on attachment, which has done more for therapy than any other scientific research' (see Section 5.5). And Suzanne Zeedyk writes that 'the operation of the attachment system is now regarded as "fact" '.[78] Even a critic, who, despite asking 'uncomfortable questions' about the attachment paradigm, seeks to maintain acceptance by the 'in-group', will be quick to reassure readers about her allegiance: 'This does not mean I have lost my admiration for the attachment framework, or my appreciation of the scientific rigour of attachment research and its many novel applications'.[79]

There is a sizeable dollop of intellectual indolence in such homage, plus a wish-fulfilling blindness to the provisionality and hard slog characteristic of any genuine scientific work. *No* scientific contribution is 'beyond all doubt', especially when it relates to so contentious a theory of human nature as attachment theory (see Appendix A.2). And however 'great' the minds that have worked on the concept of 'internal working model', this has not prevented that concept from being, in Ross Thompson's words, 'so vaguely defined that it can accommodate nearly any empirical findings' (see 5.2.4). It is easy enough for Fonagy's team to laud Ainsworth's observational work as 'meticulous'. Yet Fonagy and his colleagues show no sign of having inspected either Ainsworth's actual observational records, nor of having absorbed the scathing critiques of her data by Michael Lamb and others. Marga Vicedo, who *has* examined the archive of observational records upon which Ainsworth and her colleagues' best-known conclusions were based, found their work to be the reverse of 'meticulous':

> Although confidentiality prevents quoting directly from these data, the narrative reports from these observations that I have seen cannot be considered trustworthy scientific reports. Several of them are permeated with subjective evaluations of the mothers' personality from day one, including moral judgements. Other reports reveal tensions between the observer and the observed mothers. In addition, the reports from the different observers vary substantially in nature and quality, and most of them do not include notes taken every five minutes. In fact, one observer did not write up the observations until months later.[80]

Once we acknowledge the dubious empirical claims and the conceptual incoherencies endemic to attachment thinking (see Appendix A.2), the self-congratulatory complacency of the paradigm's insiders about its scientific credentials becomes one more symptom of its malaise.

5.3.4 Disavowal of criticism, and a casting-out of heretics

Gatekeeping rituals and idealization of the in-group have several corollaries for the dynamics maintaining the attachment paradigm: a deafness to or disavowal of criticism; strong in-group pressures to praise attachment claims, especially if one's results might cast doubt on them; and a casting-out of any heretic who should dare to flout these implicit commandments. Judi Mesman gives us a glimpse of the blindness which results from the way the attachment paradigm socializes its inmates:

> Having been academically 'raised' in one of the world's strongholds of attachment research, I was a firm believer of the universality assumptions of attachment theory and its methods. It wasn't until I started working with young scholars from the Global South, collecting video data of family life in over 20 countries, that I could not escape questioning the basis for some of these universality claims.[81]

One might wonder how a respected scholar with a PhD and a long track-record of research like Mesman had avoided absorbing *any* of the copious biological, cross-cultural, and sub-cultural evidence which challenges the universality of attachment *until she personally travelled to the Global South*. But a disavowal of contrary data and of critical research has long been endemic to the dynamics of what Mesman calls the world's 'strongholds' of attachment research.

Bowlby himself rarely addressed criticisms of his work. Neither did Ainsworth. One telling episode was when Bowlby asked Ainsworth to rebut Mead's criticisms about the cultural narrowness of the data upon which he based his claim that an attachment template was innate to every human baby (see 5.3.2). Ainsworth's resulting response to Mead entirely avoided discussing the wealth of Mead's cross-cultural data. Instead she asserted: first, that Mead had misrepresented Bowlby, who had never proposed 'an exclusive mother-child pair as the ideal'; and secondly, *though lacking any empirical support*, she claimed that dispersion of maternal care was 'not likely to be the norm in any primitive society', and hence, that it was 'entirely likely that the infant himself is innately monotropic'—which implied, contrary to her first point, that 'an exclusive mother-child pair' *was* Bowlby's ideal![82] There are more examples. Thus, Bowlby's 1982 edition of his book *Attachment* hardly ever discusses the many studies which had queried its claims since it first came out in 1969. For instance, it entirely ignores the several studies from the 1970s which proved 'stranger fear' was not the kind of universal phenomenon his theory makes it out to be.[83]

On top of simply ignoring criticism, we have also seen how editorial, methodological, and cultural forms of gatekeeping ensure that *non-approved researchers* and *non-approved kinds of evidence* are 'disappeared' from the attachment paradigm—as, for example, when findings about local conceptions and practices of childrearing are treated as inadmissible if they contradict attachment theory's Western ideal of an inborn one-to-one infant-adult template.[84] So what happens if an *insider* has the temerity to challenge the attachment perspective's paradigmatic assumptions?

In the first place, the pressures of in-group conformity usually mean that in-group critics of the attachment paradigm pull their punches. For example, as in Mesman's case, they will take pains, once they have posed some 'uncomfortable questions' about attachment claims, abjectly to assert their continued 'appreciation of the scientific rigour of attachment research'. But even this may fail, if insider criticisms become too threatening to the paradigm. Such work is liable to be 'excommunicated' from future discussions of attachment by the in-group. And likewise, its authors.

The most notable example of such excommunication attends work by the eminent researcher Michael Lamb and his colleagues. Lamb's group produced two long and meticulous critiques of attachment theory and the SSP in the mid-1980s.[85] Their critiques covered misuses of evolutionary theory in the conceptualization of attachment, flaws in the database with which Ainsworth had supported the SSP's development, the lack of discriminability of the categories and sub-categories she used to describe SSP behaviour and their lack of predictive power, the weak logic supporting attachment claims, plus, most damningly, the failure of attachment research to consider an alternative explanation for results from research using the SSP, namely that: the predictiveness of infants' behaviour classified using the SSP had not to do with their formation of a particular kind of cemented 'internal working model', or the way the workings of an infant's 'attachment behavioural system' had been shaped over many months by their mother's sensitivity. It resulted from over-time consistencies in the *kinds of care* infants were receiving between the different time-points when their 'attachment behaviour' was assessed in the SSP: '*relationships between early experiences and later outcomes have been demonstrated only when there is continuity in the circumstances that apparently produce the outcomes in question*'. That is, over-time consistency in an infant's attachment behaviour does not result from its 'internal' attachment system, but from consistent 'external' care from the group of carers who look after the baby.

Not only are the still-valid arguments that Lamb and his colleagues advanced against the attachment paradigm never discussed or referenced in such definitive volumes as the *Handbook of Attachment* (numbering 43 chapters and 1068 pages).[86] But, after publishing his critiques, many attachment researchers 'effectively ostracized Lamb'.[87]

5.3.5 Empirical overreach

We saw earlier how, despite the wealth of data to the contrary, and without citing any empirical support of her own, Ainsworth simply *asserted* that one-to-one mother-infant care was 'likely to be the norm in any primitive society'.

Similarly, Bowlby saw fit to continue to assert that infants' smiles, cries, coos, reaches, clinging, and looking simply *were* 'stereotyped' 'fixed action patterns', of the same kind as various stereotyped elements of reproductive behaviour in fish and digger wasps. He pointed to Peter Wolff's 'natural histories' of smiling and crying in support for his contention.[88] But neither Wolff's, nor *any* careful observations, back Bowlby's assertion. Bowlby and Ainsworth parroted similar claims (which are still made) about the parallel between infants' supposed 'attachment behavioural system' and those of animals like sticklebacks and herring-gulls (see Appendix A.2.1.2).

Given this background, perhaps we should not feel surprised when respected attachment figures today make unsupported empirical claims (such as those about 'infanticidal attachments' discussed earlier; Section 5.2.2). Even when attachment advocates *do* appear to support their claims with published empirical findings, appearances may mislead. Thus in 2022 Mary Sue Moore proposed that dysfunctional mothering can produce a 'dissociative' form of attachment in infants (which links to severe disorders in adulthood). She bases her proposal on what she calls 'many carefully conducted research studies' that show babies have 'an innate capacity to "dissociate" conscious awareness of bodily sensations as one of several neurologically organized survival mechanisms'.[89] To illustrate such 'careful' research, she cites three studies. But, when we get them out of the library, we find that none of these studies so much as mentions dissociation in babies.[90]

5.4 Flags of Convenience

The apparent power of the attachment paradigm in clinical work is enhanced by the frequent re-badging of existing approaches as attachment-based.[91] The promotion by policymakers and health scientists of 'evidence-based' practice, alongside the constant assertion of the unimpeachable scientific standing of the attachment paradigm, means there has been a proliferation of what might appear to be new, 'attachment-based' approaches to therapy. Clinicians nowadays find their email inboxes overflow with invitations to train in attachment-based practices, whatever initial training they may have had. 'Wisemind.com' regularly advertises these. Thus, within the context of a full-on Dialectical Behavioural Therapy (DBT) training, we find Dr Eboni Webb lecturing on what 'healthy attachment looks like', and exploring 'parenting styles' to explain later 'attachment styles'. While the growing number of like insertions into established schools of therapy may or may not be critical in terms of improving client outcomes, we will now illustrate some pitfalls.

5.4.1 Attachment-focused EMDR: healing relational trauma

Under the aegis of the procedure called Eye Movement Desensitization and Reprocessing (EMDR)—a treatment intervention which is well-established—we now find a newly labelled variety: 'Attachment-Focused EMDR'. Yet Laurel Parnell's recent book *Attachment-Focused EMDR: Healing Relational Trauma* tells us that she only *belatedly* discovered she was 'doing attachment-based work', after providing a training session attended by Daniel Siegel, a neurobiologist and exponent of attachment theory.[92]

Having talked to Siegel, she realized that she could or should re-frame her work as attachment-based, even though none of the developments and extensions of EMDR she had discovered were inspired by attachment theory.[93] So now, prior to its articulation of her innovative strategies for addressing relational trauma, Parnell's book pays tribute to Bowlby's brilliance, and to attachment theory's solid scientific credentials.

Read on and we find her book describes five pillars of effective Attachment-Focused EMDR: client safety; development and nurturing the therapeutic relationship to facilitate healing; use of a client-centred approach; create reparative neuro-networks via techniques of body-tapping; and use modified EMDR whenever client needs indicate. All five of these pillars would be familiar to most clinicians, especially EMDR clinicians—without mention of attachment theory, which has added nothing to them. Nevertheless, Parnell now labels her approach to EMDR 'attachment-focused'.

5.4.2 Couples therapy

Treatment plans and interventions which assume causal links drawn from attachment theory have become important in training couples therapists. Once we have accepted that a dyadic pair is foundational to developmental well-being, it's not surprising that there is a proliferation of attachment-based interventions for adult couples. These often link our infant-acquired 'internal working models' with how we behave as adults with our intimate partners.

Linda Cundy, Attachment Theory Consultant at London's 'Bowlby Centre' and provider of training workshops in couples counselling, is unequivocal about the origins of well-being in attachment. Her 2022 book, *Attachment, Maternal Deprivation, and Psychotherapy*, assures readers that attachment theory has been confirmed in laboratories and observational studies around the world, and can thus be safely imported into the consulting rooms of couples counsellors.[94]

Yet, at least in her workshop outlines, Cundy is careful to place less emphasis on the centrality of the mother–infant dyad than she might: 'This day is about the challenges faced by people who were ignored, criticized, rejected, or utterly neglected *within their families of origin* and who thus find it difficult to form close and lasting intimate relationships in adulthood'. This suggests a line is being blurred between grounding psychotherapy in the mother–infant dyad, and acknowledging the common-sensical notion that that's too narrow a view because *families* are the lynchpin of both mothers' and babies' well-being. Such blurring tacitly admits that Cundy's references to attachment theory have more a rhetorical than a practical value.

5.4.3 Family therapy

Family therapy has its own attachment branches. Thus Attachment-Based Family Therapy (ABFT) advertises itself as focusing on adolescent issues, and aims to repair interpersonal ruptures by rebuilding emotionally protective, secure relationships between family members. Developed and manualized by Guy Diamond and his colleagues, ABFT capitalizes on humans' 'innate, biological, and existential desire for meaningful and secure relationships' and is, it tells us, the only manualized, 'empirically supported' family therapy model specifically designed to target family and individual processes associated with adolescent suicide and depression.[95]

As with other clinical programmes, ABFT employs structured programmes which incorporate a range of techniques. And although it claims to be anchored by attachment theory, it uses attachment theory as a vehicle for ideas which are not distinctive, being common-sensical rather than derived from theory. For example, when Diamond and his colleagues argue against the idea that adolescent problems are 'intrapsychic',[96] they do so using ideas supposedly derived from attachment theory to furnish their alternative vision. These stress 'context-based' assessments and interventions—a stress aligned with what are loosely called 'environmentalist' approaches to child development, and so having no obvious tie to Bowlby's nativist, biological theory.

5.4.4 Summary

In short, with family therapy, as with other branches of clinical work, *what is true* about what clinicians hail as 'attachment theory' *is not new*, and *what*

128 Babies in Groups

is new about attachment theory *is not true*. After all, it is hardly new to say that 'context is important'; or that people are better off when they grow up surrounded by good relationships; or that severe maltreatment by parents in early childhood *may* have serious effects for psychological well-being when the abused children grow up. Conversely, it is mistaken to assume that: human sociability is primarily dyadic; early relationships are built from from stereotyped behaviours or 'fixed action patterns'; these relationships derive from an imaginary hominid evolutionary environment that prioritized infant-mother bonds in the Stone Age;[97] there is a time-defined duckling-like 'sensitive period' for specific social experiences in early infancy; and, that there is no need to examine the 'social support' surrounding a young child's caregivers to predict what will later happen to him or her (see Appendix A.2).

5.5 Seduction by Attachment Theory

From Margaret Mead onwards, many have published evidence casting doubt on the scientific validity of attachment thinking. So its continuing appeal across the professions proves that the power of the dyadic vision of infancy has roots in what we will call the feeling-structure of our Western societies, which give rise to that appeal.[98] Most obviously, the attachment vision resonates with ingrained feelings and long-standing ideas about the central importance of The Mother to children's lives. It is this non-scientific *rhetorical* appeal that we now address.

Take the idea that mental illness results from 'parental attacks' on a very young child, whether by mother, father, or anyone looking after her. Many will feel this claim makes an intuitive if chilling sense, whether or not we are psychotherapists. If we want to understand how to resolve this chill, Valerie Sinason, poet and psychoanalyst, sheds light (Figure 5.4).

Complementing her many essays and books, Sinason's lectures seek to convey her attachment views by provoking powerful emotions in us. For her, it is *our own visceral responses* which will help us to grasp the profundity of the insight attachment thinking gives—as when we are confronted by the need to imagine the experiences of a maltreated baby, and the defences which must result, and how these defences may lead later to a splintering into different identities (as in 'dissociative identity disorder' or DID).

Sinason invites us to approach the origins of fragmented identity by sharing how she as a clinician experiences the shocking outpourings of an 'abused child identity' in the speech of an adult client.[99] Sinason describes how, while

Figure 5.4 Poet and psychotherapist, Valerie Sinason.
By courtesy of Valerie Sinason.

being abused, a five- or six-year-old girl may dissociate or 'watch from above' while telling herself that the child being abused is not her, but another girl, for whom what is happening is normal. In turn, if this identity is later activated when the abuse increases—for example, through the abuser inviting several men to anally rape her—the girl's second identity may similarly 'escape', to look down creatively and see another person, 'Michael', a gay boy for whom being violently sodomized is normal.

Hearing about such a child's abuse, Sinason says, cannot help but trigger shock in us, a shock akin to our 'instinctual response' to a baby's cry. Sinason here slides our ordinary sympathetic responses to a child crying into the forbidding context derived from her story of horrific rapes. In so doing she evokes the fragility of our own attempts to defend against a lifetime of experiences of distress by getting us to think back to the dangerous time when we were at our smallest and weakest.

Referring to our instinctive reactions to a a baby screaming, Sinason portrays these screams as something no one can ignore, however much our reactions to and experiences may be moderated or changed by age or training. What happens when we pass a baby crying inconsolably in a mall?

> Do we think 'Oh, poor parents! They're tired! That baby's wearing them out. Can I help?' Or, 'Poor baby!—having a parent that's not doing something that relieves them!' Or, 'Horrible baby! Can you just shut up? I can't bear the sound!' Or, 'Horrible parents!'
>
> When I was a child psychotherapist, if I walked down the street and saw a baby crying, and a mother not looking as if she cared—to my embarrassment—I can remember frowning at the mother, adding to her hostile environment. And, when I later did adult training, and saw a baby crying, I smiled sympathetically at the mother, thinking 'Poor tired mother!' And often the poor mother, father, or, caretaker would pick the baby up or speak sympathetically—having been helped by the outside environment being less hostile.[100]

Sinason next explores the infants' complementary experiences, imagining babies as sensitively opened-up to their surroundings, gladly taking in whatever experience offers. Open like this, babies welcome the world with an expectation that everyone is thrilled to greet them, soaking up the love offered by those around them. Sinason then takes us into the feeling of being a baby exposed to *unloving* reactions. Imagine an infant with an obvious disability lying in her pram:

> And all these faces come to see the new baby and peer over the pram, and they all look excited, and then they see the baby has a disability, and they might frown, or look confused, or upset. What does it feel like if you see the peoples' faces change like that at looking at you?[101]

In this way Sinason leads us to imagine the destructive effects on an 'open' baby of these unwelcoming facial expressions. Then she invites us to go further and link these emotions with experiencing ourselves as tiny, when our smile at our parent provokes, not just confusion, but outright anger or even murderous hostility.

Of course, even the best carers will express different emotions at different times—a truism that has led psychoanalysts to propose that a crucial achievement for every baby is to find a way to combine this range of positive and negative maternal responses into an invitation to enter a world they can act upon and so gain real efficacy.[102] Melanie Klein (1882–1960) pioneered such visions.[103] For her, a key developmental hurdle is to reconcile contrasting primitive infantile experiences of what seems to be a 'split' mother: the 'good' loving mother who is always present and nurturing on the one hand, and on the other, the 'bad' neglectful mother who is vindictive or absent (cf. Section 5.1.1). In Sinason's words:

> Baby has to encompass all the visual states adult faces pass through. So all these things, *pre*-verbally, a baby is taking in. And there is an understanding somewhere within the body, within the psyche, of what you've taken in at your deepest level… a baby in fact is all in pieces. A baby is looking around everywhere, taking in things, taking in sound and vision, but not in any coherent way. And it takes some time for the baby's experience to begin to make sense…[104]

This is where Sinason starts to speculate about how the scary rejecting faces most babies see—of caregivers exhausted when tired or angry when frustrated—become integrated with the loving, accommodating faces. Her idea is that, by envisaging a small baby's conflicting and unintegrated experiences of varying parental expressions, we will catch a sense of the fractured interpersonal world an adult will experience who has *not* achieved such integration—and hence finds themselves living with DID: 'we need to think of what a shock a baby gets as slowly having to encompass all the visual states…'[105]

Sinason is building a vision of the baby's bodily-conscious-feelings-world as radically open to experiences which are compounded and multiplicitous. By now, if we have been taken up in her discourse and have identified with the baby Sinason portrays, we will be imagining ourselves absorbing countless different responses, all conflicting—some loving, some amused, some violent, some coldly dismissive, some warm and sympathetic, some silent, some loud—a 'blooming buzzing confusion'[106] of impactful events which makes us defend against feeling the reality of being 'all in pieces'. It is *this* emotional, moving, responsive, multivalent, universe that she asks us to imagine a baby acting in, acting on, trying to master, struggling to 'encompass' so that their world 'makes sense'.

Sinason's word-paintings draw us into experiencing our own vulnerabilities and our own responses to others' vulnerabilities, especially when very small and new to the world—along with our defences against these experiences, both in the 'split' normality of Klein's baby, and as produced, more intensely and catastrophically, in response to abuse. We have tentatively opened ourselves up, like the baby Sinason has sensitively been drawing for us, absorbing a flow of visceral understanding, of experiencing and re-experiencing, of pleasure and of horror.

Challenged by Sinason's several turbulent pictures of our early months, many readers will be hungry for relief. Which is when Sinason pulls a rabbit out of the hat, the rabbit being 'the brilliant research on attachment, which has done more for therapy than any other scientific research'. It is this brilliant research which, Sinason tells us, has revealed how we can be 'immunized' against a fractured identity and DID. So, now we can turn our eyes away from the stormy highs and lows of infant experience, and rest assured

> … that with a secure attachment, that where you have good-enough parenting, that a baby has got the strongest immunization for life, for all the normal ups and downs, hurdles and traumas, and would need the most unlikely sequence of experiences to develop Dissociative Identity Disorder.[107]

But no associated 'brilliant research' is cited. Nor could it be, because attachment theory hypothesizes no process which could explain how consistent parenting might bind together the shockingly fragmented experiences of young babies which Sinason has just been describing. Nor have attachment researchers ever acknowledged that all babies live in or experience a world of splits and fragments. In fact, one of Bowlby's aims in devising attachment theory was to *replace* the concepts which psychoanalysts like Klein and Sinason use to describe the subjective complexity of infant experience.[108]

The incommensurability between Sinason's description of babies' worlds and the kinds of phenomena attachment researchers research means her claims about the immunizing effects of 'good-enough parenting' do no more than echo the truism that babies brought up in a loving environment are less likely to develop problems than babies brought up in abusive environments. Sinason reiterates an easily accessed understanding of human development, ironically skating over the subjective complexity she has been describing. The way is paved again for blaming *bad-enough* 'parenting' (which largely means 'mothering' in Western societies) for causing mental illness in children.

5.6 Staying with Complexity

The jagged fault-line in Sinason's discourse illustrates the narrowed take on infancy which a dyadic focus imposes, the focus which this book challenges. Offered rich and engaging descriptions of each baby as experiencing and acting into a world which opens up to and challenges her through a multitude of different faces, feelings, and connections, we are joltingly confronted with the conclusion that this same baby's world is best understood through a theory which prioritizes just one face, that of the baby's mother[109]—a face which, thanks to two million years of evolution, will naturally mirror the baby's needs and feelings.

More generally, when we refuse dyadic spectacles, a host of new doors open, inviting us to consider afresh: how individuals become individuals when all of us start out amidst social complexity and subjective multiplicity;[110] the ways we imagine and judge our own childhoods; how we can best arrange for the care and education of our very young; how we explain pathological development; and how most effectively to assess and promote infant mental health.

Some answers are already available. To take just one example, Ruth Feldman and Miri Keren have undertaken to address the concern that, 'the application of the person-in-context perspective in infant mental health has been mainly limited to mother–child relations, and few clinicians have gone beyond the dyad'.[111]

Accordingly, Feldman and Keren have developed practices for the assessment of infant mental health which not only consider the behaviour of *both* parent–infant dyads in various different settings (home, laboratory, playground, paediatric clinic). They also observe and analyse the infant's individual disposition, the parents' mental representations of their child, their family's structure and group dynamics, the impacts on the family of its enfolding community, along with the larger envelope of cultural values, child-rearing philosophies, and norms of proper social conduct—all of which are held to contribute to the 'context' against which unusual behaviour is properly measured.

As for our own practice, more doors open. Matt's childcare and education services are implementing a group-based approach to dealing with troubling and disruptive behaviour in their infant rooms (0–2 year olds). Under Matt's direction, staff and very young children are engaged as 'spectators' in theatrical games adapted from the work of Augusto Boal.[112] Using Boal's iterative process of 'forum theatre', for example, children are encouraged to rework episodes from their rooms in ways which are likely to have better outcomes for all. Readers interested in the future progress of Matt's ongoing action research are encouraged to follow up on the website which supports and extends the work described in this book. This can be found at babiesingroups.com.

When taken up by psychotherapists, psychologists, and allied professionals, Matt's theatre-based work with babies and toddlers, like Feldman and Keren's pioneering of a genuinely context-based assessment of infants' difficulties, works towards a transformation of the limiting assumptions in dyadic therapeutic work. Such work encourages us to open our eyes to the complexity of interdependency within which every infant creates their life. But we must also ask how mental health and psychological functioning will need to be thought about, as we increasingly acknowledge that group life is the warp and weft of everyday life for both babies and their carers—as it is for us all.

6
Concluding Remarks

Figure 6.1 Belonging from the start: The herd happily welcomes a newborn baby.

Our discussion of babies as able group participants celebrates the creativity and the power of groups of humans of any age. Interdependency and multiplicity are the rule for humans, as for many other species—all of which have evolved through their participation in what Darwin called the infinitely complex 'web of relations' which makes up the natural world (Figure 6.1).[1] Each human organ combines a relative autonomy of function and bodily structure with simultaneous participation in manifold interwoven multi-organ systems—neural, digestive, locomotory, muscular, excretory, and circulatory. Similarly, every infant's awareness and interactions gain meaning through simultaneous engagement with a multi-layered presence of people and things, sensations, feelings, and actions—both of self and of others. Beyond this is an individual's 'polyadic' enmeshment within overlapping social groups and structures, endowing each of us with 'multi-subjectivity', which makes us the mercurial creatures we are. A journey which set out with the aim of incorporating babies' group capacities into contemporary visions of infancy ultimately brings us to consider the ways we create ourselves through our management of complexity and multiplicity.

The current persuasiveness of the one-to-one 'attachment' perspective derives from the intergenerational transmission of childcare practices in societies shaped by specifiable cultural, political, and economic exigencies. Accordingly, given the socio-cultural specificity of attachment theory's own origins—its close ties to the conditions of its emergence in post-(Second World) War Britain (Chapter 1.2)—it may evoke a kind of 'narrative truth' in therapists and clients who have themselves emerged from the kinds of socio-cultural conditions which attachment theorists take to be humanly universal.[2] Yet, as if to block any curiosity about such conditions, attachment advocates claim a grounding for their views in biology and a deep evolutionary past. As a result, their work cannot easily accommodate alternative cultural forms or the theoretical, clinical, and educational work which draws on the wonders, joys, and needs of infants to be in groups.

By way of context, we are reminded that in the last years of the Second World War, a political fight boiled over the provision of care versus education for very young children in post-war Britain. Prior to the adoption of the 1944 Education Act by the British government, the Nursery Schools Association issued a report which reflected the experience of many nursery and infant teachers—extolling the value of group-based education for the very young:

> No home can provide all the child needs after the period of dependent infancy, if he [or she] is to grow adequately in mind and character as well as in physique. For this period the nursery school should be the natural extension of the home and in its home-like informality provide an all-round education ... Many children who begin school at the age of five suffer considerable check in their physical and mental development—while they go through the painful process of learning, often too late, how to adjust themselves to the social life of a group of children.[3]

1944 also saw the publication of *Forty-Four Juvenile Thieves*, where John Bowlby—bypassing consideration of any possible role played by poverty, peer relations, inequality, or social alienation—argued that the lack of a secure relationship with their mother in infancy was the principal cause of delinquency among young criminals.[4] *Forty-Four Juvenile Thieves* served as an overture to Bowlby's launch of attachment theory in the 1950s.

This historical juxtaposition shows that the tension between group-based visions of our very young and the idealization of the infant–mother dyad explored in this book has a deep cultural past. Yet, as Dale Hay and her colleagues show in their extensive review of research, no contemporary theory of infancy provides a way to account for the fact that young children can develop a social life *in groups*.[5] This theoretical incapacity leads many psychologists to deny the existence of evidence for group interaction in the first year of life. Thus, as late as 2005, and despite growing evidence to the contrary, Celia Brownell and her colleagues could assert that: 'On the whole, infants and young toddlers do not appear particularly interested in social exchange with age mates, in contrast to their interest in collaborating socially with adults or even older siblings' (Figure 6.2).[6]

Whilst academics and policy advocates may fight, there is a common-sense obviousness to the need for babies and toddlers—and home-alone mothers—to spend time with friends. In post-war Australia, the government's provision of baby clinics was primarily aimed at helping individual infants deemed to be 'at risk'. But demand in Australia for playgroups, which began to be set up in the 1970s, grew rapidly in response to grassroots demand from mothers wanting their children to learn through quality play with others, and wanting adult social support for themselves.[7] Nowadays childcare and child education centres

Figure 6.2 Baby with sibling.
Laura Alzueta/Shutterstock.

are becoming commonplace in the West, providing an education and social basis for our young, as well as support for employed parents. In these settings group play is a normal part of the infants' everyday lives, making these centres a boon for our very young. Without such group experience, infants may have to rely on and develop their sense of themselves, and of others, during long days at home with just one carer, stereotypically their biological mother.

Babies' need for group experience is the same need that was underlined by the British Nursery Schools Association in 1943: preparation for a later life that will largely be lived in groups. Where our research goes beyond what teachers of infants assumed during the Second World War is in our evidence that babies can operate and thrive in groups *during their first year of life*.

The evidence and discussion which fills this book removes the need for Hay and her colleagues' theoretical puzzle about explaining how a child *becomes able* to act in a group, because—as we show—this ability grounds development from the start of life. If we look back at debates in the decades *before* the fight over infancy that followed the Second World War, we find many well-known theorists, clinicians, and philosophers arguing that the very idea of an 'individual psyche' is back-to-front—precisely because children start out integrally enmeshed in their several societal contexts—and only later begin to separate themselves out, more or less successfully, as 'an individual' who is distinct from these contexts (Figure 6.3). To take Sigmund Freud as an example, we find him writing in the early 1920s:

> Each individual is a component part of numerous groups, he is bound by ties of identification in many directions, and he has built up his ego ideal upon the most various models. Each individual therefore has a share in numerous group minds—those of his race, of his class, of his creed, of his nationality, etc.[8]

Concluding Remarks

Figure 6.3a Trivia night in a pub.
Wikimedia/CC-by-2.0.

Figure 6.3b Rugby union.
IOIO IMAGES/Shutterstock.

Figure 6.3c Men praying in mosque.
demidoff/Shutterstock.

Figure 6.3 The internet is replete with instances of the young in group formations, and of team sports.*

'The strength of the team is each individual member. The strength of each member is the team,' quoth basketball player and coach, Phil Jackson.**

* For example, Figure 6.3b
** Phil Jackson, *https://www.goodreads.com › author › 2853.Phil_Jackson*

140 Babies in Groups

Figure 6.3d Synchronized swimming team.
Pete Saloutos/Shutterstock.

Figure 6.3e Group of soldiers.
Getmilitaryphotos/Shutterstock.

Figure 6.3f Dancing boy with group of adults—screen capture from YouTube film.

APPENDIX

Intersubjectivity and Attachment: Alternatives

Attachment theory is built on a purported explanation of how crawling babies and toddlers supposedly behave when under various levels of stress or insecurity: when they feel stressed, they *seek proximity* with Mam as a 'safe haven'; when they feel unstressed, they use Mam as a 'secure base' to explore. The theory of innate intersubjectivity was proposed to explain something complementary to attachment theory: what happens when baby and mother *are already in proximity* to each other, and feeling chatty.

This Appendix presents a review of the evidential basis for these two approaches to infancy, both of which claim an innate template of one-to-one 'dyadic' sociability is the biological foundation-stone for child development.

1. Innate Intersubjectivity

The idea that babies possess an inborn faculty for intersubjectivity, that is, a capacity to read minds, has gained widespread and increasing traction with psychologists and health providers since the 1970s, inspiring a distinctive account of infant development and child psychopathology.[1] The chief source of evidence scientists adduce for this capacity remains the micro-analysis of brief face-to-face infant–mother interactions or 'conversations', usually filmed in university laboratories, starting when babies are around two months old.

Whilst there are variations in the ways discussions of infant intersubjectivity are expressed, all assume early intersubjectivity, however rudimentary, equates to a *true* reading of others: 'the infant is born with awareness specifically receptive to subjective states in other persons'.[2] Accordingly, these discussions mix up demonstrating an infant's capacity to find *a* personal significance in a m/other's conversational behaviour with finding *the* personal significance of her behaviour, as if there were no alternative to a direct and veridical form of self-other understanding.[3]

Yet, from the outset of child psychology's current engagement with the idea of intersubjectivity,[4] the go-to texts of Jürgen Habermas were stressing that intersubjectivity is impure or 'systematically distorted' unless it takes place in an 'ideal' speech situation: where all participants have symmetrical powers of expression, censure, and self-representation.[5] This ideal is far from being met in infant–mother conversations, which are highly *asymmetrical*.[6] Which raises the relevance of a lesser-known theory of infant intersubjectivity, one that holds early infant–adult interaction to be structured by a *narcissistic* dynamic, where the mother—and particularly the mother's face—is 'not yet separated off from the infant by the infant', as Donald Winnicott put it.[7]

1.1 Evaluating evidence relating to infant intersubjectivity

1.1.1 Prespeech behaviour
In the 1970s, Colwyn Trevarthen's demonstration of the recently discovered complexity of two-month-olds' contribution to filmed face-to-face 'conversations' with their mothers was *itself* held up as proof of innate intersubjectivity. The rhetorical argument went: why else would

babies show turn-taking bouts of 'listening' and 'pre-speech' (lip and tongue movements combined with speech-like breath-control and gesturing) in face-to-face 'conversations' *unless* humans had an inborn capacity for sharing states of minds with their caregivers? This argument was typically directed against psychologists who believed: either that babies lacked the power cognitively to represent other people as people before the end of their first year of life (see Chapter 3.3.1);[8] or that babies were born without complex inborn capacities and had to learn them from, or otherwise be 'scaffolded' into them, by adults (see Chapter 1.11). As mentioned, this rhetorical argument tacitly assumes intersubjectivity is inherently transparent and true or 'veridical'—typically, *without investigating what mothers' states of mind actually are* during recording sessions. And for good reason. Because a serious examination of a mother's complex mentality during early infant–adult 'conversations' would swiftly rule out any possibility of *symmetrical* infant–mother understanding (see Section 1.1.3).

1.1.2 People versus things

Those who have advocated 'innate intersubjectivity' on the grounds of observations like those just discussed have typically also claimed that babies *categorically* distinguish 'unliving physical objects as different from living intelligent objects like their mothers and behave quite differently to these two kinds of thing'.[9] This was not a claim backed up by any numerical data, being advanced largely on the grounds that it just makes sense that, if babies are born knowing about people—that they have intentions, motives, feelings, and so on—then when they face a person they must be treating that person quite differently from a thing.

When this claim is experimentally tested, however, it proves false—albeit in a way which suggests infants' interpersonal behaviour is governed in part by *their own* moods of imagination. Thus, one study filmed ten-week-olds' behaviour in two contrasting conditions: with mothers who had been asked 'to chat with and entertain' their babies; and with a small red wooden ball which moved slowly back and forth across the baby's field of vision at a reachable distance.[10] Results showed no categorical distinction in the behaviours recorded with person versus ball, though the incidence of three behaviours did differ significantly between the two conditions. (There was more 'mouth opening'—indicative of prespeech—and 'eyebrow lowering', or frowning, in the 'person-directed' condition, and more 'turning away' in the 'object-directed'.) *All* behaviours were seen in *both* conditions—including 'reaching' (which was included as hypothetically 'object-directed' condition). Further statistical analysis showed that one mode or mood of 'person-directed' infant actions occurred as a single ensemble across *both* conditions, with people *and* with things (this comprised eyebrow-raising [greeting/interest], tongue protrusion, and mouth opening [both hypothetically indicative of prespeech].[11] Which suggests that babies can sometimes treat people as things, and sometimes treat things as people just like adults.

These results undermine the claim that early infant–adult 'conversations' are generated by the infant's innate knowledge of other people: of their motives, their mental states, and their intentions. In short, we *cannot* 'look at any segment of the infant's body and detect whether he [sic] is watching an object or interacting with his mother'.[12]

1.1.3 Mirroring infants' conversational behaviour

It is now widely acknowledged that mothers and other adults, when filmed in face-to-face 'conversations' with young babies, do something that was dubbed 'mirroring' in the 1970s—or, more recently, 'affective mirroring'.[13] This is most evident in what mothers say whilst being filmed. The vast majority of mothers' speech reflects what *their babies* are doing *as they do it*: 'You a bit hot, eh?'; 'You're not looking very happy'; 'You're looking very pensive, aren't you?'; 'You've got your hand in the air'. This means changes in infant behaviour are directly matched by changes in the verbal content of 'motherese': particularly the baby's growing interest in inanimate objects over the second three months of life.

Not only does verbal content and structure—pronouns, present tense, and references—reflect or represent the baby's behaviour but the paralinguistic features of a mother's babytalk also typically echo her infant's sound-making in loudness, pitch, intonation, and phrasing. Infants' facial expressions are 'mirrored' too, right down to subtle movements of lips and eyebrows.[14] Which confirms what Donald Winnicott observed: 'when the mother is looking at the baby ... *what she looks like is related to what she sees there*'. The mother's face is 'a mirror'. So when a baby looks at a mother's face, 'what the baby sees is himself or herself'.[15] This is a highly skewed form of 'communication'.

1.1.4 Perturbation experiments

The idea that very young babies like to treat their mothers as mirrors when they 'converse' with them is supported by what are called 'perturbation experiments'. There are several examples. One is to be found in the work of Lynne Murray, who in the 1970s, invented a recording procedure in which two-month-olds and their mothers interact through closed-circuit TV. In separate rooms, each participant views a monitor showing the other. This allows two experimental conditions to be compared: 'live' and 'replay'. Murray's studies show that, when babies see their mothers 'live', they show 'normal, happy communication', 'smiling, cooing, tonguing, and gesturing'. But the delayed 'replay' condition (which perforce came second in order) 'causes the infant to show distress, puzzlement, and autistic behaviour'.[16]

Such results are typically held to have proven 'that interactions between mothers and their infants of two to three months of age are governed by mutual awareness of complex and expressive communications', and, therefore, that 'the infant possesses an innate capacity for intersubjective behaviour'.[17] But there is another explanation, which we call 'primary narcissism' (see Section 1.3): that the baby who looks away from his or her mother—whose face and voice are *not* reflecting what the baby is doing from moment to moment—is escaping feelings of impotency aroused by the mother's 'failure' to play second fiddle to the baby's lead.

1.2 Mind-reading?

The four sources of evidence just described have inspired explanations couched in terms of babies' inherent or innate comprehension of others. We are told that, if babies can be filmed responding in a comprehensible way to their mothers' talking at them, then it follows that the babies must be able to 'share and participate' in the 'motivations and purposes', 'feelings and thoughts' of their conversational partners.[18] Or, in other words, if babies can be said to converse with their Mums, there is simply no alternative to the conclusion that they manifest true intersubjectivity.

All of which bypasses the possibility of human misunderstanding. Advocates of the view that babies' have a *direct* or transparent understanding of others never mention the opacities and distortions in infant–adult, or indeed in *adult–adult* conversations.[19] Instead, they will seek to find formulations about how *best to conceive* infant–adult talk so as to prove babies capable of recognizing 'personal meaning'. For example, Vasu Reddy charmingly pictures babies as engaging adults in the kind of idealized one-to-one relating which the theologian-philosopher Martin Buber dubbed *I-Thou*, where 'in each *Thou* we address the eternal *Thou*', where 'infinity and universality are made actual', so that two people 'meet one another in their authentic existence, without any qualification or objectification of one another'.[20]

From Buber, Reddy concludes that, whenever we talk to another person *directly*, we necessarily assume he or she both 'can respond and <u>understand</u>' us, and 'deserves <u>recognition</u> *as a person*.²¹ Hence, to the extent that babies engage adults in one-to-one conversations at all, they too must recognize adults as persons who can respond to and understand them. This eye-poppingly presumes that babies and adults—in fact, all of us—just *do* habitually relate to each other in the sacred I-Thou fashion which Buber himself found to be extremely rare in today's world in which most of the inhabitants '*want* to be deceived'.²² Thus, according to Reddy, Buber's philosophy *ensures* that we only have to find evidence showing that, in face-to-face settings, very young babies *do* 'engage in conversation' with their Mum or Dad in order to conclude that babies directly recognize 'the psychological qualities' of 'persons'. In short, as in the title of her book, *How Infants Know Minds*, even two-month-old infants will have been proven to 'know [other] minds'.

In Reddy's philosophical language, babies' one-to-one engagement with adults amounts to a *cognitive* achievement, as the underlined words in the previous paragraph show: infant–adult conversations show babies are capable of 'understanding' and 'knowing [other] minds', or 'recognizing' 'the psychological qualities' of another person. Yet, in contrast with this cognitive definition, Reddy's *empirical* claim that babies do converse with adults employs twelve *non-cognitive* criteria for conversation which she calls 'structural features of dialogue'. She persuades us that two-month-old babies manifest *four* of these twelve features when *en face* with an attentive adult, namely: speech-like lip and tongue movements; non-random bodily movements and facial expressions; turn-taking; and finally, 'they express emotions which are reciprocally [i.e. comprehensibly] related to the emotions [actually emotional *expressions*] of others'. It is these *new* grounds, when viewed through the lens of her second *non-cognitive* definition, which allow her to conclude babies are capable of conversation, and that, *therefore*, by reference to her *first* definition, babies have been shown directly to understand, and recognize *the* psychological qualities of others.

This is like defining a car as a motorized vehicle that can take one from place to place, and then noting that all cars have four wheels and a windscreen. According to Reddy's logic, it would make sense to say that anyone who possesses four wheels and a windscreen has a car in which they can travel from place to place.

1.3 Primary narcissism

If we reconsider the observational evidence in Section 1.1, it squares better with an account of intersubjectivity which does not assume that all intersubjectivity is veridical. In this alternative view, young bubs are not interested in the m/other's real personal qualities, feelings, and thoughts as such. Their attraction to interacting with people like their mothers results from them enjoying a sense of empowerment and control from seeing their actions reflected back 'at twice their natural size' by the m/other.²³ Thus the reason that mothers, and all sensitive elders, typically engage in 'mirroring' when talking to babies is because mirroring proves the best way to adapt to the infant's communicative behaviour, behaviour which is governed by what is known as 'narcissism'.²⁴ Likewise, when babies turn away from their mothers in Murray's 'perturbation experiments', they do not do so out of empathy for their 'replayed' mother—who, after all, looks just as happy as she did when she was interacting with them 'live'. They turn away and get upset because they no longer feel empowered by what their mothers are (now *non*-contingently) doing. Likewise, babies do not categorically distinguish people from things because the ways they deal with the world do not slavishly reflect 'reality': how they treat both people and things depends, at least partly, on how they are feeling about the world from moment to moment.

Amongst the advantages of this alternative interpretation to conversational behaviour in young babies is that it attributes a complex subjective creativity to babies: their social behaviour is, in good part, a consequence of their own feelings and imaginings, not the fruit of a single-minded attempt to read—or of a functional 'adaptation' to—a supposedly unambiguous 'real world'. This more complex understanding of infants has another advantage: potentially explaining infant negativity as something *intrinsic* to a baby's attitude to others. Thus, several observers have noted that, by three and four months of age, babies increasingly look away from their mothers in *en face* exchanges.[25] Whilst this avoidant behaviour seldom draws comment from proponents of mind-reading, when it does, it is either explained as manifesting the baby's growing enjoyment in 'novelty and exploration'[26] or as the infant's response to his or her mother 'being too insistent', or 'unsympathetically projecting "mistaken" interpretations of the infant's feelings'.[27] Neither of these interpretations finds support in the observations they ostensibly summarize:

When four-month-olds avert their gaze from their mothers, they do not proceed to look for more interesting objects in their environment. Nor are they responding to any observed change in their mothers' behaviour: there is no evidence that the mothers of babies who look away from them have been acting unsympathetically or intrusively. When bubs look away from their Mams in recording sessions, they typically stare fixedly at some object or surface while watching and waiting (through peripheral vision, 'out of the corners of their eyes') for their Mam to look away *from them*. They then often swiftly look back at *her* averted face. Then, as soon as her head starts turning back to look at them, they immediately look away from her again, thereby continuing to avoid her gaze (these are called 'fractional glances').[28] As such, infant negativity appears to be interpersonally motivated, not due to a simple expansion of interests. The rise of fractional glances in three-and four-month-olds suggests that babies who ostentatiously look away from their mothers ('at nothing') in this manner have found a new sense of empowerment through the exertion of control over the mother's looking-behaviour.

So, it is incorrect to explain four-month-olds' negativity as the mother's 'fault'—for being 'insensitive' or 'intrusive'. Gratuitous mother-blaming of this kind is an inevitable consequence of the 'direct understanding' vision of infancy, which imagines both infants and mothers naturally possess a homogenous and univocal subjectivity, harmoniously, transparent to each other.[29]

1.3.1 Primary processes

Like cognition-first approaches, including the attachment perspective, the theory of innate intersubjectivity does not attribute an intrinsic capacity for creative imagination or fantasy to young babies. Reality is treated as something determinate and unambiguous that we—meaning, in this case, babies—just have to adapt to and learn about.

Such assumptions stand in stark contrast to an earlier theory of infant intersubjectivity, which was rooted in Sigmund Freud's theory of primary process. It is here that we find a vision of infants as beings replete with creative imagination and fantasy life. Freud's theory sets out from the viewpoint captured by the poet T.S. Eliot's line: 'humankind cannot bear very much reality'.[30] Due to babies' powerful need for self-preservation combined with their actual physical impotence, their lack of autonomy, and their vulnerability to the whims of others, any true awareness of the extent of their powerlessness would be cataclysmic. So, the first and most fundamental psychical move in humans is to deny one's actual condition via a 'primary' process of what Freud called 'hallucinatory wish-fulfilment'. Freud likens the infant's psyche to an egg which secretes a hard protective shell around a hidden yolk of 'inner' activities. Thus, infants displace any experience of their *real* vulnerability by virtue of a process which makes them feel complete, satisfied, and powerful. With time, children begin to build up reality-based 'secondary processes'—though these never entirely supplant our primitive, pleasure-governed, wish-fulfilling, primary process.

Primary processes should thus be seen partly as an escape, with the sense of their imagery being fantasy. Yet, in order for the infant to survive and thrive, the process also connects to reality by structuring representations of the ongoing satisfaction of vital needs. The baby starts sucking at the mother's proffered breast and soon feels her warm milk flooding inwards. Once the baby's stomach is full, the milk will have satisfied his or her physiological need. But any satisfaction the baby *immediately feels* upon sucking cannot be directly related to physiological satisfaction, because, until the feed is finished, the baby's physiological need remains unmet. Hence baby's *experience* of satisfaction at 'getting fed' is related to a reality *which it simultaneously distorts*. Jacques Lacan (1949) found an image of this mismatch between reality and imaginary satisfaction in infants' jubilant control over their own image in a mirror. The mirror offers a complete, bounded, and integrated image of the self which is both real and unreal—in that it faithfully reflects what the baby looks like yet shows no sign of the baby's felt fears, confusions, needs, demands, and vulnerabilities. It was Lacan's metaphor of the mirror which was taken up by Winnicott into the annals of psychotherapy and, from there, into laboratory-based infant research.

Winnicott extended Lacan's notion of the mirror dynamic in infancy to what he called the 'holding' function of maternal behaviour. 'Holding' captures a crucial aspect of the individual's relationship with others. In infancy, it is comprised of the m/other giving back to the baby what the baby feels and needs but can, when left to his or her own devices, only hallucinate. The mother's role is to complete *in reality* what the baby can only wish for. It is in this way that, when it comes to face-to-face interaction, the mother undertakes to make of herself and her face 'a mirror'. So when a baby looks at a mother's face, the baby will see what she or he is doing being reflected back and elaborated 'live' by the mother. In this, the mother's 'holding' or 'mirroring' role serves to reassure the baby that it is safe to accept a limited amount of reality, even while ignoring many aspects of his or her immediate need.

This approach, which highlights the active imagination and creativity of the narcissistic infant, provides quite a different story of development from that of a psyche directly imbibing or adapting to an unambiguous reality which is presumed to be perceived accurately and without difficulty. Such presumption finds advocates of babies' capacity for direct understanding of other people also assuming a capacity for direct understanding in themselves. Thus, such scientists feel no need to examine different interpretations of the interactions they observe; nor to question the grounds of their own participation in what has for centuries been called the hermeneutic 'circle' of interpretation.[31] Nor do they acknowledge a need to consider what psychoanalysts call the contribution of the counter-transference to their reading of others.[32]

There is always likely to be some self-serving element in general observations about babies.[33] Thus, the best-known scientific visions of infancy have all been elaborated by theorists who use infancy as a canvas upon which to draw—or as a kind of proving-ground for—the key features of *their own* vision of humanity. Freud pictured infancy as a time dominated by sexual passions, instancing the faces flushed with pleasure of babies sucking at their mothers' breasts and the erections of baby boys. The 'genetic epistemologist' Jean Piaget imagined a baby whose primary goal was to build a science-like conceptual representation of the physical world: for example, by constructing a realistic 'object concept' (e.g. so that it can recognize that things continue to exist even when out of sight). No talk of breasts or erections for Piaget! The grammarian Noam Chomsky argued babies were born endowed with a 'language acquisition device' that was (like Chomsky) sensitive to the fundamental rules of grammar. And proponents of the view that infants need a 'theory of mind' before they can understand others, model babies on the ideal of the hypothetico-deductive scientist they themselves aspire to be.[34]

Such a history shows that it is imperative for psychologists to recognize how their visions of infancy may be partial: a form of *situated* knowledge, coloured by *their own participation* in the groups to which *they* belong.[35] Interpretation always starts out as a more or less plausible attempt to incorporate an act or event into a specific culture of understanding.

1.4 Intersubjectivity in groups

Meanwhile, more recent formulations of intersubjectivity theory have been converging with our findings about babies in groups. Stephen Malloch and Colwyn Trevarthen have pounced with gusto on the idea that baby humans have an inborn 'communicative musicality' which allows them to join with or enrol others both in shared rhythmic forms of pulse and variations of quality (i.e. in the pitch, contour, and volume) of sound-making. Such forms of shared agency are by no means limited to two-person interactions (cf. Chapter 4). Music and dance as easily engage 'many with many'[36] as one with one—as anyone knows who has enjoyed a corroboree, ceilidh, or concert.

2. The attachment perspective

Bowlby's attachment theory holds that all human babies are born with the raw materials to construct an 'attachment behavioural system' over their first three years of life.[37] By a child's third birthday, this attachment system will have gained a stable form. This form will either be secure or insecure, depending on how the child's mother looked after the child during infancy.[38] Henceforth, the social and emotional life of the child—and the adult she or he becomes—will be strongly influenced by the form of his or her primary attachment system.

These claims about babies remain what the current *Handbook of Attachment* calls the undisputed 'core'[39] of today's attachment theory. *none* of them has a credible grounding in evidence, as we now show.

2.1 The infant's 'attachment behavioural system' does not exist.

In the 1950s and 1960s, Bowlby argued that babies are born with an *instinct* to attach themselves to their mothers, resulting in behaviour parallel to the lamb in the poem 'Mary had a little lamb'. However, the term 'instinct' underwent significant critique in the study of animal behaviour (ethology) during the 1960s and 1970s, because instincts were too often attributed to animals, and humans, without any distinctive observable criteria. It would be better, argued ethologists, if rigid sequences of the highly stereotyped behaviours they called 'fixed action patterns' (or FAPs) were no longer called *instincts*. Instead, repeated sequences of FAPs—like the 16 FAPs which constitute the stereotyped nest-building behaviour of digger wasps, or the 20 FAPs which comprise parental incubation of herring-gull eggs—should be understood as the output of hierarchically-organized 'behavioural systems'.[40] So Bowlby changed his language, and claimed that, when he wrote of attachment formation as 'instinctive', what he meant was that all human babies were born biologically programmed to develop a thermostat-like 'attachment behavioural system' over the first three years of life—a system which had proximity-to-mother as its 'set-goal' (just as the eggs of the herring gull are the 'set-goal' of their parents' twenty incubational FAPs). But this claim has no basis in evidence:

2.1.1 Infant social behaviour does not comprise 'fixed action patterns' and is not solely dyadic

Bowlby said babies begin the process of attachment formation with a limited range of inborn proximity-promoting behaviours or signals: babbling, clinging, crying, following (with their eyes), grasping, looking, orienting, reaching, rooting, smiling, and sucking. These are emitted[41] towards others indiscriminately from birth until 12 weeks of age. From 3 to 7 months, babies continue to 'emit' these so-called attachment behaviours to all-comers but, increasingly, in a more marked fashion towards their mother-figure than towards anyone else. Bowlby called these attachment behaviours fixed action patterns (FAPs), as they are '*highly stereotyped* and, once initiated, follow their typical course to its completion *almost irrespective of what is happening in the environment*.'[42]

In fact, the attachment behaviours Bowlby lists have little in common with FAPs. From birth onwards, actions like rooting, sucking, reaching, and grasping are all goal-directed, in that they can be altered to gain advantages, and hence *are flexible*, in form, function, and duration—antithetically to FAPs.[43] Unaccountably, Bowlby even called *smiling* and *crying* FAPs, despite only citing articles containing evidence to the contrary (cf. Chapter 5.3.5)! As any parent knows from a baby's first days on, smiles take many subtly variable forms, varying in length, occasion, and intensity.[44] And crying is a *continuous* system for coding distress, cries varying gradually from being quiet and discontinuous to loud and continuous.[45] Gaze is also complex from birth—integrating both focal and peripheral vision (see Chapter 2)—and highly variable in target and duration. Babbling is highly variable too, not fixed, and it is not a neonatal behaviour, first occurring around four months of age.[46]

Conversely, there are other *obviously variable* behaviours which promote proximity to caregivers in the first three months of life. These Bowlby ignores. Both touch and interactional synchrony are important for maintaining infant–adult proximity.[47] Defecation also advantageously promotes caregiver-infant proximity[48]—especially where, as in the African regions where our ancestors are thought to have evolved, smell-drawn disease vectors are likely to had an impact on infants' survival.

Leaving aside the flexibility and underestimated numbers of the 'proximity-promoting or maintaining' behaviours which Bowlby dubbed 'attachment behaviours'—any unblinkered vision of infancy must also consider the meaning and function of the *full* range of social skills and social capacities manifest in young babies (see Chapter 2.3 for a sketch-map). Most notable here—given the adherence of attachment theory to a dyadic vision of infant 'attachments' and 'relationships'[49]—are the demonstrations reviewed in this book that infants act in *supra-dyadic* ways, before attachments have even begun to form. The fact that infants' evolved interactive repertoire does not fit Bowlby's dyadic formula queries the entire conception of an evolved 'attachment behavioural system' which has one 'mother figure' as set goal.[50] And it entirely refutes the idea that all human social behaviour—including with peers—is generated by a 'top priority' 'dyadic programme', namely that of 'attachment'.[51]

2.1.2 'Attachment behaviours' do not occur in stable sequences

When Mary Ainsworth and her colleagues designed the method of assessing infant–mother attachments known as the 'strange situation procedure' (or SSP), they assumed the infant's attachment behaviours would vary in a tightly inter-correlated way under different circumstances—as do the FAPs making up the reproductive behaviour systems of digger wasps, herring gulls, and stickleback fish. Whilst they ignored the fact that the 'attachment behaviours' Bowlby called FAPs are neither stereotyped nor insensitive to context (see Section 2.1.1), they could not escape finding attachment behaviours do not tightly inter-correlate: both their occurrence and sequencing show little stability over time.[52] In fact, all attachment behaviours, and attachment-relevant behaviours (e.g. resisting the mother), change form during infancy, in ways that alter their significance vis-à-vis contexts and caregivers. Conversely, new behaviours—like language use and locomotion—become pertinent to proximity promotion as a child matures. It is partly for this reason that coding of the SSP has moved from counting discrete behaviours to making stylistic assessments about different styles, organizations, or patterns of behaviour (cf. Chapter 5.2.4).[53]

2.1.3 Stranger fear and separation anxiety cannot function as milestones of development

Two behavioural phenomena were held by Bowlby to mark an infant's passage from Phase II (3–7 months) to Phase III (8–30 months) of attachment formation: fear of strangers and separation anxiety. He believed that, around eight months of age, all securely attached babies will show fear of strangers, though secure infants will be more sociable to strangers than insecure infants. But stranger fear and separation anxiety are not reliably observed in babies. So they cannot serve as universal markers of socio-emotional development.

The *fear of strangers* phenomenon appears to be a consequence of *how* strangers behave towards a baby. If strangers behave in the passive, stilted manner dictated by the SSP, babies may treat them more cautiously than if a stranger actively approaches and engages with the infant in a friendly way.[54] Hence, contrary to Bowlby's theory, it appears that Phase 3 infants *do not typically show a fear of strangers*—positive responses predominating when a stranger behaves in an ordinary friendly way.[55] Indeed, after a few minutes of interaction with a friendly stranger, one-year-olds have been found to direct behaviour towards the stranger which, had it been shown to the mother, would have been termed attachment behaviour.[56] And 10-month-olds follow strangers as often as their mothers in a novel environment.[57]

Like fear of strangers, Bowlby saw *separation anxiety*—expressed by following, clinging, and crying when a mother leaves her baby—as an indispensable sign of a child's entry into Phase 3 of attachment formation. For this reason, a 'separation' from the baby's mother was included by Ainsworth and colleagues as the fourth episode in the SSP. But, despite being attachment enthusiasts, their results refuted Bowlby's claim. At the start of Episode 4, only one in five babies cried when their mother departed (leaving them alone in an unfamiliar room with an unfamiliar person), and just one in ten followed their mother to the door as she left. Around 30% showed no change in behaviour when Episodes 3 (baby with mother and stranger) and 4 were compared. More infants played with the stranger in Episode 4 than in Episode 3, when both mother and stranger were present. For this reason, separation anxiety cannot be used as a diagnostic of attachment.[58]

Note that Bowlby's principal evidence for 'separation anxiety' came from: research on caged baby rhesus monkeys brought up alone; observations of the effects of parent-deprivation on infants in hospital or other forms of institutional care, alone for several weeks or longer; and foster children undergoing a change of mother figure. Such extreme experiences confound separation with a host of other socio-emotional and environmental circumstances.

2.1.4 'Attachment behaviours' do not have a distinctive evolutionary provenance

Bowlby claimed that attachment behaviours, like wasp and gull FAPs, all have well-defined *activating* and *terminating* conditions which serve to promote proximity to a baby's mother-figure. He said this was because they had evolved to have the function of protecting the baby against danger. However, each one of the behaviours Bowlby calls 'attachment behaviours' has a function *other than* promoting proximity to caregivers: the baby's need for milk makes sucking essential; rooting serves as a feeding cue;[59] babbling is an important step in the development of language;[60] looking informs infants about their entire environment and helps direct any intentional action; reaching is directed at anything a baby wants to grasp, not just mothers;[61] and 'following' (by looking and later by locomotion) also has several functions (e.g. exploration).[62] Bowlby did (mistakenly) propose that some attachment behaviours (namely, sucking) had *two separate* functions (one being nutrition, as in 'nutritive sucking', and a second non-nutritive 'soothing' function, as in 'non-nutritive sucking'—which was supposedly related to attachment).[63] But this is seldom the most parsimonious proposal: one explanation for the evolution of a behaviour is better than two.

Not surprisingly, therefore, it has been shown that 'proximity-seeking' behaviours have no single specialized 'attachment' function of 'protection-by-mother'. They have *multiple* functions—reflecting their multiple *non-attachment* roles.[64] Furthermore, because each purported attachment behaviour has a primary function which is *not* proximity-promotion, *their activating and terminating conditions are not primarily governed by proximity*, contrary to Bowlby. For example, Bowlby wrote that, up to four months, a baby's smile 'appears to be a fixed action pattern elicited mainly by sight of his mother's face (full face, not profile), to be intensified by social interaction, and to be terminated when he is picked up'.[65] Evidence shows that babies often smile without external stimulation, for example when asleep, and when *already held* by parents, for example, when feeding.[66] They also smile when they experience control, whether in social or non-social situations, as when neonates successfully solve a problem (detecting an arbitrary rule linking the sounds of a bell or a buzzer with the provision of milk on one side of their head or the other), or when three-month-olds are given control over the movements of a mobile hanging above their crib.[67]

2.1.5 The evolutionary rationale for an 'attachment behavioural system' is redundant

Bowlby argued that the 'attachment behavioural system' of modern infants first evolved to protect infants against danger: when a Stone Age baby was endangered two million years ago, its best chance at survival was to stay close to its mother—hence the evolution and inheritance of a set of 'attachment behaviours' which serve to maintain babies' proximity to their mothers in times of stress. Yet the behavioural system responsible for an infant's survival *cannot be* or have been the attachment system, because, according to Bowlby, this has not fully formed until *after* a child turns two: it was only from 30 months of age onwards that Bowlby dated the onset of a stable 'goal-corrected partnership' between toddler and mother-figure. *None* of the so-called attachment behaviours 'emitted' during the first nine months is goal-corrected, according to Bowlby. Hence, even by his own lights, what must have ensured the baby's survival in prehistoric times was what Bowlby calls 'the caregiving system', as it does in ours, not 'the attachment behavioural system' (see 'signals' in Section 2.3.1 below). Which makes redundant Bowlby's entire evolutionary rationale for the existence of an 'attachment behavioural system'.

2.1.6 The evidence from primates said to support infant attachment does not

Bowlby said care of the young in baboons, chimps, gorillas, and rhesus macaques gives us the best model for how our ancestors cared for babies two million years ago. He particularly drew on Harry Harlow's experiments on the effects of deprivation in rhesus monkeys. For Bowlby, Harlow's key result was that caged infants who had been deprived of mothering during their own infancy grew up to be pathological. But Bowlby sidelined some key Harlow findings, stressing only the disastrous effects of the infant's being deprived of an attachment to a mother-figure.[68] Harlow's deprivation experiments did not just deprive baby monkeys of their mothers, however, they *also* denied caged baby monkeys of contact *with peers*. This led Harlow to test the part played *by peers* in monkey upbringing. And, contrary to Bowlby's claims, he found that, 'in the monkey, at least, it would appear that under favourable circumstances, *real mothers can be bypassed but early peer experiences cannot*'.[69] This suggests that group relations are more important for a baby monkey's well-being than having a relationship with its mother—a finding which, if extrapolated to humans à la Bowlby, would suggest groupness is the most essential form of sociability for human babies.[70]

As discussed in Chapter 1 (Section 1.5), Sarah Blaffer Hrdy argues that humans are, and stem from, *cooperative* breeders.[71] We are more like marmosets and tamarins (*Callitrichidae*)—who care for infants collectively—than rhesus macaques or great apes, who do not. She backs her claim by demonstrating several parallels between Callitrichids and humans: willingness of mothers to let others hold their newborns; multiple caregivers for each infant; calculating attitudes to infanticide; a willingness to feed other mothers' babies; helpfulness to others; swift rate of reproduction; and a capacity for speedy colonization of new territory. None of these features is found in the four primate species Bowlby takes as models for early humans.

Like most scientists, Bowlby presumed our prehistoric proto-human ancestors lived in small stable social groups comprising individuals of both sexes and all ages. Such groups would have served two functions, said Bowlby: protection from predators; and facilitating food-getting by cooperative hunting. However, Bowlby *also* claimed (without backup evidence) that, when members of such groups are threatened, the mature males, *whether monkeys or humans*, (would) combine to drive off the predator whilst the mothers retire with their babies. From this made-up scenario, he extrapolated the adaptiveness of a unique bond between mother and child. Unfortunately for attachment theory, however, Bowlby's made-up scenario is refuted by observational evidence from Shirley Strum and her colleagues showing that scared infants tend to go with *any* group member prepared to pick them up, not exclusively their mother, in group-living primates like olive baboons.[72]

2.2 Measures of infant attachment have weak to non-existent predictive power

The fundamental assumption of attachment theory's explanations of human behaviour is that what happens early in one's life has a strong and long-lasting influence over one's well-being, or, in short, that *early is deep*. Research refutes this assumption, twice over. Measures of attachment security in infants prove unstable in the short term. And they do not predict adult functioning strongly, or (often) at all.

The most widely used means of diagnosing the security or insecurity of infant attachments is the SSP.[73] This 20-minute procedure is designed to reflect how a crawling or toddling infant, when under different levels of stress, interacts with their mother-figure in stress-related situations during everyday life. So the question arises: do SSP ratings reflect the *current state* of child–parent *interaction*—something which may vary from day to day or month to month? Or do SSP ratings reflect the stable *underlying structure* of the infant's *attachment* to his or her mother figure? Attachment researchers claim a Yes answer to the second question. But research continues to refute their claim: stability of infant–mother behaviour in the SSP reflects the stability of external circumstances, not the existence of an 'internal working model' or 'attachment behavioural system' *inside* the baby—as we now show.

2.2.1 Over-time reliability of the Strange Situation Procedure depends on non-infant factors

Studies relevant to the over-time *reliability* of the SSP test the same infant-adult pair twice in the SSP, a few weeks or months apart. Such studies find that temporal reliability in SSP classifications of infant-adult attachment is most strongly linked to continuity in each pair's 'background variables': their socio-economic status; the degree of marital harmony at home; whether living arrangements change; continuity of childcare provision; and whether or not caregivers have reliable social support. Conversely, short-term *variations* in attachment classifications in the SSP correlate with short-term variations in background variables.[74]

This means the proportions of the variance in studies of social behaviour (infant or parental) explained by the different types of 'attachment security' the SSP constructs are seldom if ever 'strong' in attachment research, especially where studies sample children other than volunteer middle-class children from intact families.[75] Equally, because almost all attachment studies are correlational, even a powerful correlation between two indicators, of say infant security and maternal sensitivity, may be the result of a third *unstudied* variable (e.g. social support for the dyad) which has produced related effects in *both* indicators, implying that: when over-time correlational results are hailed as proving the 'effects' of infantile attachments, the results are serving as proxies for the over-time effects of unstudied background variables. Thus the exclusion of *any* background characteristic may have inflated even the moderate effect-sizes attachment research claims. For example, while some analyses of attachment stability factor in *some* forms of environmental 'risk status', they often do *not* include social support—a powerful co-correlate of caregiving behaviour, even in high-risk families.[76] Furthermore, when we inspect the few studies held up as having shown (from the effects of therapeutic interventions) a non-correlational *directly-causal* influence of maternal care on infant attachment security, we find *none* of these studies has controlled for placebo effects.[77]

In short, just as Michael Lamb and his colleagues showed in the mid-1980s, diagnoses of attachment in/security constructed using the SSP do not primarily reflect an 'internal' structure in the child. They primarily reflect what is going on in the social environment external to the child and his or her caregiver(s).[78]

2.2.2 Classifications of infant attachments do not predict adult behaviour

Unsurprisingly, given the results just reviewed, none of the major longitudinal studies which have examined the long-term correlates of early infant–adult attachments have found any large direct effect of primary attachments on grown-up functioning—especially if they have controlled for background variables like social support for mothers. The so-called Minnesota study found that, if socio-contextual variables were controlled, attachment security in infancy was a very weak predictor of adult functioning (accounting for 5% of the variance in global social competence at age nineteen). Neither of two German longitudinal studies found a significant relationship of security of attachment in the SSP at either twelve or eighteen months with *any* measure of attachment or relationship beyond the age of ten. An Israeli longitudinal study on attachment representations showed that continuity in representation was significantly tied to stability, and discontinuity from instability, in the *caregiver's* environment. Taken together, findings from such studies show that, when attachment measures *are combined with* measures of an infant–mother dyad's social background, a far stronger association with later outcomes results—explaining 50% versus 5% of the variance in the Minnesota study—than do attachment measures alone.[79]

All of which suggests that, contrary to Bowlby's theory, the primary cause of different developmental outcomes is not an infant's primary attachment per se, but the manner in which the infant–mother dyad's social context supports their two lives. Hence the failure of attachment security to correlate directly with grown-up competence has been repeatedly found in recent years, *especially* in studies which include and assess infant–mother couples from diverse social environments.[80] Conversely, studies which recruit homogenous *low*-risk dyads from intact middle-class families, and/or which *do not* include measures of dyads' social environment, *do* sometimes report infants' attachment classifications associate significantly with later outcomes.[81] Contrary to their authors' claims, however, such studies cannot tell us if the significant associations they report are attributable to infants' attachment security, or whether both earlier and later measures symptomatically reflect continuities in 'background' differences in children's everyday lives.[82]

In this context, the most notable use of Bowlby's idea that primary attachments create a template or formative precursor for all later relationships has been to explain correlations between (early) infant–mother attachments and (later) behaviour *with peers*. On average, studies which report such associations first measure 'attachment security' around two years of age (in infants from stable families), then measure inter-peer interaction two years later.[83] Significant correlations between the two measures may then be held to show a causal link from attachment to peer competence. But to assume correlations show causes is an elementary logical error. Moreover, this kind of study rarely reports social background variables like social support. Finally, the design of these studies tacitly assumes babies are incapable of peer-peer interaction *before they are well past their third birthday*. Hence they never consider measuring attachment security *and* peer competence *at the same age* in infancy.[84]

Until we know how competent infants are with peers *from early in life*, the relative contribution of infant-adult relationships to later peer competence will remain unknown. And, as this book shows, babies are capable of supra-dyadic peer interaction before babies have *even begun* to form what Bowlby called 'attachments'. This raises the possibility that both peer and infant–adult interaction are the product of the same (supra-dyadic) relational capacity.[85] Alternatively, it is possible that good early experience with peers may shape the later formation of so-called attachment relationships—as in Harlow's monkeys.

2.3 Attachment theory is a theory of caregiving, not of infant social behaviour

All the evidence reviewed in this Appendix proves 'attachment theory' to be a misnomer. Attachment theory *does not* explain infants' social and emotional development in terms of data generated by an infant's *internal* 'attachment system'. The data it theorizes are primarily generated by the growing child's *external* caregiving environment. Insofar as attachment theory applies to babies, it is a theory of caregiving, not a theory of the infant's 'attachment system' or 'internal working model'. In fact, Bowlby's evolutionary rationale for all human babies possessing an 'attachment behavioural system' *refutes itself—because*, according to Bowlby, that system has not formed until the child is approaching his or her third birthday. Even the SSP, whilst supposedly focused on infant behaviour, is, as Marga Vicedo observes, today primarily used as a tacit way of identifying better and worse kinds of maternal care.[86]

To underline this conclusion, consider three further points:

2.3.1 The infant's smiles and cries are signs not 'signals'
Bowlby refers to attachment behaviours as 'signals'. Yet, as with sucking, reaching, and rooting, few of them are 'sent' as signals, given their non-attachment functions (see Section 2.1.3). Smiles and cries seem to function more as flexible symptoms of the baby's varying state or mood than as other-directed displays.[87] Of course, this does not stop such behaviours being *interpreted by others as signs* relevant to an infant's current caregiving needs.

Thus, when infant behaviours like smiles and cries *do* trigger effective care from others, this is because a potential caregiver *reads* a behaviour as having a certain kind of meaning. Smiles and cries only promote proximity to a caregiver if they serve to prompt caregiving behaviour. A *willingness to care for babies* in adults and older children, plus *a drive to interpret others' expressions*,[88] is thus both necessary and sufficient to account for the development of early infant-adult relationships. It is therefore superfluous to hypothesize an *additional* 'behavioural system'—that is, an innate 'attachment behavioural system'—in babies, to account for the formation of the kinds of behaviour attachment theorists theorize.

2.3.2 Caregiving behaviour varies historically and cross-culturally
Anyone who inspects the copious cross-cultural evidence on child-rearing available today must acknowledge that human caregiving behaviour rarely corresponds to the pattern attachment theorists hold to be natural or normal. This evidence proves to be nonsense the idea that all human caregiving has a biological template which evolved two million years ago and is best manifested by intact middle-class families from the UK and USA in the 1950s.[89]

2.3.3 Equating dyadic maternal care to the baby's effective environment is misogynistic

Despite evidence showing the dependence of child outcomes on the social environment surrounding those who care for the child, Bowlby largely treated 'the mother' as the entirety of an infant's environment, thus rhetorically desert-islanding both mother and child from their social circumstances.[90] Unsurprisingly then, Bowlby's confidence that 'the very great influence that a child's mother has on his development' would not lead to blame but be understood as a consequence of 'the amount of emotional support, or lack of it, she herself is receiving' has proven void.[91] The idea that mothers (or other 'dyadic' caregivers) are to blame for children's difficulties proves endemic to attachment-based explanations, and to attachment-inspired policy.[92] Witness the swarm of new infant–mother attachment 'types' devised by attachment-inspired clinicians—without any backing from observational research on children—to explain various forms of adult psychopathology. As we have seen, one such is Brett Kahr's empirically unsupported account of schizophrenia as mainly produced by young children's 'infanticidal attachments' to mothers (or fathers) who 'transmit death-related messages to their children, sometimes consciously, but often unconsciously' (Chapter 5.2.2).[93]

2.4 Is attachment theory scientific?

Mary Ainsworth and her colleagues described attachment theory as something which could not be refuted. They called it a 'perspective'—a term which seemingly classes it with the views of flat-earthers and scientologists—not a hypothetico-deductive theory.[94] If it is really irrefutable, this, for many people, including John Bowlby, would make it *unscientific*. Bowlby undoubtedly believed attachment theory *was* scientific.[95] So: who is right?

Ainsworth is right.[96] To subscribe to attachment theory today is to be unscientific or, more precisely, *pseudo-scientific*, insofar as the theory is claimed to be 'scientific' *despite* all the criticisms documented here. Anyone who wishes to check the extent to which attachment theory is pseudo-scientific today should turn to the introductory chapter in the current *Handbook of Attachment*, where we read: 'Bowlby and Ainsworth's original ideas have held up well ... nothing that has emerged from the thousands of studies produced over the past 40 years has led to a serious challenge to the core theory'.[97] Apparently, the attachment paradigm remains impervious to all the evidence this Appendix reviews.[98] It is hence justly now called *a perspective—on* a par with the denial of climate-change. Nor is it a neutral perspective. It is culturally biased, mother-blaming, misogynistic, and, as such deeply unethical.[99]

2.5 Babies do best in groups

Fortunately, given the scientific demise of attachment theory, there is another show in town which *can be refuted*. A great deal of the evidence accumulated by ethnographers shows that babies do best when they are brought up—not by just one desert-islanded mother—but by a *group* of people. Babies do better in groups when in quality centre-based childcare—as we argued from the evidence discussed in Chapter 4. And research has repeatedly shown that, even when living in 'high-risk' conditions, babies do better in extended families than in isolated 'nuclear' families.[100] The importance of groups for healthy child development is also reflected in the proven importance of social support for children's *and mothers'* well-being—and by whatever therapeutic successes 'the Circle of Security' has (see Chapter 5.2.3).

Even attachment research suggests babies do better in groups, or with 'multiple caregivers'. The attempt to shoehorn this finding back into the dyadic fold explains the value-adding of multiple caregivers as being the consequence of 'multiple attachments'. But the ways in which such group care supposedly helps infants, that is, how being integrated into a group of caregivers impacts a baby's putative 'internal working model', remains so vague as to be unscientific.[101] Worse, attachment theory provides no way to theorize genuinely group-based (that is, *supra-dyadic*) behaviour.[102] Which means it cannot explain findings that third-party relationships (e.g. marital discord) can have a *direct* (supra-dyadic) impact on infants' socio-emotional development.[103,104]

All such findings, which seem anomalous from the attachment perspective, make good scientific sense if we take up Darwin's hypothesis—that babies grow up most securely if they are integrated into a group of caring people—and then set about testing that hypothesis.

Notes

Preface

1. For further discussion, see Solomon, Samuel. 2013. 'Denise Riley's Socialized Biology'. *Journal of British and Irish Innovative Poetry* 5: 167–199.

Chapter 1

1. See Bradley, Ben S. 2020. *Darwin's Psychology: The Theatre of Agency*. Oxford: Oxford University Press.
2. Hay, Dale, Marlene Caplan, and Alison Nash. 2011. 'The Beginnings of Peer Relations'. In *Handbook of Peer Interactions, Relationships, and Groups*, edited by Kenneth Rubin, William Bukowski, and Brett Laursen, pp. 121–142. New York: Guilford Press.
3. 'The human being is in the most literal sense *zoon politikon*: not merely a gregarious animal, but an animal which can individuate itself only in the midst of society'. From Marx, Karl. 1973. *Grundrisse: Foundations of the Critique of Political Economy*. Penguin: Harmondsworth, p. 18. Quoted by Riley, Denise. 1983, *War in the Nursery: Theories of Child and Mother*. London: Virago, p. 16. See also Selby, Jane. 1985. 'Feminine Identity and Contradiction: Women Research Students at Cambridge University'. PhD thesis. Cambridge University.
4. Spock, Benjamin. 1946. *The Common Sense Book of Baby and Child Care*. New York: Duell, Sloan & Pearce.
5. Dickens, Charles. 1838. *Oliver Twist; or, The Parish Boy's Progress*. London: Bentley's Miscellany.
6. Anon. 1911. 'Baby-farming'. In online *Encyclopaedia Britannica*. 11th edn. Accessed 11 September 2022. https://en.wikisource.org/wiki/1911_Encyclop%C3%A6dia_Britannica/Baby-Farming
7. Dickens, Charles. 1839. *The Life and Adventures of Nicholas Nickleby*. London: Chapman and Hall; Renton, Alex. 2018. *Stiff Upper Lip: Secrets, Crimes and the Schooling of a Ruling Class*. London: Weidenfeld and Nicholson.
8. Waugh, Auberon. 1977. 'Suffer the Little Children', *The Spectator*, September 30th, p. 6; quoted in Renton, *Stiff Upper Lip*.
9. Holmes, Jeremy. 1993. *John Bowlby and Attachment Theory*. London: Routledge, p. 16.
10. Quoted in Schwartz, Joseph. 1999. *Cassandra's Daughter: A History of Psychoanalysis*. London: Routledge, p. 225.
11. N.B. Bowlby, John. 1982. *Attachment and Loss, Vol.1: Attachment*, 2nd edn. New York: Basic Books never refers to 'infant–mother attachment' because, according to his theory, children only *start* forming attachments around the age of nine months and do not establish a stable attachment until around thirty months of age (see Appendix A.2)—that is, after they have

ceased being infants. (The American Medical Association defines infancy as the period of life which lasts from birth to twelve months of age.) Nevertheless, his theory is *nowadays* typically *called* a theory of 'infant–mother attachment'—because it is blurred together with Mary Ainsworth's theory of 'infant–mother attachment' (which clashes with Bowlby's theory on this and other counts). For two seminal examples of such blurring, see: pp. 765–766 in Inge Bretherton. 1992. 'The Origins of Attachment Theory: John Bowlby and Mary Ainsworth'. *Developmental Psychology*, 28: 759–775; and Cassidy, Jude. 2016. 'The Nature of the Child's Ties'. In *Handbook of Attachment: Theory, Research and Clinical Applications*, edited by Jude Cassidy and Philip Shaver, pp. 3–24. London: Guilford Press, p. 17. We adopt current usage by referring to Bowlby's theory as one of 'infant-mother attachment'.

12. Holmes, *John Bowlby*, pp. 40–41.
13. See Appendix (A.2.5).
14. Campbell, Donald. 1958. 'Common Fate, Similarity, and Other Indices of the Status of Aggregates of Persons as Social Entities'. *Behavioural Science*, 3: 14–25. For discussion, see Bradley, Ben S. and Michael Smithson. 2017. 'Groupness in Preverbal Infants: Proof of Concept'. *Frontiers of Psychology*, 8. https:// doi.org/ 10.3389/ fpsyg.2017.00385.
15. Hrdy, Sarah Blaffer. 2009. *Mothers and Others: The Evolutionary Origins of Mutual Understanding*. Cambridge, MA: Harvard University Press, p. 128.
16. Coontz, Stephanie. 2016. *The Way We Never Were: American Families and the Nostalgia Trap*. New York: Basic Books.
17. Riley, *War in the Nursery*, passim.
18. E.g. Spieker, Susan, and Lillian Bensley. 1994. 'Roles of Living Arrangements and Grandmother Social Support in Adolescent Mothering and Infant Attachment'. *Developmental Psychology*, 30: 102–111; Olds, David L., JoAnn Robinson, Ruth O'Brien, Dennis Luckey, Lisa Pettitt, Charles Henderson, Rosanna Ng, Karen Sheff, Jon Korfmacher, Susan Hiatt, and Ayelet Talmi. 2002. 'Home Visiting by Paraprofessionals and by Nurses: A Randomized Control Trial'. *Paediatrics*, 110: 486–496; Olds, David, Lois Sadler, and Harriet Kitzman. 2007. 'Programs for Parents of Infants and Toddlers: Recent Evidence from Randomized Trials'. *Journal of Child Psychology and Psychiatry*, 48: 355–391.
19. Al Awad, Ahmed, and Edmund Sonuga-Barke. 1992. 'Childhood Problems in a Sudanese City: A Comparison of Extended and Nuclear Families'. *Child Development*, 63: 906–914.
20. Coontz, *The Way We Never Were*.
21. Hrdy, *Mothers and Others*, p. 68.
22. Hewlett, Barry. 1989. *Diverse Contexts of Human Infancy*. Englewood Cliffs, NJ: Prentice Hall.
23. Behar, Doron, R. Villems, H. Soodyall, J. Blue-Smith, L. Pereira, E. Metspalu, R. Scozzari, H. Makkan, S. Tzur, D. Comas, J. Bertranpetit, L. Quintana- Murci, C. Tyler-Smith, R. Spencer Wells, S. Rosset, and the Genographic Consortium. 2008. 'The Dawn of Human Matrilineal Diversity'. *American Journal of Human Genetics*, 82: 1–11; Harpending, Henry, M.A. Batzer, M. Gurven, L.B. Jourde, A. Rogers, and S.T. Sherry. 1996. 'Genetic Traces of Ancient Demography'. *Proceedings of the National Academy of Sciences (USA)*, 95: 1961–67; Hrdy, 2011; Ingman, Max, H. Kaessmann, Svante Pääbo, and U. Gyllensten. 2000. 'Mitochondrial Genome Variation and the Origin of Modern Humans'. *Nature*, 408: 708–713.
24. Hrdy, *Mothers and Others*, pp. 75–76, quoting Konner, Melvin. 1972. 'Aspects of the Developmental Ecology of a Foraging People'. In *Ethological Studies of Child Behaviour*, edited by Nick Blurton-Jones, pp. 285–304. Cambridge: Cambridge University Press.

25. Hrdy, *Mothers and Others*, p. 111.
26. Dunbar, Robin and S. Schultz. 2007. 'Understanding Primate Brain Evolution'. *Philosophical Transactions of the Royal Society B*, 362: 649–658.
27. Darwin, Charles. 1874. *The Descent of Man and Selection in Relation to Sex*, 2nd edn. London: Murray, pp. 588–589. (We edited out the word 'barbarous' before 'tribe'.)
28. Darwin, Charles. 1877. 'A Biographical Sketch of an Infant'. *Mind: A Quarterly Review of Psychology and Philosophy*, 2: 285–294; Darwin, Charles. 1890. *The Expression of the Emotions in Man and Animals*, 2nd edn. London: Murray, pp. 154–185.
29. Bradley, Ben S. and C. Trevarthen. 1978. 'Babytalk as an Adaptation to the Infant's Communication'. In *The Development of Communication*, edited by Natalie Waterson and Catherine Snow, pp. 75–92. London: Wiley; Selby, Jane. 1977. 'An Observational Study of Interactions between Human Mothers and their Babies during Baby's Feed: The Structure of the Feed, Individual Differences and Possible Important Precursors for Language and Social Behaviour. Review of Literature on Pre-Linguistic Development and its Inherent Problems of Description'. MA thesis, University of St. Andrews (128 pp. + 80 Figures).
30. Paul, Campbell and Frances Thomson-Salo. 1996. 'Infant-Led Innovations in a Mother-Baby Therapy Group'. *Journal of Child Psychotherapy*, 6: 118–136.
31. Quoted from Paul and Thomson-Salo, 'Infant-Led Innovations', p. 226.
32. Fivaz–Depeursinge, Elisabeth and Antionette Corboz-Warnery. 1999. *The Primary Triangle: A Developmental Systems View of Mothers, Fathers and Infants*. New York: Basic Books; Nadel, Jacqueline and Heléne Tremblay-Leveau. 1999. 'Early Perception of Social Contingencies and Interpersonal Intentionality: Dyadic and Triadic Paradigms'. In *Early Social Cognition: Understanding Others in the First Months of Life*, edited by Philippe Rochat, pp. 189–212. Mahwah, NJ: Lawrence Erlbaum. See also Gordon, Ilanit and Ruth Feldman. 2008. 'Synchrony in the Triad: A Microlevel Process Model of Coparenting and Parent-Child Interactions'. *Family Process*, 47: 465–479—who studied infant–mother–father trios.
33. Anna, Freud. 1960. 'Discussion of Dr. John Bowlby's Paper'. *Psychoanalytic Study of the Child*, 15: 53–62.
34. E.g. Stone, L.J., H.T. Smith, and L.B. Murphy, eds. 1973. *The Competent Infant: Research and Commentary*. London: Taylor & Francis.
35. Bower, Tom and Jennifer Wishart. 1972. 'The Effects of Motor Skill on Object Permanence'. *Cognition*, 1: 165–172.
36. Bower, Tom, John Broughton and Michael Moore. 1970. 'Demonstration of Intention in the Reaching Behaviour of Neonates'. *Nature*, 228: 679–681.
37. Bower, Tom. 1974. *Development in Infancy*. New York: Freeman.
38. Schaffer, Rudolph. 1971 *The Growth of Sociability*. Harmondsworth: Penguin, p. 1.
39. Fantz, Robert. 1961. 'The Origin of Form Perception'. *Scientific American*, 204: 66–73.
40. Bowlby, *Attachment*, pp. 262–267.
41. Trevarthen, Colwyn. 1974. 'Conversations with a Two-Month-Old'. *New Scientist*, 62: 230–235.
42. In 1976, *New Scientist* put out a spoof article sending up Colwyn's 'overblown' claims from his film-studies. Written by 'Ed Start' (a humorous pseudonym, supposed to chime with the USA's 'Head Start' programme), 'Is Politeness Innate?' re-used a photo Colwyn had taken to illustrate infants' intersubjective 'prespeech' (in his 1974 *New Scientist* article 'Conversations with a two-month-old') to debate the risible hypothesis that young babies

cover their mouths when burping. See Start, Ed. 1976. 'Is Politeness Innate?' *New Scientist*, 71: 586–587.
43. See Bradley, Ben S. (in press). 'The Evidence for Innate Intersubjectivity'. In *Intersubjective Minds*, edited by Vasu Reddy and Jonathan Delafield-Butt. Oxford: Oxford University Press.
44. Bradley and Trevarthen, 'Babytalk as an Adaptation'; Bradley, Ben S. 2010. 'Jealousy in Infant-Peer Trios: From Narcissism to Culture'. In *Handbook of Jealousy: Theories, Principles and Multidisciplinary Approaches*, edited by Sybil Hart and Maria Legerstee, pp. 192–234. Hoboken, NJ: Wiley-Blackwell.
45. Winnicott, Donald. 1967. 'Mirror-Role of Mother and Family in Child Development'. In *Playing and Reality*, pp. 130–138. Harmondsworth: Penguin. 1974.
46. Virginia Woolf. 1935. *A Room of One's Own*. London: Hogarth, p. 53.
47. E.g. Murray, Lynne and Colwyn Trevarthen. 1985. 'Emotional Regulation of Interactions between Two-Month-Olds and their Mothers'. In *Social Perception in Infants*, edited by Tiffany Field and Nathan Fox, pp. 177–197. Norwood, NJ, Ablex; Trevarthen, Colwyn, Murray, Lynne and Penelope Hubley. 1981. 'The Psychology of Infants'. In *Scientific Foundations of Paediatrics*, 2nd edn., edited by John Davis and Joseph Dobbing, pp. 211–274. London: Heinemann Medical. See also Appendix (section A.1).
48. E.g. Kaye, Kenneth. 1984. *The Mental and Social Life of Babies: How Parents Create Persons*. Brighton: Harvester; Shotter, John and Susan Gregory. 1976. 'On First Gaining the Idea of Oneself as a Person'. In *Life Sentences: Aspects of the Social Role of Language*, pp. 3–9, edited by Rom Harré. New York: Wiley; Newson, John. 1979. 'The Growth of Shared Understandings between Infant and Caregiver'. In *Before Speech: The Beginning of Interpersonal Communication*, pp. 207–222, edited by Margaret Bullowa. Cambridge: Cambridge University Press.

Chapter 2

1. Throughout this chapter, when 'we' refers to the authors of this book, it refers specifically to Ben and Jane.
2. Ainsworth, Mary, Mary Blehar, Everett Waters, and Sally Wall. 2015. *Patterns of Attachment: A Psychological Study of the Strange Situation*. London: Routledge; Bretherton, Inge and Mary Ainsworth. 1974. 'Responses of One-Year-Olds to a Stranger in a Strange Situation'. In *The Origins of Fear*, edited by Michael Lewis and Leonard Rosenblum, pp. 131–164. New York: Wiley; Lamb, Michael, Ross Thompson, William Gardner, Eric Charnov, and David Estes. 1984. 'Security of Infantile Attachment as Assessed in the "Strange Situation": Its Study and Biological Interpretation'. *Behavioural and Brain Sciences*, 7: 127–147; Lamb, Michael, Ross Thompson, William Gardner, Eric Charnov, Eric and James Connell. 1985. *Infant-Mother Attachment: The Origins and Developmental Significance of Individual Differences in Strange Situation Behaviour*. Hillsdale, NJ: Erlbaum.
3. The idea that *smiling* is a single facial expression is mistaken. Babies make many different kinds of smile. Oster, Harriet. 1978. 'Facial Expression and Affect Development'. In *The Development of Affect: Genesis of Behaviour*, Vol. 1, edited by Michael Lewis and Lewis Rosenblum. Boston, MA: Springer, pp. 43–75; Bradley, Ben S. 1980. 'A Study of Young Infants as Social Beings'. PhD thesis Department of Psychology, Edinburgh University.
4. Crying, vocalizing and orienting are also have a multiplicity of forms and potential meanings see Section 2.3.

5. Argyle, Michael, and Mark Cook. 1976. *Gaze and Mutual Gaze*. Cambridge: Cambridge University Press.
6. All babies' identities disguised and parental permissions obtained.
7. I.e. foot-holding plus looking. For a definition of initiation, see p. 149 in Tremblay-Leveau, H. and Nadel, J. 1996. 'Exclusion in Triads: Can It Serve "Meta-Communicative" Knowledge in 11- and 23-Month-Old Children?.' *British Journal of Developmental Psychology*, 14: 145–158.
8. Nichols, Austin and Jon Maner. 2008. 'The Good-Subject Effect: Investigating Participant Demand Characteristics'. *Journal of General Psychology*, 135: 151–166; Orne, Martin. 1962 'On the Social Psychology of the Psychological Experiment: With Particular Reference to Demand Characteristics and Their Implication'. *American Psychologist*, 17: 776–783; Morawski, Jill. 1988. 'Impossible Experiments and Practical Constructions: The Social Bases of Psychologists' Work'. In *The Rise of Experimentation in American Psychology*, edited by Jill Morawski, pp. 72–93. New Haven, CT: Yale University Press.
9. Suls, Jerry and Ralph Rosnow. 1988. 'Concerns about Artifacts in Psychological Experiments'. In *The Rise of Experimentation in American Psychology*, edited by Jill Morawski, pp. 163–187. New Haven, CT: Yale University Press.
10. Niko Tinbergen was another example. See his remarks on experimental psychology in Tinbergen, Niko. 1963. 'On Aims and Methods of Ethology'. *Zeitschrift für Tierpsychologie*, 20: 410–433.
11. Bradley, Ben S. 2020. *Darwin's Psychology: The Theatre of Agency*. Oxford: Oxford University Press. Ch. 2.
12. Often, the nearest students get to a discussion of description in their nationally accredited introductory course on 'research methods and statistics in psychology' is half a lecture on 'measurement and measurement error'. You can only measure something if you already know what it is. Yet neither 'methods' courses nor prescribed textbooks discuss how students might best observe and describe 'what something is'.
13. Geertz, Clifford. 1973. *The Interpretation of Cultures: Selected Essays*. London: Hutchinson; Ardener, Edwin. 1989. 'Some Outstanding Problems in the Analysis of Events'. In *The Voice of Prophecy and Other Essays*, edited by Malcolm Chapman, pp. 86–104. Oxford: Basil Blackwell; Flyvbjerg, Bent. 2006. 'Five Misunderstandings of Case-Study Research'. *Qualitative Inquiry*, 12: 219–245.
14. See Flyvbjerg, 'Five Misunderstandings'; Strum, Shirley. 1989. *Almost Human: A Journey into the World of Baboons*. London: Elm Tree Books; Strum, Shirley. 2012. 'Darwin's Monkey: Why Baboons Can't Become Human'. *Yearbook of Physical Anthropology*, 55: 3–23; Maddox, Brenda. 2003. *Rosalind Franklin: The Dark Lady of DNA*. New York: Harper-Collins.
15. Heidi Keller defines 'polyadic' as meaning 'that several communication partners interact with each other at the same time. Polyadic is supposed to contrast to dyadic where two partners communicate with each other'. See Keller, Heidi. 2021. *The Myth of Attachment Theory: A Critical Understanding for Multicultural Societies*. London: Routledge, pp. 46, 66. She argues that many non-Western children grow up in multi-person settings where polyadic communication is the norm.
16. Geertz, Clifford. 1983. *Local Knowledge: Further Essays in Interpretive Anthropology*. New York: Basic Books, pp. 320–321: 'such inference begins with a set of (presumptive)

signifiers and attempts to place them within an intelligible frame'. In our case the 'presumptive signifiers' are all the details of Paula's behaviour and their circumstances.

17. This phrase is, we believe, a known figure of speech in ordinary conversation. It is also a key term in the psychoanalysis of collectives, best traced through the work of Wilfred Bion and Isabel Menzies-Lyth, e.g. *Containing Anxiety in Institutions. Selected Essays, Vol.1* 1988. London: Free Association Press. Obviously, it is also a common-sense idea that an eight-month-old may feel anxiety on being left by her mother in a strange situation—especially since this has been erected into a cornerstone of attachment theory. But it should be noted that Paula was the only one of the three babies in this trio who struck us as showing anxiety when their mothers exited the studio.
18. Geertz, *Interpretation of Cultures*, p. 321.
19. Bowlby, John. 1988. *A Secure Base*. London: Basic Books.
20. Cassidy, Jude. 2016. 'The Nature of the Child's Ties'. In *Handbook of Attachment: Theory, Research and Clinical Applications*, edited by Jude Cassidy and Philip Shaver, pp. 3–24. London: Guilford Press, p. 8.
21. Mueller, E. and Brenner, J. 1977. 'The Origins of Social Skills and Interaction among Playgroup Toddlers'. *Child Development*, 48: 854–861.
22. Trevarthen, Colwyn. 1968. 'Two Mechanisms of Vision in Primates'.' *Psychologische Forschung*, 31: 299–337., p. 328.
23. Bradley, Ben S. 2009. Early Trios: Patterns of Sound and Movement in the Genesis of Meaning between Infants'. In *Handbook of Communicative Musicality: Exploring the Basis of Human Companionship*, edited by Stephen Malloch and Colwyn Trevarthen, pp. 263–280. Oxford: Blackwell-Wiley.
24. Draghi-Lorenz, R., Reddy, V., and Costall, A. 2001. 'Rethinking the Development of "Nonbasic" Emotions: A Critical Review of Existing Theories'. *Developmental Review*, 21: 261–304. N.B. Darwin's understanding of facial expressions makes them *all* social; see Bradley, *Darwin's Psychology*.
25. E.g. Watson, J.S. 1972. 'Smiling, Cooing and "The Game"'. *Merrill-Palmer Quarterly*, 18: 323–339; Bretherton and Ainsworth, 'Responses of One-Year-Olds to a Stranger'.
26. See Appendix 2.1.1; Oster, 'Facial Expression and Affect Development'.
27. Oster, Harriet. 2005. 'The Repertoire of Infant Facial Expressions: An Ontogenetic Perspective'. In *Emotional Development: Recent Research Advances*, edited by J. Nadel and D. Muir, pp. 261–292. Oxford: Oxford University Press.
28. Bradley, 'A Study of Young Infants', pp. 112–122.
29. Trevarthen, Colwyn. 1986. 'Development of Intersubjective Motor Control in Infants'. In *Motor Development in Children: Aspects of Coordination and Control*, edited by M.G. Wade and H.T.A. Whiting, pp. 209–261. Dordrecht: Martinus Nijhof.
30. Trevarthen, Colwyn. 1986. 'Form, Significance and Psychological Potential of Hand Gestures of Infants'. In *The Biological Foundation of Gestures: Motor and Semiotic Aspects*, edited by J.-L. Nespoulous, P. Perron, and A.R. Lecours, pp. 149–202. Hillsdale, NJ: Lawrence Erlbaum.
31. E.g. Oster, 'Facial Expression and Affect Development'; Oller Kimbrough, Eugene Buder, Heather Ramsdell, and Roger Bakeman. 2013. 'Functional Flexibility of Infant Vocalization and the Emergence of Language'. *Proceedings of the National Academy of Sciences*, 110: 6318–6323. (doi:10.1073/pnas.1300337110); Liszkowski, Ulf. 2014. 'Two Sources of Meaning in Infant Communication: Preceding Action Contexts and Act-Accompanying

Characteristics'. *Philosophical Transactions of the Royal Society B*, 369: 20130294: https://doi.org/10.1098/rstb.2013.0294.
32. The number given for 'being looked at' is the sum of the looking by the two other babies, some of whose looks overlapped.
33. See pp. 213–216 in Selby, Jane and Bradley, Ben S. 2003 'Infants in Groups: A Paradigm for the Study of Early Social Experience. *Human Development*, 46: 197–221.
34. E.g. Hart, Sybil, Carrington, Heather A., Tronick, E.Z., and Carroll, Sebrina R. 2004. 'When Infants Lose Exclusive Maternal Attention: Is It Jealousy?' *Infancy*, 6: 57–78.
35. Inclusive infant behaviour like this surprised Helene Tremblay-Leveau and Jacqueline Nadel in an experiment where an adult stooge was instructed to sit with two older infants (11–23 months of age) and to focus exclusively on one baby while ignoring the other. Despite the adult's undivided attention, 'included' infants sometimes made overtures to 'bring in' the excluded infant. Tremblay-Leveau, Helene and Nadel, Jacqueline. 1995. 'Young Children's Communicative Skills in Triads'. *International Journal of Behavioural Development*, 18: 227–242.
36. If you would like to see statistical evidence for this claim, see Chapter 3.
37. Some researchers have tried to cheat this blindness by equating 'simultaneous' interaction with *sequential* interaction: claiming infant behaviour in baby–mother–father trios is simultaneous whenever a baby shows 'a rapid shift of gaze and affect between partners' over a period of anything from 3 to 30 seconds. See Chapter 3.
38. This phrase is ambiguous. It *might* apply to our research if babies like Joe, Mona and Ann were deemed to see each other as 'particular'. But we guess it does not as, presumably, Bowlby means 'familiar' by 'particular', and is gesturing towards what are nowadays called 'multiple' dyadic 'attachments': to mother, father, educator, etc.
39. Bowlby, John. 1982. *Attachment and Loss, Vol. I: Attachment*, 2nd edition. New York: Basic Books, pp. 228–232.
40. Bowlby, *Attachment*, p. 306.
41. Bowlby, *Attachment*, Ch. 14.
42. Cassidy, 'The Nature of the Child's Ties', pp. 9–10 and p. 19 n. 1.
43. Ainsworth, Mary. 1989. 'Attachments beyond Infancy'. *American Psychologist*, 44: 709–716; Feldman, Ruth. 2012. 'Bio-behavioral Synchrony: A Model for Integrating Biological and Microsocial Behavioral Processes in the Study of Parenting'. *Parenting*, 12: 154–164, p. 42; See also Zeifman, D. and Hazan, C. 2016. 'Pairbonds as Attachments: Mounting Evidence in Support of Bowlby's Hypothesis'. In *Handbook of Attachment*, n. 17, pp. 418–420.
44. Cassidy, 'The Nature of the Child's Ties', n. 17, p. 10. 'Separation anxiety' is a topic that has hardly been studied at all. Yet it is still a cornerstone of attachment theory—as current treatments of 'the affiliative system' show. Ainsworth et al., *Patterns of Attachment*, pp. 262ff, report that the 'strange situation procedure' *does sometimes* elicit distress from infants, 'when briefly separated from the mother in the unfamiliar environment of the laboratory', but such distress is '*not as ubiquitous as anticipated*'. 'Separation protest ... [is] by no means invariably activated by the baby's realization of the mother's departure', continue Ainsworth et al.—nor does 'separation from the mother ... significantly lower the total number of smiles, nor those directed to the stranger'. See Appendix A.2.
45. 'Contemporary studies' is a loaded phrase. Very often psychologists only cite—and only read—'contemporary studies' very selectively, limiting their review to studies that conform to their own theoretical preferences. For example—and this is only one of many possible

examples—attachment researchers typically do not cite or discuss studies that challenge the basic assumptions of attachment theory (e.g. the latest *Handbook of Attachment*; Cassidy and Shaver, eds., 2016, n. 17). See Chapter 5 for more on this.
46. See Trevarthen, Colwyn. 2012. 'Finding a Place with Meaning in a Busy Human World: How Does the Story Begin, and Who Helps?' *European Early Childhood Education Research Journal*, 20: 303–312; Joynson, Robert. 1974. *Psychology and Common Sense*. London: Routledge.
47. See e.g. Menzies-Lyth, Isabel. 1959. 'The Functioning of Social Systems as a Defence Against Anxiety'. *Human Relations*, 13: 95–121; Bion, Wilfred. 1961 *Learning from Experience*. New York: Basic Books; Bick, Elizabeth. 1968. 'The Skin in Early Object Relations'. *International Journal of Psycho-Analysis*, 49: 484–486. For synonyms like 'hold' see: Winnicott, Donald W. 1965. *The Maturational Processes and the Facilitating Environment: Studies in the Theory of Emotional Development*. London: Hogarth. Bradley, Ben S., Jane Selby, and Cathy Urwin. 2012. 'Group Life in Babies: Opening up Perceptions and Possibilities'. In *Infant Observation and Research: Emotional Processes in Everyday Lives*, edited by Cathy Urwin and Janine Sternberg, pp. 137–148. Hove: Routledge.
48. As in a court of law, our approach does not aim for proof 'beyond all shadow of doubt'. See Bradley, 'A Study of Young Infants', Ch. 2, for discussion.
49. Bradley, *Darwin's Psychology*, Ch. 2.
50. Murray, Joseph. Ed. 2014. *Labelling Theory: Empirical Tests*. New York: Routledge.
51. Wagoner, Brady. Ed. 2010. *Symbolic Transformations: Toward an Interdisciplinary Science of Symbols*. London: Routledge.

Chapter 3

1. Both these concepts remain central to attachment theory, having been first highlighted by Mary Ainsworth in the 1970s. See: *Handbook of Attachment: Theory, Research and Clinical Applications*, 3rd edn, edited by Jude Cassidy and Philip Shaver. New York: Guilford Press;; Duschinsky, Robbie. 2020. *Cornerstones of Attachment Research*. Oxford: Oxford University Press. Neither concept has empirical warrant (see Appendix A.2.1.3).
2. Popper, Karl 1957. *The Poverty of Historicism*. Oxford: Routledge & Kegan Paul, p. 76.
3. Bion, Wilfred. 2014. *The Complete Works of W.R. Bion, Vol. 4*, edited by Chris Mawson, pp. 97–98. London: Karnac Books.
4. Hart, Sybil, Tiffany Field, and Claudia Del Valle. 1998. 'Infants Protest their Mothers' Attending to an Infant-Size Doll'. *Social Development*, 7: 54–61; Miller, Alison, Brenda Volling, and Nancy McElwain. 2000. 'Sibling Jealousy in a Triadic Context with Mothers and Fathers'. *Social Development*, 9: 433–457; Dunn, Judy and Carol Kendrick. 1982. 'Social Behaviour of Young Siblings in the Family Context: Differences between Same-Sex and Different-Sex Dyads'. *Child Development*, 52: 1265–1273.
5. Tremblay-Leveau, Heléne and Jacqueline Nadel. 1996. 'Exclusion in Triads: Can it Serve "Meta-Communicative" Knowledge in 11- and 23-Month-Old Children?' *British Journal of Developmental Psychology*, 14: 145–158; Tremblay, Heléne and Katia Rovira. 2007. 'Joint Visual Attention and Social Triangular Engagement at 3 and 6 Months'. *Infant Behaviour and Development*, 30: 366–379; Selby, Jane and Ben S. Bradley. 2003. 'Infants in Groups: A Paradigm for the Study of Early Social Experience'. *Human Development*, 46: 197–221.

6. The importance of history in preverbal communication has been argued for babies a few months older than ours, based on experimental findings rather than case-analysis. See Liszkowski Ulf. 2014. 'Two Sources of Meaning in Infant Communication: Preceding Action Contexts and Act-Accompanying Characteristics'. *Philosophical Transactions of the Royal Society B*, 369: 20130294: https://doi.org/10.1098/rstb.2013.0294
7. E.g. Bauer, Patricia, Marina Larkina, and Joanne Deocampo. 2011. 'Early Memory Development'. In *The Blackwell Handbook of Childhood Cognitive Development*, edited by Usha Goswami, pp. 153–179. Oxford: Blackwell.
8. Bion, Wilfred. 2013. 'Attacks on Linking'. *The Psychoanalytic Quarterly*, 82: 285–300; Britton, Ronald. 1989. 'The Missing Link: Parental Sexuality in the Oedipus Complex'. In *The Oedipus Complex Today*, edited by Ronald Britton, M. Feldman, and E. O'Shaughnessy, pp. 83–101. London: Karnac Books.
9. As argued by Britton, 'The Missing Link'.
10. See Walkerdine, Valerie. 1988. *The Mastery of Reason: Cognitive Development and the Production of Rationality*. London: Routledge, for her analysis of 'forgetting' detail in Western rationality and Selby, Jane. 1985. 'Feminine Identity and Contradiction: Women Research Students at Cambridge University'. PhD thesis. Cambridge University, for a theorization of individuation.
11. Liddle, Mitzi-Jane, Ben Bradley, and Andrew McGrath. 2015. 'Baby Empathy and Peer Prosocial Responses'. *Infant Mental Health Journal*, 36: 446–458.
12. See Fivaz references in Fivaz, Elisabeth. 2017. 'The Present Moment in the Primary Triangle'. *Psychoanalytic Inquiry*, 37: 242–250. Fivaz uses a 3-second time period. For a 30-second time period see: Ishikawa, Fumiko and Dale Hay. 2006. 'Triadic Interaction among Newly-Acquainted 2-Year-Olds'. *Social Development*, 15: 145–168.
13. The looks of the eight-month-olds in our own studies range from 0.1 to 40 seconds in length, having an average look-length of 2.3 seconds—with 43% of babies' looks lasting less than one second. Our babies changed direction of gaze every 3.7 seconds on average. Given that the obvious target of an infant's change-of-gaze—when she or he is sitting in a tight triangular group of three people and currently looking at one group member—is the other group member, chance would predict that a high proportion of infants' looks over a three-second time period (let alone over a period of 30 seconds!) will be switches of gaze between its two fellow group members.
14. Campbell, Donald. 1958. 'Common Fate, Similarity, and Other Indices of the Status of Aggregates of Persons as Social Entities. *Behavioural Science*, 3: 14–25. For discussion, see Bradley, Ben S. and Michael Smithson. 2017. 'Groupness in Preverbal Infants: Proof of Concept'. *Frontiers of Psychology*, 8. https:// doi.org/ 10.3389/ fpsyg.2017.00385.
15. A study somewhat along these lines was published by Gordon, Ilanit and Ruth Feldman. 2008. 'Synchrony in the Triad: A Microlevel Process Model of Coparenting and Parent-Child Interactions'. *Family Process*, 47: 465–479. Gordon and Feldman retain dyadic looking as a hallmark of social behaviour—and studied an asymmetrical group of two adults (mother and father) with a baby. Nevertheless, they showed a significant tie between shifts in infants' 'social focus' (switching gaze direction between mother and father or vice versa) and *preceding* 'coparental' behaviour or 'microlevel signals' *between the two parents*.
16. Emery, Nathan. 2000. 'The Eyes Have It: The Neuroethology, Function and Evolution of Social Gaze'. *Neuroscience and Biobehavioural Reviews*, 24: 581–604. doi: 10.1016/ S0149-7634(00)00025-7

17. Beier, Jonathan and Elizabeth Spelke. 2012. 'Infants' Developing Understanding of Social Gaze'. Child Development, 83: 486–496. doi: 10.1111/j.1467-8624.2011.01702.
18. Brooks, Rechele and Andrew Meltzoff. 2005. 'The Development of Gaze-Following and its Relation to Language'. *Developmental Science*, 8: 535–543. doi: 10.1111/j.1467-7687.2005.00445.x
19. Bowlby, John. 1982. *Attachment and Loss, Vol.1: Attachment*, 2nd edn. New York: Basic Books, pp. 376–377.
20. Bowlby, *Attachment*, p. 353.
21. Thompson, Ross. 2017. 'Twenty-First Century Attachment Theory: Challenges and Opportunities'. In *The Cultural Nature of Attachment: Contextualizing Relationships and Development*, edited by Heidi Keller and Kim Bard, pp. 301–320. Cambridge, MA: MIT Press, p. 304.
22. See e.g. Lamb, Michael and Alison Nash. 1989. 'Infant-Mother Attachment, Sociability, and Peer Competence'. In *Peer Relationships in Child Development*, edited by T. Berndt and G. Ladd, pp. 217ff. New York: Wiley; *Handbook of Attachment*, Cassidy and Shaver eds.
23. A similar concept-first view of human sociability underpinned Schaffer's claim that at birth an infant 'is essentially an asocial being' who takes over a year to become social, through a slow process of so-called *socialization*. See Schaffer, Rudolph. 1971. *The Growth of Sociability*, p. 1. Harmondsworth: Penguin. Like Bowlby, Schaffer was channelling Piaget's view that before a baby had developed an object concept (around 9–18 months of age), he or she would be incapable of having real social relationships because a parent would cease to exist in the baby's mind whenever out of view.
24. Bradley, Ben S. 1993. 'A Serpent's Guide to Children's "Theories of Mind"'. *Theory & Psychology*, 3: 497–521.
25. Hobson, Peter. 1991. 'Against the Theory of "Theory of Mind"'. British Journal of Developmental Psychology, 9: 33–51, p. 45; Trevarthen, Colwyn. 1979. 'Communication and Cooperation in Early Infancy: A Description of Primary Intersubjectivity'. In *Before Speech: The Beginning of Interpersonal Communication*, pp. 321–347, edited by Margaret Bullowa. Cambridge: Cambridge University Press; Reddy, Vasu. 2008. *How Infants Know Minds*. Cambridge, MA: Harvard University Press, p. 89.
26. For a book-length elaboration of this view, see Reddy's engaging *How Infants Know Minds*—which develops what Reddy calls a 'second-person' approach to understanding infants, drawing heavily on Martin Buber's *I and Thou* (discussed at length in Appendix, A.1). Like Hobson and Trevarthen, Reddy draws on J.J. Gibson's 'direct' theory of perception. Gibson proposed that we need no higher cognitive input to know what we see before us, the 'external' data are enough. Even exponents of 'theory of mind' assume that babies are born with a 'primary' form of representation or perception which has 'direct semantic relations' with the 'actual situation' in the world (see Bradley, 'Serpent's Guide'). This works well for all aspects of the world, they say, *except other people*. To deal with other people, so the argument for 'theory of mind' goes, we need a second form of 'meta'-representation, namely, *our own* 'theory of mind'. And this takes time to develop.
27. Reddy, *How Infants Know Minds*, p. 68. Cf. Fivaz, 'The Present Moment in the Primary Triangle'; Stern, Daniel. 2005. 'Le Désir d'Intersubjectivité. Pourquoi? Comment?' *Cahiers Critiques de Thérapie Familiale et de Pratiques de Réseaux*, 35: 29–42.
28. Salmon, Peter. 2021. *An Event, Perhaps: A Biography of Jacques Derrida*. London: Verso, p. 192.

29. Derrida, Jacques. 1987. *The Post Card: From Socrates to Freud and Beyond*. Chicago, IL: University of Chicago Press.
30. Freud, Sigmund. 1922. *Group Psychology and Analysis of the Ego*. London: Hogarth Press, p. 92.
31. For Darwin, tribal dynamics *transcended* one-to-one relations: witness his view that a clan's cohesion results from members' obedience to group-held norms, 'the wishes and judgement of *the community*'. Darwin, Charles. 1874. *The Descent of Man and Selection in Relation to Sex*, 2nd edn. London: Murray, p. 99, our italics.
32. Burnes, Bernard and Bill Cooke. 2013. 'Kurt Lewin's Field Theory a Review and Re-evaluation'. *International Journal of Management Reviews*, 15: 408–425; Gergen, Kenneth. 1989. 'Social Psychology and the Wrong Revolution'. *European Journal of Social Psychology*, 19: 463–484; (1989); Hinshelwood, Robert. 2007. 'Bion and Foulkes: The Group-as-a-Whole'. *Group Analysis*, 40: 344–356.
33. Bonebright, Denise. 2010. '40 Years of Storming: A Historical Review of Tuckman's Model of Small Group Development'. *Human Resource Development International*, 13: 111–120.
34. Hinshelwood, 'Bion and Foulkes', p. 350
35. Trevarthen, Colwyn and Kenneth Aitken. 2001. 'Infant Intersubjectivity: Research, Theory and Clinical Applications'. *Journal of Child Psychology and Psychiatry and Allied Disciplines*, 42: 3–48; Stern, 'Le Désir d'Intersubjectivité'; Fivaz, 'The Present Moment'; Reddy, *How Infants Know Minds*.
36. Cowan, Philip. 1997. 'Beyond Meta-Analysis. A Plea for a Family Systems View of Attachment'. Child Development, 68: 601–603; Lamb, Michael and Alison Nash. 1989. 'Infant-Mother Attachment, Sociability, and Peer Competence'. In *Peer Relationships in Child Development*, edited by T.J. Berndt and G.W. Ladd, pp. 219–245. New York: Wiley; Lewis, Michael, and Keiko Takahashi. 2005. 'Beyond the Dyad'. *Human Development*, 48: 5–111; Lewis, Michael. 2010. 'Beyond the Dyad'. In *The Cambridge Handbook Environment in Human Development: A Handbook of Theory and Measurement*, edited by Linda Mayes and Michael Lewis, pp. 103–117. Cambridge: Cambridge University Press; Nash, Alison. 1995. 'Beyond Attachments: Toward a General Theory of the Development of Relationships in Infancy'. In *Behavioural Development*, edited by K.E. Hood, G. Greenberg, and E. Tobach, pp. 287–326. New York: Garland Publishing; Rutter, Michael. 1995. 'Clinical Implications of Attachment Concepts: Retrospect and Prospect'. *Journal of Child Psychology and Psychiatry*, 36: 549–571.
37. E.g. Howes, Carollee and Susan Spieker. 2016. 'Attachment Relations in the Context of Multiple Caregivers'. In *Handbook of Attachment*, edited by Cassidy and Shaver, pp. 314–329.
38. Lewis and Takahashi, 'Beyond the Dyad'; Lewis, 'Beyond the Dyad'.
39. Lewis and Takahashi, 'Beyond the Dyad', pp. 21–22
40. Williams, Raymond. 2015. 'Structures of Feeling'. In *Structures of Feeling: Affectivity and the Study of Culture*, edited by Devika Sharma and Frederik Tygstrup, pp. 20–25. Berlin: De Gruyter.
41. The idea that a scientific theory could ever be 'beyond all doubt' neatly captures Kahr's unscientific attitude.
42. Kahr, Brett. 2012. 'The Infanticidal Origins of Psychosis: The Role of Trauma in Schizophrenia. In *Shattered States: Disorganized Attachment and Its Repair*, edited by Judy Yellin and Kate White, pp. 7–126. London: Karnac Books, p. 8.

43. Cassidy, Jude. 2016. 'The Nature of the Child's Ties'. In *Handbook of Attachment*, edited by Cassidy and Shaver, pp. 3–24, p. 11.
44. This is also true of Gordon, Ilanit and Ruth Feldman. 2008. 'Synchrony in the Triad: A Microlevel Process Model of Coparenting and Parent-Child Interactions'. *Family Process*, 47: 465–479. But Gordon and Feldman *do* show that, in infant–mother–father trios, interspousal behaviour does affect later infant behaviour.
45. Hay, Dale, Marlene Caplan, and Alison Nash. 2008. 'The Beginnings of Peer Relations'. In *Handbook of Peer Interactions, Relationships and Groups*, edited by K.H. Rubin, W.M. Bukowski, and B. Laursen, pp. 121–142. London: Guildford Publications, p. 122.
46. E.g. Reddy, Vasu, and Gina Mireault. 2015. 'Teasing and Clowning in Infancy'. *Current Biology*, 25: R20-R23.
47. E.g. Field, Tiffany. 1979. 'Infant Behaviours Directed Toward Peers and Adults in the Presence and Absence of Mother'. *Infant Behaviour and Development*, 2: 179–184.
48. Bion, Wilfred. 1948, 'Group Methods of Treatment'. In *The Complete Works of W.R. Bion, Vol.4*, p. 68.
49. Rees, Roger, and Mady Weiss. 1984. 'Role Differentiation: The Relationship between Instrumental and Expressive Leadership'. *Small Group Behaviour*, 15: 109–123; Price, Melissa, and Maureen Weiss. 2013. 'Relationships among Coach Leadership, Peer Leadership, and Adolescent Athletes' Psychosocial and Team Outcomes: A Test of Transformational Leadership Theory'. *Journal of Applied Sport Psychology*, 25: 265–279.
50. Especially if these are identified with verbal plans, as by Bion.

Chapter 4

1. Find at https://www.centresupport.com.au/.
2. Department of Education, Employment and Workforce Relations (DEEWR). 2009. *Belonging, Being and Becoming: The Early Years Learning Framework for Australia* [EYLF]. Canberra: Commonwealth of Australia. https://www.education.gov.au/child-care-package/resources/belonging-being-becoming-early-years-learning-framework-australia
3. Egs. Little, Helen and Matthew Stapleton. 2022. 'Exploring toddlers' rituals of "belonging" through risky play in the outdoor environment'. *Contemporary Issues in Early Childhood*: https://doi.org/10.1177/1463949120987656; Selby, Jane, Bradley, Ben S., Stapleton, Matthew, and Harrison, Linda. 2018. 'Is Infant Belonging Observable? A path through the maze'. In *Contemporary Issues in Early Childhood*, 19, 404–416.
4. See Australia's *National Quality Frameworks*: https://www.acecqa.gov.au/nqf/snapshots.
5. A thick, dark brown Australian food spread made from leftover brewers' yeast extract with various vegetable and spice additives.
6. Liddle, Mitzi-Jane, Ben Bradley, and Andrew McGrath. 2015. 'Baby Empathy and Peer Prosocial Responses'. *Infant Mental Health Journal*, 36: 446–458.
7. On analogical thinking see e.g. Ferry, Alissa, Susan Hespos, and Dedre Gentner. 2015. 'Prelinguistic Relational Concepts: Investigating Analogical Processing in Infants'. *Child Development*, 86: 1386–1405.
8. See e.g. Lewis. Michael. 2011. 'The Origins and Uses of Self-Awareness or the Mental Representation of Me'. *Consciousness and Cognition*, 20: 120–129.

9. N.B. Heidi Keller describes the nature of the needed change of role well: In a group-oriented education centre, such as in Japan, 'the teacher's task would be to moderate the group activities instead of concentrating on individual children. In several of the Japanese kindergartens, studied by Tobin et al. (2013), the teachers are the attentive observers who only interfere when the situation is overburdening the children. This kind of pedagogy needs different qualifications from what is stressed today with the focus on the individual child and the dyadic responsivity'. See p. 109 in Keller, Heidi. 2021. *The Myth of Attachment Theory: A Critical Understanding for Multicultural Societies*. London: Routledge. See also Friezer, Belinda. 2022. 'How do Infants Interact in Groups in Long Day Care Across the First Two Years of Life?' Charles Sturt University: PhD dissertation; Tobin, Joseph, Yeh Hsueh, and Mayumi Karasawa. 2009. *Preschool in Three Cultures Revisited: China, Japan, and the United States*. Chicago, IL: Chicago University Press.
10. See the video at the book's companion website: babiesingroups.com, namely: https://vimeo.com/616566958/86e67c01e5.
11. Heidi Keller reports a recent study from Germany which showed that all but four of the 198 early education professionals she surveyed 'stressed the importance of attachment theory for the pedagogical work in kindergarten'; see pp. 82ff in Keller, *The Myth of Attachment Theory*.
12. Mercer, Jean. 2006. *Understanding Attachment: Parenting, Child Care, and Emotional Development*. Westwood, CT: Greenwood.
13. Awarded a CBE by Queen Elizabeth II in 2022.
14. Leach, Penelope. 2008. 'EYFS best practice: All about ... relationships and feelings in the nursery'. *Nursery World*, 4 Nov: https://www.nurseryworld.co.uk/features/article/eyfs-best-practice-all-about-relationships-and-feelings-in-the-nursery.
15. DEEWR. 'EYLF', p. 17; see also p. 106 in Australian Children's Education and Care Quality Authority (ACECQA). 2017. *Guide to the National Quality Framework (GNQF)* https://www.acecqa.gov.au/sites/default/files/2018-03/Guide-to-the-NQF_0.pdf.
16. Australian Children's Education and Care Quality Authority (ACECQA). 2022. *Guide to the National Quality Framework*, p. 226: https://www.acecqa.gov.au.
17. ACECQA, *GNQF*, p. 163.
18. ACECQA, *GNQF*, p. 228.
19. Australian Department of Education. 2021. Child Care in Australia Report March Quarter 2021: https://www.education.gov.au/child-care-package/early-childhood-data-and-reports/quarterly-reports/child-care-australia-report-march-quarter-2021#toc-introduction.
20. Woods, Danielle. 2022. 'Cheaper Childcare is a Win-Win-Win Policy'. 4 July: https://grattan.edu.au/news/cheaper-childcare-is-a-win-win-win-policy/.
21. Pre-2012 in the state of New South Wales, there were room-size caps for the number of children in the regulations, and the maximum number of children in a single service was capped at ninety places per day.
22. This was exacerbated by the government's introduction of a minimum qualification requirement for working in early education (Certificate III in Early Childhood Education and Care). This created an exodus of mature, experienced women who were not prepared to study for the qualifications.
23. ACECQA, *National Quality Standards*: https://www.acecqa.gov.au/national-quality-framework.

24. Cf. the change described above by Heidi Keller of the educator role required for group-oriented practice rather than dyad-focused practice.

Chapter 5

1. The discovery of physiological and neuropsychological links, between mothers' social settings during pregnancy and their babies' later behaviour, sustains significant research energy, e.g. Verdult, Rien. 2021. 'Prenatal Roots of Attachment'. In *Handbook of Prenatal and Perinatal Psychology: Integrating Research and Practice*, edited by Klaus Evertz, Ludwig Janus, and Rupert Linder, pp. 227–246. Cham (Switzerland): Springer; Takács, Lea, Jiří Stipl, Maria Gartstein, Samuel Putnam, and Catherine Monk. 2021. 'Social Support Buffers the Effects of Maternal Prenatal Stress on Infants' Unpredictability'. *Early Human Development*, 157: 105352.
2. Freud, Sigmund. 1993. 'Observations on Transference-Love: Further Recommendations on the Technique of Psycho-Analysis III'. *Journal of Psychotherapy Practice and Research*, 2: 173–180. First published in 1915.
3. See also Chodorow, Nancy. 2010. 'Beyond the Dyad: Individual Psychology, Social World'. *Journal of the American Psychoanalytic Association*, 58: 207–230.
4. See Britton, Ronald. 1989. 'The Missing Link: Parental Sexuality in the Oedipus Complex'. In *The Oedipus Complex Today*, edited by R. Britton, M. Feldman, and E. O'Shaughnessy, pp. 83–101. London: Karnac Books.
5. Freud, Sigmund. 1922. *Group Psychology and Analysis of the Ego*. London: Hogarth Press; Bion, Wilfred. 2014. *The Complete Works of W.R. Bion, Vol.4*, edited by Chris Mawson. London: Karnac Books
6. Bion, Wilfred. 1961. *Experiences in Groups and Other Papers*. London: Tavistock Publications, p. 143.
7. Liddle, Mitzi-Jane, Ben S. Bradley, and Andrew McGrath. 2015. 'Baby Empathy and Peer Prosocial Responses'. *Infant Mental Health Journal*, 36: 446–458.
8. For additional evidence that babies joining in with other babies recognize the existing relationships between their peers and what they are playing with, and their social position within the group, see Friezer, Belinda. 2022. 'How do Infants Interact in Groups in Long Day Care Across the First Two Years of Life?' Charles Sturt University: PhD dissertation.
9. Bion, *Experiences in Groups*, p. 169.
10. E.g. Bowlby, John. 1982. *Attachment and Loss, Vol.1: Attachment*, 2nd edn. Basic Books, p. 31.
11. E.g. Paul, Campbell and Frances Thomson-Salo. 2014. 'Babies in Groups: The Creative Roles of the Babies, the Mothers, and the Therapists'. In *The Baby as Subject*, pp. 134–153. London: Routledge.
12. Lyons-Ruth, Karlen and Eda Spielman. 2004. 'Disorganized Infant Attachment Strategies and Helpless-Fearful Profiles of Parenting: Integrating Attachment Research with Clinical Intervention'. *Infant Mental Health Journal*, 25: 318–335. While later we criticize Moore's claim that Lyons-Ruth and Spielman's account *proves* infant dissociation has a basis in neurobiology, Moore's orientation is consistent with the contemporary development of Interpersonal Neurobiology (IPNB), as advocated by Daniel Siegel (2001) for example. Bringing together the 'materiality' of the mind with psychotherapy has a solid history which has been critically assessed, due to what the philosopher Donald Davidson

called the incommensurability of—or untranslatability of the languages relating to—the material and mental worlds (see Davidson, Donald.1980. *Essays on Actions and Events.* Oxford: Clarendon.) Thus, Ari Natinsky (e.g. 2021) reviews Louis Cozolino's (2014) *The Neuroscience of Human Relationships: Attachment and the Developing Social Brain,* 2nd edn. New York: Norton. Natinsky documents the rhetorical devices Cozolino, an influential theorist in this area, has to use to make apparent links between the material and the mental: including 'analogy, ambiguity, speculative language, and figures of speech such as metaphor and personification'. p.v. See Siegel, Daniel. 2001. 'Toward an Interpersonal Neurobiology of the Developing Mind: Attachment Relationships, "Mindsight" and Neural Integration'. *Infant Mental Health Journal,* 22: 67–94; Natinsky, Ari. 2021. 'Psychotherapy and the Embodiment of Neuronal Identity'. In *Hermeneutics and the Blooming of Mavericks,* edited by Philip Cushman. New York: Routledge.
13. Moore, Mary Sue. 2022. 'Importance of Attachment in the Presence of a Perceived Threat'. In *Treating Children with Dissociative Disorders Attachment, Theory, Trauma and Practice,* edited by Valerie Sinason and Renée Marks, Chapter 3. London: Routledge.
14. Lyons-Ruth and Spielman, 'Disorganized Infant Attachment', p. 330
15. Lyons-Ruth and Spielman, 'Disorganized Infant Attachment', p. 332.
16. A focus they prefer to what they call 'libidinal and aggressive drives': Lyons-Ruth and Spielman, 'Disorganized Infant Attachment', p. 319.
17. Note their slippage from the word 'parent' to the word 'mother'.
18. Wylie, Mary Sykes. 2011. 'Do We Still Need Attachment Theory? Jerome Kagan, Daniel Siegel, and Salvador Minuchin Weigh In'. *Psychotherapy Networker*: https://www.psychotherapynetworker.org/blog/details/1103/do-we-still-need-attachment-theory
19. Kahr, Brett. 2007. 'The Infanticidal Attachment'. *Attachment: New Directions in Psychotherapy and Relational Psychoanalysis,* 1: 117–132.
20. Kahr, 'Infanticidal Attachment', p. 119. It is of course impossible for anyone *veridically* to 'experience' the consequences *of accounts of* events *recalled by others* from *their* pasts – especially when these imputed consequences (babies' 'infanticidal' attachments) also supposedly occurred *decades ago,* in the pasts *of others.* Even the term 'infanticidal attachment' makes no conceivable *prima facie* sense: implying that babies themselves are *infanticidal,* i.e. that they (like their parents, supposedly) *want to* or do *kill babies*!
21. Lidz, Theodore, Robert Orrill, and Robert Boyers. 1971. 'Schizophrenia, R. D. Laing, and the Contemporary Treatment of Psychosis: An Interview with Dr. Theodore Lidz'. Salmagundi, 16: 105–136, p. 107.
22. Lidz, Theodore. 1973. *The Origin and Treatment of Schizophrenic Disorders.* New York: Basic Books, pp. 99–100.
23. Kahr, 'Infanticidal Attachment', pp. 120–121. Regarding the validity of this reading of the mother's remark about Woolf, see: Clark, Heather. 2020. *Red Comet: The Short Life and Blazing Art of Sylvia Plath.* New York: Vintage Books. (Thanks to Michaela Chamberlain for suggesting this reading.)
24. Lidz, *Schizophrenic Disorders,* pp. 26, 99–100.
25. Note that this confusion parallels a confusion in the broader attachment literature: Bowlby himself carefully confined the term 'attachment' to *the child's* side of his or her tie to a primary caregiver, something which only comes into force *after two years of age.* Yet, apparently, as with many who now use ideas of attachment styles during clinical practice and theory, the 'infanticidal' component of what Bowlby called the 'attachment–caregiving

bond' *belongs to the parent or caregiver* (i.e. to what Bowlby defined as the 'caregiving system', not the 'attachment system'), who feels like killing her baby long before s/he is two years old. See Appendix A.2.

26. E.g. Fairbrother, Nichole, Fanie Collardeu, Sheila Woody, David Wolfe, and Jonathan Fawcett. 2022. 'Post-Partum Thoughts of Infant-Related Harm and Obsessive-Compulsive Disorder'. *Journal of Clinical Psychiatry*, 83: e1–17: https://www.psychiatrist.com/jcp/ocd/postpartum-thoughts-infant-related-harm-obsessive-compulsive-disorder-relation-maternal-physical-aggression-toward-infant/
27. Winnicott, Donald. 1949. 'Hate in the Counter-Transference'. *International Journal of Psycho-Analysis*, 30: 69–67; Bradley, Ben S. 1991. 'Infancy as Paradise'. *Human Development*, 34: 35–54.
28. If 1 in 2 babies have mothers who harbour infanticidal thoughts and only 1 in 300 become schizophrenic, infanticidal thoughts cannot be the cause of schizophrenia.
29. Marvin, Robert, Glen Cooper, Kent Hoffman, and Bert Powell. 2002. 'The Circle of Security Project: Attachment-Based Intervention with Caregiver–Pre-School Child Dyads'. *Attachment & Human Development*, 4: 107–124, p. 108.
30. Marvin et al., 'The Circle of Security'.
31. Marvin et al., 'The Circle of Security', p. 115, our italics.
32. A like plea occurs on p. 354 in Sroufe, Alan. 2005. 'Attachment and Development: A Prospective, Longitudinal Study from Birth to Adulthood'. *Attachment & Human Development*, 7: 349–367.
33. Marvin et al., 'Circle of Security', p. 116. Note the symptomatic disturbance of grammar in this formulation, which makes a group 'process' equate to an individual 'skill'.
34. See for example research showing how poverty and societal context affects early development, research which bypasses the behaviour of 'the mother': e.g. Centre on the Developing Child. 2013. *Early Childhood Mental Health*. Retrieved from www.developingchild.harvard.edu.
35. Whilst few attachment theorists dispute his heroism in this regard, the extent to which Bowlby himself *caused* this shift is hotly debated among historians. See e.g. Van der Horst, Frank, and René van der Veer. 2009. 'Changing Attitudes towards the Care of Children in Hospital: A New Assessment of the Influence of the Work of Bowlby and Robertson in the UK, 1940–1970'. *Attachment & Human Development*, 11: 119–142.
36. See e.g. Lewontin, Richard, Steven Rose, and Leon Kamin. 1984. *Not in Our Genes: Biology, Ideology and Human Nature*. New York: Pantheon; Bradley, Ben S. 2020. *Darwin's Psychology: The Theatre of Agency*. Oxford: Oxford University Press; Bradley, Ben S. 2022. 'Natural Selection according to Darwin: Cause or Effect?' *History and Philosophy of the Life Sciences*, 44: https://doi.org/10.1007/s40656-022-00485-z
37. Fonagy, Peter, Patrick Luyten, Elizabeth Allison, and Chloe Campbell. 2016. 'Reconciling Psychoanalytic Ideas with Attachment Theory'. In *Handbook of Attachment: Theory, Research and Clinical Applications*, 3rd edn, edited by Jude Cassidy and Philip Shaver, pp. 780–804. New York: Guilford Press, p. 781.
38. For more on this, see Appendix, Section A.2.1.2
39. Ainsworth et al., *Patterns of Attachment*, pp. 262ff.
40. Ainsworth et al., *Patterns of Attachment*, pp. 295–298.
41. Or 'models' plural: theorists disagree.

42. Thompson, Ross. 2017. 'Twenty-First Century Attachment Theory: Challenges and Opportunities'. In *The Cultural Nature of Attachment: Contextualizing Relationships and Development*, edited by Heidi Keller and Kim Bard, pp. 301–320. Cambridge: MIT Press, pp. 303–304.
43. See e.g. Bretherton, Inge, and Kristine Mullholland. 2008. 'Internal Working Models in Attachment Relationships: Elaborating a Central Concept in Attachment Theory'. In *Handbook of Attachment: Theory, Research, and Clinical Implications*, 2nd edn, edited by Jude Cassidy and Phillip Shaver, pp. 346–426. New York: Guilford Press.
44. Cf. Devereux, George, ed. 1953. *Psychoanalysis and the Occult*. New York: International Universities Press.
45. Kahr, 'Infanticidal Attachment', p. 119.
46. This usage of 'paradigm' remains common. See e.g. Robbie Duschinsky, 2020. *Cornerstones of Attachment Research*. Oxford: Oxford University Press, (*passim*).
47. Kuhn, Thomas. 1962. *The Structure of Scientific Revolutions*. Chicago, IL: University of Chicago Press.
48. E.g. Smith, Fred and Rebecca Bace. 2003. *A Guide to Forensic Testimony: The Art and Practice of Presenting Testimony as an Expert Technical Witness*. Boston, MA: Addison-Wesley, p. 130.
49. Ainsworth et al., *Patterns of Attachment*, pp. 3ff.
50. Anon. 'Paradigm'. *Wikipedia*: accessed on 25 July 2022. https://en.wikipedia.org/wiki/Paradigm
51. In 2021, a recognized clinician told Jane that attachment theory's validity is a 'no brainer'.
52. See e.g. Angell, James. 1909. 'The Influence of Darwin on Psychology'. *Psychological Review*, 16: 152–169; Bradley, *Darwin's Psychology*, Chs.1 and 2.
53. Howell, Jennifer, Brian Collisson, and Kelly King. 2014. 'Physics Envy: Psychologists' Perceptions of Psychology and Agreement About Core Concepts'. *Teaching of Psychology*, 4: 330–334.
54. Koch, Sigmund. 1981. 'The Nature and Limits of Psychological Knowledge: Lessons of a Century of Psychology *qua* "Science"'. *American Psychologist*, 36: 257–269.
55. For critiques of the scientific value of statistical significance in disciplines like psychology see e.g.: Greenhalgh, Trisha. 1998. 'Narrative-Based Medicine in an Evidence-Based World'. In *Narrative-Based Medicine: Dialogue and Discourse in Clinical Practice*, edited by Trisha Greenhalgh and Brian Hurwitz, pp. 247–265. London: BMJ Books; Maxwell, Scott, Michael Lau, and George Howard. 2015. 'Is Psychology Suffering from a Replication Crisis?: What Does "Failure to Replicate" Really Mean?' *American Psychologist*, 70: 487–498; Munafo, Marcus and John Sutton. 2017. 'There's this Conspiracy of Silence around How Science Really Works'. *The Psychologist*, 30: 46–49; Ferguson, Christopher. 2015. 'Everybody Knows Psychology Is Not a Real Science'. *American Psychologist*, 70: 527–542. On the mathematical construction of statistical 'significance', 'confidence levels' and related concepts, see Smithson, Michael. 2002. *Confidence Intervals*. London: Sage.
56. Tinbergen, Niko. 1963. 'On Aims and Methods of Ethology'. *Zeitschrift für Tierpsychologie*, 20: 410–433, (p. 412). Cf. Baumeister, Roy, Kathleen Vohs, and David Funder. 2007. 'Psychology as the Science of Self-Reports and Finger Movements: Whatever Happened to Actual Behavior?' *Perspectives on Psychological Science*, 2: 396–403.; Gergen, Kenneth. 1989. 'Social Psychology and the Wrong Revolution'. *European Journal of Social Psychology*, 19: 463–484.

57. Tinbergen, Elisabeth and Niko Tinbergen. 1972. 'Early Childhood Autism – An Ethological Approach'. *Advances in Ethology*, Supplement 10: 1–53.
58. E.g. Bowlby, *Attachment*, p. 250, reports that infant smiling 'appears to be a fixed action pattern'. But this can be disproved in minutes by anyone who observes a baby carefully. See Appendix A.2.1.3.
59. An invention paradoxically *applauded* by Bowlby, see: Bowlby, *Attachment*, pp. 334ff.
60. Vicedo, Marga. 2017. 'Putting Attachment in its Place: Disciplinary and Cultural Contexts'. *European Journal of Developmental Psychology*, 14: 684–699.
61. See Vicedo, Marga. 2017. 'The Strange Situation of the Ethological Theory of Attachment: A Historical Perspective'. In *The Cultural Nature of Attachment: Contextualizing Relationships and Development*, edited by Heidi Keller and Kim Bard, pp. 13–51. Cambridge: MIT Press, p. 30: 'Ainsworth's twenty-minute procedure to categorize infants and mothers undoubtedly became central to the successful spread of Bowlby's views. In the context of post-World War II views of science, the operationalization of attachment research via the Strange Situation played a key role in the rise and expansion of attachment theory. Having an easy, short, and cheap laboratory tool to study attachment was crucial to [attachment theory's] enormous appeal in American psychology'.
62. Fonagy et al., 'Reconciling Psychoanalytic Ideas', p. 785. On 'failures to replicate' attachment-based research, see: van IJzendoorn, Marius and Marian Bakermans-Kranenburg. 2021. 'Replication Crisis Lost in Translation? On Translational Caution and Premature Applications of Attachment Theory'. *Attachment & Human Development*, 23: 422–437
63. Ravitz, Paula, Robert Maunder, Jon Hunter, Bhadra Sthankiya, and William Lance. 2010. 'Adult Attachment Measures: A 25-Year Review'. *Journal of Psychosomatic Research*, 69: 419–432. (29 such measures are reviewed.)
64. Keller, Heide. 2018. 'Universality Claim of Attachment Theory: Children's Socioemotional Development'. *Proceedings of the National Academy of Sciences*, 115: 11414–11419; Henrich, Joseph, Steven Heine, and Ara Norenzayan. 2010. 'The Weirdest People in the World?' *Behavioural and Brain Sciences*, 33: 61–135.
65. Keller, 'Universality Claim', p. 11415; Jeffrey, Arnett. 2008. 'The Neglected 95%: Why American Psychology Needs to Become Less American'. *American Psychologist*, 63: 602–614.
66. 'What about multiple attachments', some will cry: 'All attachment theorists nowadays acknowledge multiple attachments!' No, they do not. Witness Kahr, 'Infanticidal Attachment'. Witness Lyons-Ruth and Spielman, 'Disorganized Infant Attachment'. Moreover, when they do, they end up in an intractable theoretical muddle if they try to explain how those 'multiple attachments' end up producing one consolidated 'internal working model' as would conform to Bowlby's stated theory in *Attachment*—built to prioritize just one 'primary' attachment figure, the 'mother-figure' (see Appendix A.2.5). Generally, they do not try.
67. Keller, Heidi and Kim Bard, eds. 2017. *The Cultural Nature of Attachment: Contextualizing Relationships and Development*. Cambridge: MIT Press; Otto Hiltrud and Heidi Keller, eds. 2014. *Different Faces of Attachment: Cultural Variations on a Universal Human Need*. Cambridge: Cambridge University Press; Naomi Quinn and Jeanette Mageo, eds. 2013. *Attachment Reconsidered: Cultural Perspectives on a Western Theory*. New York: Palgrave Macmillan; Erdman, Phyllis and Nok-Mun Ng, eds. 2010. *Attachment: Expanding the*

Cultural Connections. New York: Routledge; Keller, Heidi. 2021. *The Myth of Attachment Theory: A Critical Understanding for Multicultural Societies*. London: Routledge, especially Ch.5; Vicedo, 'Putting Attachment in its Place'.
68. Mesman, Judi, Marius van IJzendoorn, and Abraham Sagi-Schwartz. 2016. 'Cross-Cultural Patterns of Attachment Universal and Contextual Dimensions'. In *Handbook of Attachment: Theory, Research, and Clinical Applications*, 3rd edition, edited by Jude Cassidy, and Phillip Shaver, pp. 852–877. New York: Guilford Publications, 2016 et al. (p. 871).
69. Mesman et al., 'Cross-Cultural Patterns', p. 871.
70. See Keller, *The Myth of Attachment Theory*.
71. The study in question was: Agrawal, Priyanka and Jatinder Gulati. 2005. 'The Patterns of Infant-Mother Attachment as a Function of Home Environment'. *Journal of Human Ecology*, 18: 287–293. This study reported 100% securely attached babies—and explained the finding in terms of cultural differences between the home environments and kinds of care experienced by the Indian babies studied versus the kinds experienced by the middle-class babies typically studied in the USA.
72. Cassidy and Shaver, *Handbook of Attachment*, 3rd edn, p. 871.
73. This kind of gatekeeping mostly escapes scrutiny. Heretical papers seldom see the light of day. Or their authors have to change their tune if they want to get published—like Fraley and Spieker, (we also speak from experience).
74. Duschinsky, *Cornerstones of Attachment*, p. 146.
75. Fraley, Chris and Susan Spieker. 2003. 'Are Infant Attachment Patterns Continuously or Categorically Distributed? A Taxometric Analysis of Strange Situation Behaviour'. *Developmental Psychology*, 39: 387–404
76. Kahr, Brett. 2012. 'The Infanticidal Origins of Psychosis: The Role of Trauma in Schizophrenia'. In *Shattered States: Disorganized Attachment and Its Repair*, edited by Judy Yellin and Kate White, pp. 7–126. London: Karnac Books, p. 8.
77. Fonagy et al., 'Reconciling Psychoanalytic Ideas with Attachment Theory'.
78. Zeedyk, Suzanne. 2016. 'Attachment'. https://suzannezeedyk.com/attachment-suzanne-zeedyk/
79. Mesman, Judi. 2021. 'Attachment Theory's Universality Claims: Asking Different Questions'. In *Attachment: The Fundamental Questions*, edited by Ross Thompson, Jeffrey Simpson, and Lisa Berlin, pp. 245–251. New York: Guilford.
80. Vicedo, 'Strange Situation', p. 34.
81. Mesman, 'Attachment Theory's Universality Claims', p. 245.
82. Vicedo, 'Strange Situation', p. 17.
83. Ainsworth et al. *Patterns of Attachment* (this 1978 book confirmed that a minority of infants reliably show fear of strangers); Harriet Rheingold and Carol Eckerman. 1973. 'Fear of the Stranger: A Critical Examination'. *Advances in Child Development and Behaviour*, 8: 185–222; Hildy Ross and Barbara Goldmann. 1977. 'Infants' Sociability toward Strangers'. *Child Development*, 48: 638–642; Solomon, Ruth and Therese Décarie. 1976. 'Fear of Strangers: A Developmental Milestone or an Overstudied Phenomenon?' *Canadian Journal of Behavioural Science*, 8: 351–362. N.B. All these studies were published well before Bowlby produced his revised edition of *Attachment* in 1982.
84. See p. 233 in Keller, Heidi. 2021. 'Attachment Theory: Fact of Fancy?' In *Attachment: The Fundamental Questions*, edited by Ross Thompson, Jeffrey Simpson, and Lisa Berlin, pp. 229–236. New York: Guilford.

85. Lamb, Michael, Ross Thompson, William Gardner, Eric Charnov, and David Estes. 1984. 'Security of Infantile Attachment as Assessed in the "Strange Situation": Its Study and Biological Interpretation'. *Behavioural and Brain Sciences*, 7: 127–47; Lamb, Michael, Ross Thompson, William Gardner, Eric Charnov, and James Connell. 1985. *Infant-Mother Attachment: The Origins and Developmental Significance of Individual Differences in Strange Situation Behaviour*. Hillsdale, NJ: Erlbaum.
86. Lamb et al., 1984. 'Security of Infantile Attachment', is not mentioned at all. Lamb et al., *Infant-Mother Attachment* is mentioned twice in Cassidy and Shaver, *Handbook of Attachment*: once in an endnote to refute Lamb et al.'s claim that Bowlby ever pushed an exclusive 'monotropism' (p. 20); and once to note Lamb et al.'s argument that 'an early secure attachment provides a stronger foundation for subsequent psychosocial achievements if the sensitive, supportive parental care initially contributing to attachment security is maintained over time' (p. 334). Neither even registers Lamb's team's critiques.
87. Vicedo, 'Strange Situation', p. 33. See Appendix A.2.
88. Wolff, Peter. 1963. 'Observations on the Early Development of Smiling'. In *Determinants of Infant Behaviour, Vol. 2*, edited by Brian Foss. London: Methuen; Wolff, Peter. 1969. 'The Natural History of Crying and Other Vocalizations in Early Infancy'. In *Determinants of Infant Behaviour, Vol. 4*, edited by Brian Foss. London: Methuen.
89. See Appendix, Section A.1.3.1, for an alternative account of dissociation in infants.
90. One never mentions infants, being a study of child abuse recalled by 18–60 year olds (Chu, Ja. and David Dill. 1990. 'Dissociative Symptoms in Relation to Childhood Physical and Sexual Abuse'. *American Journal of Psychiatry*, 147: 887–892). One only mentions dissociation once, in passing, when it refers to dissociation *in mothers* (Lyons-Ruth and Spielman, 'Disorganized Infant Attachment'). And, while the third discusses the 'defensive *behaviour*' of babies who are routinely hurt by their caregivers, it avoids attributing any kind of 'internal' defensive process to babies, thus denying the very possibility of infant 'dissociation' – a word which it never uses (Selma Fraiberg. 1982. 'Pathological Defenses in Infancy'. *Psychoanalytic Quarterly*, 51, 612–635). See Moore, 'Importance of Attachment'.
91. As when ships fly flags of convenience, financial motives are involved here. For, with the rise of a need for clinicians to maintain, renew, or update the currency of their professional memberships and credentials by means of 'professional development', a competitive market has grown up in which training courses for many different types of clinical approach contend for market share.
92. Parnell, Laura. 2013. *Attachment-Focused EMDR: Healing Relational Trauma*. New York: Norton,
93. Siegel, Daniel. 2013. 'Foreword'. In Parnell, *Attachment-Focused EMDR*, p. xiii.
94. Cundy, Linda. 2022. *Attachment, Maternal Deprivation, and Psychotherapy: Surviving or Thriving*. London: Confer Books.
95. Diamond, Guy, Jody Russon, and Suzanne Levy. 2016. 'Attachment-Based Family Therapy: A Review of the Empirical Support'. *Family Process*, 55: 595–610.
96. Diamond et al., 'Attachment-Based Family Therapy', p. 595.
97. For a critique of Bowlby's use of evolutionary evidence and theory, see: Bradley, 'Natural Selection'; Hinde, Robert. 1983. 'Ethology and Child Development'. In *Handbook of Child Psychology, vol. 2: Infancy and Developmental Biology*, edited by Marshall Haith and James Campos, pp. 27–94. New York: Wiley; Hinde, Robert. 1991. 'Relationships, Attachment, and Culture: A Tribute to John Bowlby'. *Infant Mental Health Journal*, 12: 154–163; Lamb

et al., 'Security of Infantile Attachment'; Lamb et al., *Infant-Mother Attachment*; Ch.1 and Appendix, A.2.
98. On 'structures of feeling', see Davika Sharma and Frederik Tygstrup, eds. 2015. *Structures of Feeling: Affectivity and the Structure of Culture*. Berlin: De Gruyter.
99. Sinason, Valerie. 2021. 'The Truth about Trauma and Dissociation; Part II' (Confer Events, Strype St., London. 21 July).
100. Sinason, 'Truth about Trauma'.
101. Sinason, 'Truth about Trauma'.
102. Klein, Melanie. 1952. 'On Observing the Behaviour of Young Infants'. In *Developments in Psycho-Analysis*, edited by Melanie Klein, Paula Heimann, Susan Isaacs, and Joan Rivière, pp. 237–270. London: Hogarth Press; Klein, Melanie. 1952. 'Some Theoretical Conclusions regarding the Emotional Life of the Infant'. In *The Writings of Melanie Klein, Volume 8: Envy and Gratitude and Other Works*, pp. 61–94. London: Hogarth Press.
103. Bowlby was trained by Melanie Klein and another Kleinian analyst, Joan Rivière. See Holmes, Jeremy. 1993. *John Bowlby and Attachment Theory*. London: Routledge, p. 5.
104. Sinason, 'Truth about Trauma'.
105. Sinason, 'Truth about Trauma'.
106. William James. 1890. *Principles of Psychology*, Vol.1. New York: Norton, p. 488: 'The baby, assailed by eyes, ears, nose, skin, and entrails at once, feels it all as one great blooming, buzzing confusion …' William James' description, though out of sync with the contemporary science of infant psychology, is here recovered in the arena of emotional meaning-making.
107. Sinason, 'Truth about Trauma'.
108. Bowlby, *Attachment*, pp. 11ff.
109. Or 'mother-figure'.
110. We might find internet links to illustrate most ideas, and this link takes us to the joy of dancing with others, the same rhythm for all, yet we discern the arising of each individuality. Check out https://www.youtube.com/watch?v=Uk_G1-qM-2U
111. Feldman, Ruth and Miri Keren. 2004. 'Expanding the Scope of Infant Mental Health Assessment: A Community-Based Approach'. In *Handbook of Infant Mental Health Assessment*, edited by Rebecca DelCarmen-Wiggins and Alice Carter, pp. 443–465. Oxford: Oxford University Press (p. 445)
112. Boal, Augusto. 1985. *Theatre of the Oppressed*. New York: Theatre Communications Group; Boal, Augusto. 1992. *Games for Actors and Non-Actors*. London: Routledge.

Chapter 6

1. See Bradley, Ben S. 2020. *Darwin's Psychology: The Theatre of Agency*. Oxford: Oxford University Press, p. 72.
2. For more on the ideas that attachment discourse may sometimes prove to have efficacy as 'narrative truth' with some clients—even though it does not have reliable or generalizable 'historical truth', see Spence, Donald. 1984. *Narrative Truth and Historical Truth: Meaning and Interpretation in Psychoanalysis*. New York: Norton.
3. Nursery Schools Association. 1943. *The First Stage in Education*: quoted in Whitbread, N. 1972. *The Evolution of the Nursery-Infant School: A History of Infant and Nursery Education, 1800–1970*. London: Routledge & Kegan Paul, pp. 103–104.

4. Bowlby's claims were later refuted by Rutter, Michael. 1972. *Maternal Deprivation Reassessed*. Harmondsworth: Penguin.
5. Hay, Dale, Marlene Caplan, and Alison Nash. 2011. 'The Beginnings of Peer Relations'. In *Handbook of Peer Interactions, Relationships, and Groups*, edited by Kenneth Rubin, William Bukowski, and Brett Laursen, pp. 121–142. New York: Guilford Press.
6. Brownell, Celia, Sara Nichols, and Margarita Svetlova. 2005. 'Early Development of Shared Intentionality with Peers'. *Behavioural and Brain Sciences*, 28: 693–694
7. Townley, C. 2018 'Playgroups: Moving in from the Margins of History, Policy and Feminism'. *Australasian Journal of Early Childhood*, 43 (2): 64–71.
8. Freud, Sigmund. 1922. *Group Psychology and Analysis of the Ego*. London: Hogarth Press, p. 101.

Appendix

1. Trevarthen, Colwyn and Kenneth Aitken. 2001. 'Infant Intersubjectivity: Research, Theory and Clinical Applications'. *Journal of Child Psychology and Psychiatry and Allied Disciplines*, 42: 3–48.
2. Trevarthen and Aitken, 'Infant Intersubjectivity', p. 4.
3. Murray, Lynne. 1998. 'Contributions of Experimental and Clinical perturbations of Mother–Infant Communication to the Understanding of Infant Intersubjectivity'. In *Intersubjective Communication and Emotion in Early Ontogeny*, edited by Steiner Bråten, pp. 127–143. Cambridge: Cambridge University Press, p. 147; Reddy, Vasu. 2008. *How Infants Know Minds*. Cambridge, MA: Harvard University Press, p. 89.
4. For an earlier engagement, see George F. Stout. 1903. *The Groundwork of Psychology*. London: Tutorial Press, pp. 170–187.
5. Habermas, Jürgen. 1970. 'Towards a Theory of Communicative Competence'. In *Recent Sociology, No.2*, edited by Hans Dreitzel, pp. 115–148. London: Macmillan; Habermas, Jürgen. 1970. 'On Systematically Distorted Communication'. *Inquiry*, 13: 205–218; Ryan, Joanna. 1974. 'Early Language Development: Towards a Communicational Analysis'. In *The Integration of a Child into a Social World*, edited by Martin Richards, pp. 185–214. Cambridge: Cambridge University Press.
6. Bradley, Ben S. 1989. 'The Asymmetric Involvement of Infants in Social Life: Consequences for Theory'. *Revue Internationale de Psychologie Sociale*, 2: 61–81; Bradley, Ben S. 2010. 'Jealousy in Infant-Peer Trios: From Narcissism to Culture'. In *Handbook of Jealousy: Theories, Principles and Multidisciplinary Approaches*, edited by Sybil Hart and Maria Legerstee, pp. 192–234. Hoboken, NJ: Wiley-Blackwell.
7. Winnicott, Donald. 1967. 'Mirror-Role of Mother and Family in Child Development'. In *Playing and Reality*, pp. 130–138. Harmondsworth: Penguin.; Lacan, Jacques. 1949. 'The Mirror Stage as Formative of the Function of the I'. In *Écrits: A Selection*, edited and translated by Alan Sheridan, pp. 1–7. London: Tavistock; Lacan, Jacques. 1981. *Speech and Language in Psychoanalysis*, edited and translated by Anthony Wilden. Baltimore, MD: Johns Hopkins University Press; Selby, Jane. 1993. 'Primary Processes: Developing Infants as Adults'. *Theory & Psychology*, 3: 523–544.
8. E.g. Schaffer, Rudolph. 1971. *The Growth of Sociability*. Harmondsworth: Penguin Books.

9. Trevarthen, Colwyn. 1974. 'Conversations with a Two-Month-Old'. *New Scientist*, 62: 230–235; Richards, Martin. 1974. 'First Steps in Becoming Social'. In *The Integration of a Child into a Social World*, edited by Martin Richards, pp. 83–99. Cambridge: Cambridge University Press; Brazelton, Berry, Barbara Koslowski, and Mary Main. 1974. 'The Origins of Reciprocity'. In *The Effect of the Infant on Its Caregiver*, edited by Michael Lewis and Lawrence Rosenblum, pp. 49–76. New York: Wiley; Bruner, Jerome. 1975. 'The Ontogenesis of Speech Acts'. Journal of Child Language, 2: 1–19; Hobson, Peter. 2007. 'Communicative Depth: Soundings from Developmental Psychopathology'. Infant Behavior and Development, 30: 267–277.
10. Bradley, Ben S. 1985. 'Failure to Distinguish between People and Things in Early Infancy'. *British Journal of Developmental Psychology*, 3: 281–292.
11. Cf. Frye, D., Rawling, P., Moore, C., and Myers, I. 1983. 'Object-Person Discrimination and Communication at 3 and 10 months'. *Developmental Psychology*, 19: 303–309; Legerstee, Maria. 1997. 'Contingency Effects of People and Objects on Subsequent Cognitive Functioning in Three-Month-Old Infants'. *Social Development*, 6: 307–321.
12. Brazelton et al., 'The Origins of Reciprocity'.
13. Bradley, Ben S. and Colwyn Trevarthen. 1978. 'Babytalk as an Adaptation to the Infant's Communication'. In *The Development of Communication*, edited by Natalie Waterson and Catherine Snow, pp. 75–92. London: Wiley. A host of authors have since argued the importance of mothers' 'affect mirroring' for infant development. Indeed, even where 'affect mirroring' is not mentioned as such, the most effective form of 'natural' mothering is tacitly equated with affect mirroring. E.g. Gergely, Gyorgy and John Watson. 1996. 'The Social Biofeedback Theory of Parental Affect-Mirroring: The Development of Emotional Self-Awareness and Self-Control in Infancy'. *International Journal of Psycho-Analysis*, 77: 1181–1212; Legerstee, Maria and Jean Varghese. 2001. 'The Role of Maternal Affect Mirroring on Social Expectancies in 3-Month-Old Infants'. *Child Development*, 72: 1301–1313. See Bradley, 'Jealousy in Infant-Peer Trios', for a review.
14. Bradley and Trevarthen, 'Babytalk as an Adaptation'.
15. Winnicott, 'Mirror-Role of Mother'.
16. Murray, Lynne. 1980. 'The Sensitivities and Expressive Capacities of Young Infants in Communication with their Mothers'. Unpublished Ph.D. thesis, University of Edinburgh; Trevarthen, Colwyn, Lynne Murray and Penelope Hubley. 1981. 'The Psychology of Infants'. In *Scientific Foundations of Paediatrics*, 2nd edn., edited by John Davis and Joseph Dobbing, pp. 211–274. London: Heinemann Medical; Murray, Lynne and Colwyn Trevarthen. 1985. 'Emotional Regulation of Interactions between Two-Month-Olds and their Mothers'. In *Social Perception in Infants*, edited by Tiffany Field and Nathan Fox, pp. 177–197. Norwood, NJ: Ablex; cf. Tronick, Edward, Heidelise Als, Lauren Adamson, Susan Wise, and Berry Brazelton. 1978. 'The Infant's Response to Entrapment between Contradictory Messages in Face-to-Face Interaction'. *Journal of the American Academy of Child Psychiatry*, 17: 1–13.
17. Trevarthen et al., 'Psychology of Infants'.
18. E.g. Trevarthen, Colwyn. 1998. 'The Concept and Foundations of Infant Intersubjectivity'. In *Intersubjective Communication and Emotion in Early Ontogeny*, edited by Steiner Braten, pp. 15–46. Cambridge: Cambridge University Press, p. 16; Reddy, *How Infants Know Minds*.
19. See e.g. Habermas, 'On Systematically Distorted Communication' and 'Towards a Theory of Communicative Competence'; Lacan, *Speech and Language*; Selby, Jane. 'Primary

Processes'; also Bradley, Ben S. 1981. 'Negativity in Early Infant-Adult Exchanges and its Developmental Significance'. *European Monographs in Social Psychology*, 24: 1–38; Bradley, Ben S. (in press). 'The Evidence for Innate Intersubjectivity'. In *Intersubjective Minds*, edited by Vasu Reddy and Jonathan Delafield-Butt. Oxford: Oxford University Press.
20. Buber, Martin. 1937. *I and Thou*. Edinburgh: T. & T. Clark, p. 6; Anon. 2022. 'Martin Buber'. *Wikipedia*: https://en.wikipedia.org/wiki/Martin_Buber (accessed 18 Sept. 2022). Other philosophers recruited for the same purpose by earlier advocates of intersubjectivity include John Macmurray (1891–1976) and David Hamlyn (1924–2012).
21. Reddy, *How Infants Know Minds*, p. 27.
22. Kaufmann, Walter. 1970. 'I and You: A Prologue'. In *I and Thou* by Martin Buber, pp. 9–48. New York: Scribner, pp. 9–10. To the extent that babies show primary narcissism in *en face* conversations with adults, theirs is more an I-It relationship, than an I-Thou relationship.
23. Virginia Woolf. 1935. *A Room of One's Own*, p. 53. London: Hogarth.
24. Lacan 'Mirror Stage'; Winnicott, 'Mirror-Role of Mother'.
25. Bradley, 'Negativity'; Bradley, Ben S. 1991. 'Infancy as Paradise'. *Human Development*, 34: 35–54.
26. Reddy, *How Infants Know Minds*, p. 116
27. Trevarthen et al., 'Psychology of Infants', p. 246; Trevarthen, Colwyn. 1988. 'Universal Cooperative Motives: How Infants Begin to Know Language and Skills of Culture'. In *Acquiring Culture: Ethnographic Perspectives on Cognitive Development*, edited by Gustav Jahoda and Ioan Lewis, pp. 37–90. London: Croom Helm, p. 43.
28. Bradley, 'Negativity'. 'Fractional glances' were first described as occurring in the behaviour of autistic children; see Corinne Hutt and Christopher Ounsted. 1966. 'The Biological Significance of Gaze Aversion with Particular Reference to the Syndrome of Infantile Autism'. *Behavioural Science*, 11: 346–356.
29. Bradley. 'Infancy as Paradise'; Riley, Denise. 1983. *War in the Nursery: Theories of Child and Mother*. London: Virago; Bradley, Ben S. *Visions of Infancy: A Critical Introduction to Child Psychology*. Cambridge: Polity Press
30. Freud, Sigmund. 1914. 'On Narcissism: An Introduction'. In *On Metapsychology: The Theory of Psychoanalysis (Pelican Freud Library, Vol.11)*, edited by Angela Richards, pp. 59–98. London: Penguin Books, 1984. For a full-blown psychoanalytic theory of intersubjectivity from the 1950s, see Lacan, *Speech and Language*.
31. Eliot, Thomas Stearns. 1936. 'Burnt Norton'. In *Collected Poems, 1909–1935*. London: Faber & Faber.
32. Palmer, Richard. 1969. *Hermeneutics: Interpretation Theory in Schleiermacher, Dilthey, Heidegger, and Gadamer*. Evanston: Northwestern University Press
33. Devereux, George. 1968. *From Anxiety to Method in the Behavioural Sciences*. The Hague: Mouton.
34. Especially if these observations are *ex cathedra* rather than being based on carefully-triangulated observations *of babies*—about which, see Ch.2 in Bradley, Ben S., 2020. *Darwin's Psychology: The Theatre of Agency*. Oxford: Oxford University Press.
35. See Bradley, *Visions of Infancy*; Bradley, Ben S. 1993. 'A Serpent's Guide to Children's "Theories of Mind"'. *Theory & Psychology*, 3: 497–521.
36. Haraway, Donna. 1988. 'Situated Knowledges: The Science Question in Feminism and the Privilege of Partial Perspective'. *Feminist Studies*, 14: 575–599.

37. Malloch, Stephen and Colwyn Trevarthen. 2009. 'Musicality: Communicating the Vitality and Interests of Life'. In *Handbook of Communicative Musicality: Exploring the Basis of Human Companionship*, edited by Stephen Malloch and Colwyn Trevarthen, pp. 1–11. Oxford: Blackwell-Wiley, p. 6.
38. N.B. In this Appendix, we focus primarily on the work of John Bowlby, as this is still treated as the undisputed core of attachment theory (see e.g. Cassidy quote in Section A.2.4). Furthermore, because Bowlby was sloppy with definitions and changed his 'position' to suit occasions, we will focus our critique on his most extensive and considered formulation of attachment theory *as it relates to infants*: Bowlby, John. 1982. *Attachment and Loss, Vol.1: Attachment*, 2nd edn. New York: Basic Books.
39. It is nowadays fashionable in attachment writings to refer to 'mother figures' or '(primary) caregivers', not 'mothers', as primary attachment figures. But the term 'mother figure' still makes 'mothers' the template for understanding caregiving. And Bowlby certainly referred far more frequently to 'mothers' than 'mother figures'. Even contemporary writers like Marvin et al., who ostensibly focus on 'caregivers' in their article, go on to call out 'mothers' *thirty-three* times as against naming 'fathers' just once: Marvin, Robert, Glen Cooper, Kent Hoffman, and Bert Powell. 2002. 'The Circle of Security Project: Attachment-Based Intervention with Caregiver–Pre-School Child Dyads'. *Attachment & Human Development*, 4: 107–124.
40. See Cassidy, Jude. 2016. 'The Nature of the Child's Ties'. In *Handbook of Attachment: Theory, Research and Clinical Applications*, 3rd edn, edited by Jude Cassidy and Philip Shaver, pp. 3–24. New York: Guilford Press, 2016, p. 17.
41. Baerends, Gerard. 1976. 'Functional Organization of Behaviour. *Animal Behaviour*, 24: 726–738.
42. Bowlby, *Attachment*, pp. 244ff
43. Bowlby, *Attachment*, p. 65.
44. Von Hofsten, Claes and Kerstin Rosander. 2019. 'The Development of Sensorimotor Intelligence in Infants'. *Advances in Child Behaviour and Development*, 55: 73–106.
45. E.g. Messinger, Daniel and Alan Fogel. 2007. 'The Interactive Development of Social Smiling'. *Advances in Child Development and Behaviour*, 35: 327–366; Bradley, Ben S. 1980. 'A Study of Young Infants as Social Beings'. Unpublished Ph.D. thesis, University of Edinburgh.
46. Pratt, Chris. 1981. 'Crying in Normal Infants'. In *Communicating with Normal and Retarded Children*, edited by William Fraser and Robert Grieve, pp. 3–23. London: Wright & Sons
47. Ollers, Kimbrough and Rebecca Eilers. 1988. 'The Role of Audition in Infant Babbling'. *Child Development*, 59: 441–449.
48. Botero, Maria, Hillary Langley, and Amanda Venta. 2020. 'The Untenable Omission of Touch in Maternal Sensitivity and Attachment Research'. *Infant and Child Development*: https://doi.org/10.1002/icd.2159; Feldman, Ruth. 2007. 'Parent–Infant Synchrony and the Construction of Shared Timing; Physiological Precursors, Developmental Outcomes, and Risk Conditions'. *Journal of Child Psychology and Psychiatry*, 48: 329–354.
49. Jordan, Geraldine, Kelly Arbeau, Denise McFarland, Kelly Ireland, and Alescia Richardson. 2020. 'Elimination Communication Contributes to a Reduction in Unexplained Infant Crying'. *Medical Hypotheses*, 142, 109811.
50. 'Attachments' and 'Relationships' are often treated as the same thing by attachment researchers, albeit incorrectly, according to Bowlby's book *Attachment*.

51. Nash, Alison. 1995. 'Beyond Attachments: Toward a General Theory of the Development of Relationships in Infancy'. In *Behavioural Development*, edited by Kathryn Hood, Gary Greenberg, and Ethel Tobach, pp. 287–326. New York: Garland Publishing.
52. Bowlby, *Attachment*, pp. 376–377.
53. Ainsworth, Mary, Mary Blehar, Everett Waters, and Sally Wall. 2015. *Patterns of Attachment: A Psychological Study of the Strange Situation*. New York: Routledge, p. 33. (First published 1978); Waters, Everett. 1978. 'The Reliability and Stability of Individual Differences in Infant–Mother Attachment'. *Child Development*, 49: 483–494.
54. Ainsworth et al., *Patterns of Attachment*, pp. 17–19, 289–293; Waters. 'The Reliability and Stability of Individual Differences in Infant–Mother Attachment, p. 483:' The reliability of discrete-behaviour variables was typically very low, and there was little evidence of temporal stability'.
55. Rheingold, Harriet, and Carol Eckerman. 1973. 'Fear of the Stranger: A Critical Examination'. *Advances in Child Development and Behaviour*, 8: 185–222; Ross, Hildy, and Barbara Goldmann. 1977. 'Infants' Sociability toward Strangers'. *Child Development*, 48: 638–642; Solomon, Ruth and Therese Décarie. 1976. 'Fear of Strangers: A Developmental Milestone or an Overstudied Phenomenon?' *Canadian Journal of Behavioural Science*, 8: 351–362.
56. Ainsworth et al., *Patterns of Attachment*.
57. Bretherton, Inge. 1978. 'Making Friends with One-Year-Olds: An Experimental Study of Infant-Stranger Interaction'. Merrill-Palmer Quarterly, 24: 29–51
58. 'Hay, Dale. 1977. 'Following Their Companions as a Form of Exploration for Human Infants'. *Child Development*, 48: 1624–1632.
59. Ainsworth et al., *Patterns of Attachment*.
60. Glodowski, Kathryn, Rachel Thompson, and Lauren Martel. 2019. 'The Rooting Reflex as an Infant Feeding Cue'. *Journal of Applied Behaviour Analysis*, 52: 17–27.
61. Ollers and Eilers, 'Infant Babbling'.
62. Von Hofsten and Rosander. 'The Development of Sensorimotor Intelligence in Infants'.
63. Hay, Dale. 1977. 'Following Their Companions as a Form of Exploration for Human Infants'. *Child Development*, 48: 1624–1632.' with 'Hay, 'Following Their Companions'.
64. Lappi, Hanne, Minna Valkonen-Korhonen, Stefanos Georgiadis, Mika Tarvainen, Ina Tarkka. Pasi Karjalainen, and Johannes Lehtonen. 2007 'Effects of Nutritive and Non-Nutritive Sucking on Infant Heart Rate Variability during the First 6 months of Life'. *Infant Behaviour and Development*, 30: 546–556; Lehtonen, Johannes, Minna Valkonen-Korhonen, Stefanos Georgiadis, Mika P. Tarvainen, Hanne Lappi, Juha-Pekka Niskanen, Ari Pääkkönen, and Pasi Karjalainen. 2016. 'Nutritive Sucking Induces Age-Specific EEG-Changes in 0-24-Week-Old Infants'. *Infant Behaviour and Development*, 45: 98–108.
65. Hay, Dale. 1980. 'Multiple Functions of Proximity-Seeking in Infancy'. *Child Development*, 51: 636–645.
66. Bowlby, *Attachment*, p. 250.
67. Messinger and Fogel, 'Infant Smiling'.
68. Selby, 'Primary Processes'; Papousek, Hanus. 1969. 'Individual Variability in Learned Responses in Human Infants'. In *Brain and Early Behaviour: Development in the Fetus and Infant*, edited by Roger Robinson, pp. 251–266. New York: Wiley; Watson, John. 1972. 'Smiling, Cooing and "The Game"'. *Merrill-Palmer Quarterly*, 18: 323–339.
69. Bowlby, *Attachment*, pp. 164, 218.

70. Harlow, Harry. 1962. 'Affectional Systems of Monkeys, Involving Relations between Mothers and Young'. *International Symposium on Comparative Medicine Proceedings*, pp. 6–10. Eaton Laboratories, p. 10.
71. 'Peer experience during early development is the *sine qua non* for adequate adolescent and adult monkey behaviour': Harlow, Harry and Billy Seay. 1964. 'Affectional Systems in Rhesus Monkeys'. *Journal of the Arkansas Medical Society*, 61: 107–110. See discussion in Marga Vicedo. 2013. *The Nature and Nurture of Love: From Imprinting to Attachment in Cold War America*. Chicago, IL: University of Chicago Press.
72. Hrdy, Sarah Blaffer. 2009. *Mothers and Others: The Evolutionary Origins of Mutual Understanding*. Cambridge, MA: Harvard University Press.
73. Strum, Shirley. 2012. 'Darwin's Monkey: Why Baboons Can't Become Human'. *Yearbook of Physical Anthropology*, 55: 3–23.
74. The SSP is also used to validate the other main means of assessing infant attachments: the Attachment Q-Sort.
75. The classic critiques here are by Michael Lamb and his colleagues: Lamb, Michael, Ross Thompson, William Gardner, Eric Charnov, and David Estes. 1984. 'Security of Infantile Attachment as Assessed in the "Strange Situation": Its Study and Biological Interpretation'. *Behavioural and Brain Sciences*, 7: 127–147 (e.g. 'When rearing conditions change, early events may have no predictive value at all', p. 137); Lamb, Michael, Ross Thompson, William Gardner, Eric Charnov, Eric and James Connell. 1985. *Infant–Mother Attachment: The Origins and Developmental Significance of Individual Differences in Strange Situation Behaviour*. Hillsdale, NJ: Erlbaum. For more recent research, meta-analyses, and reviews of research, see, for example: Booth-LaForce, Cathryn and Glenn Roisman. 2021. 'Stability and Change in Attachment Security'. In *Attachment: The Fundamental Questions*, edited by Ross Thompson, Jeffrey Simpson, and Lisa Berlin, pp. 154–160. New York: Guilford; De Wolff, Marianne and Marinus Van IJzendoorn. 1997. 'Sensitivity and Attachment: A Meta-Analysis on Parental Antecedents of Infant Attachment'. *Child Development*, 68: 571–591; Fraley, Chris. 2013. 'Interpersonal and Genetic Origins of Adult Attachment Styles: A Longitudinal Study from Infancy to Early Adulthood'. *Journal of Personality and Social Psychology*: doi:10.1037/a0031435; Grossman, Klaus, Karin Grossman, and Everett Waters, eds. 2005. *Attachment from Infancy to Adulthood: The Major Longitudinal Studies*. New York: Guilford Press; Raikes, Abigail and Ross Thompson. 2005. 'Links between Risk and Attachment Security: Models of Influence'. *Applied Developmental Psychology*, 26: 440–455.
76. E.g. van IJzendoorn, Marinus, and Marian Bakermans-Kranenburg. 2021. 'Replication Crisis Lost in Translation? On Translational Caution and Premature Applications of Attachment Theory'. *Attachment & Human Development*, 23: 422–437; Woodhouse, Susan, Julie Scott, Allison Hepwoth, and Jude Cassidy. 2020. 'Secure Base Provision: A New Approach to Examining Links between Maternal Caregiving and Infant Attachment'. *Child Development*, 91: e249-e265
77. See refs in endnote #75 and Cowan, Philip. 1997. 'Beyond Meta-Analysis. A Plea for a Family Systems View of Attachment'. *Child Development*, 68: 601–603
78. E.g. Bakermans-Kranenberg, Marian, Marinus Van IJzendoorn, and Femmie Juffer. 2003. 'Less is More: Meta-Analyses of Sensitivity and Attachment Interventions in

Early Childhood'. *Psychological Bulletin*, 129: 195–215; Belsky, Jay, Kate Rosenberger, and Keith Crnic. 1995. 'The Origins of Attachment Security: "Classical" and Contextual Determinants'. In *Attachment Theory: Social, Developmental and Clinical Perspectives*, edited by Susan Goldberg, Roy Muir, and John Kerr, pp. 1253–1183. Hillsdale, NJ: Analytic; Boldt, Lea, Kathryn Goffin, and Grazyna Kochanska. 2020. 'The Significance of Early Parent-Child Attachment for Emerging Regulation: A Longitudinal Investigation of Processes and Mechanisms from Toddler Age to Preadolescence'. *Developmental Psychology*, 56: 431–443; Fearon, Pasco and Jay Belsky. 2016. 'Precursors of Attachment Security'. In Cassidy and Shaver, eds., *Handbook of Attachment*, pp. 291–313.

79. Lamb et al., 'Security of Infantile Attachment'; Lamb et al., *Infant Mother Attachment*.
80. Grossman et al., *Attachment from Infancy to Adulthood*; Rutter, Michael. 2006. 'Critical Notice'. *Journal of Child Psychology and Psychiatry*, 47: 974–977.
81. E.g. Kochanska, Grazyna and Sanghag Kim. 2012. 'Toward a New Understanding of the Legacy of Early Attachments for Future Antisocial Trajectories: Evidence from Two Longitudinal Studies'. *Developmental Psychopathology*, 24: 783–806; Pinquart, Martine, Cristina Feusner, and Lieselotte Ahnert. 2013. 'Meta-Analytic Evidence for Stability in Attachments from Infancy to Early Adulthood'. *Attachment & Human Development*, 15: 189–218.
82. E.g. Hsiao, Celia, Nina Koren-Karie, Heidi Bailey, and Greg Moran. 2015. 'It Takes Two to Talk: Longitudinal Associations among Infant–Mother Attachment, Maternal Attachment Representations, and Mother–Child Emotion Dialogues'. *Attachment & Human Development*, 17: 43–64; Shahar-Maharik, Tali, David Oppenheim, and Nina Koren-Karie. 2018. 'Adolescent Insightfulness toward a Close Friend: Its Roots in Maternal Insightfulness and Child Attachment in Infancy'. *Attachment & Human Development*: https://doi.org/10.1080/14616734.2018.144673
83. Lamb et al., 'Security of Infantile Attachment', *Infant–Mother Attachment*; Booth-LaForce and Roisman, 'Stability and Change in Attachment Security'.
84. This average is taken from Groh, Ashley, Pasco Fearon, Marian Bakermans-Kranenburg, Marinus van IJzendoorn, Ryan Steele, and Glenn Roisman. 2014. 'The Significance of Attachment Security for Children's Social Competence with Peers: A Meta-Analytic Study'. *Attachment & Human Development*, 6: 103–136: in this meta-analysis, attachment security was, on average, measured at 31 months of age, and peer competence was measured at 54.3 months of age. See also Grossman et al., *Attachment from Infancy to Adulthood*.
85. Lamb, Michael and Alison Nash. 1989. 'Infant–Mother Attachment, Sociability, and Peer Competence'. In *Peer Relationships in Child Development*, edited by Thomas Berndt and Gary Ladd, pp. 219–245. New York: Wiley.
86. Nash. 'Beyond Attachments'
87. Vicedo, Marga. 2017. 'Putting Attachment in its Place: Disciplinary and Cultural Contexts'. *European Journal of Developmental Psychology*, 14: 684–699; Vicedo, Marga. 2017. 'The Strange Situation of the Ethological Theory of Attachment: A Historical Perspective'. In *The Cultural Nature of Attachment: Contextualizing Relationships and Development*, edited by Heidi Keller and Kim Bard, pp. 13–51. Cambridge: MIT Press.
88. Messinger and Fogel, 'Infant Smiling'; Pratt, 'Infant Crying'.
89. Darwin, Charles. 1890. *The Expression of the Emotions in Man and Animals*, 2nd edn. London: Murray p. 378.

90. E.g. Keller, Heidi. 2021. *The Myth of Attachment Theory: A Critical Understanding for Multicultural Societies*. London: Routledge; Keller, Heidi and Kim Bard, eds. 2017. *The Cultural Nature of Attachment: Contextualizing Relationships and Development*. Cambridge: MIT Press; Otto Hiltrud and Heidi Keller, eds. 2014. *Different Faces of Attachment: Cultural Variations on a Universal Human Need*. Cambridge: Cambridge University Press; Naomi Quinn and Jeanette Mageo, eds. 2013. *Attachment Reconsidered: Cultural Perspectives on a Western Theory*. New York: Palgrave Macmillan; Phyllis Erdman and Nok-Mun Ng, eds. 2010. *Attachment: Expanding the Cultural Connections*. New York: Routledge. See also, Harris, Judith. 2011. *The Nurture Assumption: Why Children Turn Out the Way They Do*, 2nd edn. New York: Free Press.
91. Riley, *War in the Nursery*.
92. Bowlby, John. 1988. *A Secure Base*. New York: Basic Books, p. 125 N.B. Contemporary attachment theorists continue to echo Bowlby's ineffectual protests that they are not intentionally mother-blaming, even though they do blame mothers for poor child outcomes. Such protests are hypocritical, given the way the theory they advocate has mother-blaming built into it. See e.g. Sroufe, Alan. 2005. 'Attachment and Development: A Prospective, Longitudinal Study from Birth to Adulthood'. *Attachment & Human Development*, 7: 349–367; Marvin et al., 'The Circle of Security Project', p. 116.
93. Bradley, 'Infancy as Paradise'; Granqvist, Pehr et al. 2017. 'Disorganized Attachment in Infancy: A Review of the Phenomenon and its Implications for Clinicians and Policy-Makers'. *Attachment & Human Development*, 19: 534–558; Granqvist et al., 2017; Keller, Heide. 2018. 'Universality Claim of Attachment Theory: Children's Socioemotional Development'. *Proceedings of the National Academy of Sciences*, 115: 11414–11419; Keller, *The Myth of Attachment Theory*.
94. See p.119 in Kahr, Brett. 2007. 'The Infanticidal Attachment'. *Attachment: New Directions in Psychotherapy and Relational Psychoanalysis*, 1: 117–132.
95. Ainsworth et al., *Patterns of Attachment*, p. 4: 'Attachment theory might be described as "programmatic" and open-ended. It does not purport to be a tight network of propositions on the basis of which hypotheses may be formulated, any one of which, in the event of an adequate but unsuccessful test, could invalidate the theory as a whole ... Despite its lack of resemblance to a mathematico-physical theory, both the general theory of behaviour and attachment theory amount to what Kuhn (1962) termed a paradigm change for developmental psychology—a complete shift of perspective ... '
96. Bowlby was an advocate of Sir Karl Popper's view that a theory or hypothesis which cannot be empirically tested and so refuted is not scientific: see Bowlby, *Attachment*, *passim*; Bowlby, John. 1982. 'A Case of Mistaken Identity'. *Higher Education Quarterly*, 36: 328–332.
97. For some recent analyses refuting the scientific status of attachment theory see: Harkness, Sara. 2015. 'The Strange Situation of Attachment Research: A Review of Three Books'. *Reviews in Anthropology*, 44: 178–197; Keller, Heidi. 2021. 'Attachment Theory: Fact or Fancy?' In *Attachment: The Fundamental Questions* Thompson et al., eds, pp. 229–236; Keller, *The Myth of Attachment Theory*; Vicedo, Marga. 2020. 'On the History, Present, and Future of Attachment Theory'. *European Journal of Developmental Psychology*, 17: 147–155.
98. Cassidy, 'The Nature of the Child's Ties', p.17. The current *Handbook of Attachment* either ignores or palliates *all* the criticisms summarized here. Thus, *nowhere* in its 1068 pages does it discuss the exemplary critiques made by the team led by Michael Lamb, nor those

of Marga Vicedo, or Rheingold and Eckerman. Over the decades, attachment theorists' unwillingness to confront criticism has become legendary: see comments to this effect in Lamb et al., 'Security of Infantile Attachment', p. 161; Keller, *The Myth of Attachment Theory*; Keller, 'Attachment Theory: Fact of Fancy?'; Mesman, Judi. 2021. 'Attachment Theory's Universality Claims: Asking Different Questions'. In *Attachment: The Fundamental Questions*, edited by Ross Thompson, Jeffrey Simpson, and Lisa Berlin, pp.245–251. New York: Guilford; Rutter, 'Critical Notice'; Vicedo, 'Putting Attachment in its Place'.

99. Which this Appendix has merely sketched. Another interchange which shows attachment advocates' continuing incapacity to respond constructively to criticism is contained in a recent dispute between Marga Vicedo and Robbie Duschinsky and colleagues: see Vicedo, 'Putting Attachment in its Place'; Duschinsky, Robbie, Marinus Van Ijzendoorn, Sarah Foster, Sophie Reijman, and Francesca Lionetti. 2020. 'Attachment Histories and Futures: Reply to Vicedo's 'Putting Attachment in Its Place'. *European Journal of Developmental Psychology*, 17: 138–146 https://doi.org/10.1080/17405629.2018.1502 916; and, Vicedo, 'On the History, Present, and Future of Attachment Theory'. Over the decades, attachment theorists' unwillingness to confront criticism has become legendary: see Lamb et al., 'Security of Infantile Attachment', p.161; Keller, *The Myth of Attachment Theory*; Keller, 'Attachment Theory: Fact of Fancy?'; Mesman, 'Attachment Theory's Universality Claims'; Rutter, 'Critical Notice'.

100. See for example, Riley, *War in the Nursery*; Keller, 'Universality Claim'; Keller, *The Myth of Attachment Theory*.

101. E.g. Howes, Carollee and Alison Wishard Guerra. 2009. 'Networks of Attachment Relationships in Low-Income Children of Mexican Heritage'. *Social Development*, 18: 896–914.

102. Thompson, Ross. 2017. 'Twenty-First Century Attachment Theory: Challenges and Opportunities'. In *The Cultural Nature of Attachment: Contextualizing Relationships and Development*, edited by Heidi Keller and Kim Bard, pp. 301–320. Cambridge: MIT Press, pp. 303–304.

103. Even where there are said to be 'multiple attachments', these are still conceived dyadically: each attachment reputedly having an adult as set-goal. E.g. Howes, Carollee and Susan Spieker. 2016. 'Attachment Relations in the Context of Multiple Caregivers'. In *Handbook of Attachment*, edited by Cassidy and Shaver, pp. 314–329

104. See e.g. Cowan, 'Beyond Meta-Analysis. A Plea for a Family Systems View of Attachment'.

Index

For the benefit of digital users, indexed terms that span two pages (e.g., 52-53) may, on occasion, appear on only one of those pages.

Tables and figures are indicated by t and f following the page number

abuse 128–30
affective mirroring 142–43
affiliative system 44; *see also* attachment system
agency 13, 14–15, 45, 74, 88, 103, 147
Ainsworth, M. 113–14, 115–16, 118, 121–22, 123, 124–25, 148, 149, 154
alloparents 10
apes 10, 103, 104f
Ardener, E. 28–29
Aristotle 3, 28, 29
attachment
  attachment-based therapy 125–28
  attachment behaviours 1–2, 44, 113–14, 124, 147–51, 153
  Attachment Q-Sort 120
  attachment system 124, 147, 150, 153
  attachment theory 4–6, 18–19, 113–25, 153–54
    categories of 120–21, 152–53
      disorganized 109
      dissociative 125
      infanticidal 109–11, 115, 154
      secure/insecure 31, 44, 69, 95–96, 109, 119, 120–21, 132, 136, 147, 149, 151–52
    criticisms of 115–32, 147–54
    denies subjective complexity 113–15
    Handbook of Attachment 119, 120, 124, 147, 154
    longitudinal studies of 152–53
    multiple attachments 68–69, 154–55
    'paradigm' 69, 115–25, 154
    'perspective' 147–55
    see also Ainsworth; affiliative system; behavioural systems; Bowlby; Circle of Security; internal working models; Strange Situation Procedure (SSP)

babbling 34, 36, 79, 147–48, 149
baby farms 3–4
behavioural systems 44, 65–66, 124–25, 147–48, 150, 153
belonging 74–75, 79, 135f
binocular view 49–52
Bion, W. 50, 68, 71–72, 103
Boal, A. 133
boarding schools 4–5
Bower, T. 18
Bowlby, J. 4–6, 18–19, 44, 65, 69, 113, 115–16, 118, 121, 123, 124–25, 136, 147–48, 149, 150, 151, 153, 154
Bradley, B.S. 15–16
brain size 13–15
Breuer, J. 102
Brownell, C. 137
Buber, M. 143
Bussey, K. 71

Callitrichids 11–12, 150–51
care-and-contact mothering 10
case studies 28–30, 105
cats' chorus 34, 39
Centre Support 74–75
chimpanzees 10, 14, 104f, 150
Chomsky, N. 146
Circle of Security 111–13, 154
cognition-first approach 65–66; *see also* infants
common fate 61–62
communicative behaviours, *see* infants
'the competent infant' 17–18; *see also* infants
complexity of infant experience 49–60, 67, 70, 86, 87–88, 103–5, 111, 113–15, 132–34; *see also* multiplicity of infant worlds
conversation in infancy 19–20, 21–22, 39–43, 52, 66–67, 87

Coontz, S. 10
cooperative breeding 10–12, 13, 150–51
countertransference 103, 146
couples therapy 126–27
cross-cultural studies 12–13, 119–20, 153
crying 3, 93–95, 130, 148, 153
cultural differences 12–13, 119–20, 153
Cundy, L. 126–27
curiosity 31, 34, 93, 96, 136

dance 140f, 147
Darwin, C. 2, 15, 27–28, 67–68, 117, 135–36, 155
defecation 148
depression 16, 127
description, *see* methods
Dialectical Behavioural Therapy (DBT) 125
Diamond, G. 127
Dickens, C. 3–4
'Dimensions of Disrupted Maternal Affective Communication' 108t
direct understanding 66–67, 141–47; *see also* infants
disorganized attachment, *see* attachment: categories of
dissociative attachment, *see* attachment: categories of
dissociative identity disorder (DID) 107–9, 128–32
DNA 12
dyadic programme of human sociability, *see* infants: 'dyadic'

Early Childhood Education and Care (ECEC) centres 74–82
  educators in ECEC 68–69, 74, 75–76, 77–80, 81–82, 88–98
  policy in ECEC 8, 74, 91, 95–100, 125, 154
Early Years Learning Framework (EYLF) 74–75, 79, 91
Eliot, T.S. 145
ethnography 28–29, 30, 88, 119–20, 154
ethology 118, 147; *see also* behavioural systems; fixed action patterns (FAPs)
evolution 2, 12–13, 150
extended families, *see* families
Eye Movement Desensitization and Reprocessing (EMDR) 126; *see also* therapies

facial expressions 35–36; *see also* infants: means of communication
families 7–10, 107–11
  background variables 151–53
  extended 7–10, 154
  nuclear, traditional 7–10, 154
  see also social support
family therapy 127
Fantz, R. 18–19
Feldman, R. 133
field theory 68
Fivaz, E. 17, 61, 70
fixed action patterns (FAPs) 124–25, 147–48, 149
Flyvbjerg, B. 28–29
focal vision, *see* vision
Fonagy, P. 121–22
Foulkes, S. 68
fractional glances 145
Fraley, C. 120–21
Freud, A. 17–18
Freud, S. 67–68, 102, 103, 138, 145, 146
Freud in North Queensland (FINQ) conference 15–16

Galileo 29
Gandhi, M. 69
gatekeeping 118–21, 123
gaze 25–26, 39–40, 54, 63–64, 148; *see also* infants: means of communication, vision
Geertz, C. 28–29, 30
gestures 36, 39–43, 45–46, 55
gorillas 10, 150
gravitational theory 29
groups
  group analysis 68
  group animals 68–69, 103
  group conversation 52
  group dynamics 7, 16, 38, 51–52, 56, 68, 88, 115–25
  groups, primacy of 65–69
  group therapy 15–16, 102–3, 111–13
  history in infant groups 55–57
  routines in infant groups 53–60, 87–88
  see also Bion; Darwin; Foulkes; Freud, S and A.; groupness; Lewin; Tuckman
groupness 6–7, 47, 60–64, 68–69, 71, 87–88, 115, 150

Habermas, J. 141
Handbook of Attachment 119, 120, 124, 147, 154
Harlow, H. 150, 153
Harrison, L. 74–75
Hay, D. 137
hermeneutics, *see* methods
history in infant groups 55–57
'holding' function 146
Hrdy, S.B. 6, 11–13, 150–51
hypothetico-deductive method 27

imitation 26–27, 34, 38
individuation 3, 59
Industrial Revolution 3–4
infanticide 4, 11–12, 111, 150–51; *see also* attachment: infanticidal
infants
   approaches to studying
     cognition-first 65–66
     the competent infant 17–18
     direct understanding 66–67, 141–47
     dyadic 1–2, 18–20, 29–30, 44, 61, 63–64, 65–66, 68–69, 71, 103–15, 141
     scaffolding 17, 20–21
   meaning-making in 26–27, 30–31
   means of communication 31–38, 52, 147–48; *see also* vocalization
   work, capacity for 60, 71–72, 93–95
   see also complexity of infant experience; multiplicity of infant worlds
in-group idealization 121–22
insecure attachment, *see* attachment, categories of
intentional action 18, 33, 63, 149
internal working models (IWMs) 44–45, 65–66, 107, 112, 113–15, 118, 121–22, 124, 126, 154–55; *see also* attachment
intersubjectivity 19–20, 61, 68–69, 141–47
I-Thou 143–44

jealousy 11, 42–43, 46–47, 49, 50–51

Kahr, B. 69–70, 109–11, 115, 121, 154
Keren, M. 133
Klein, M. 130–32
Kung Bushpeople 12–13, 13*f*

labelling theory 47
Lacan, J. 145–46

Lamb, M. 121–22, 124, 152
language acquisition device 146
Lausanne Trilogue Play procedure 17, 61
Leach, P. 95
learning stories 91–93
Leonardo da Vinci 69
Lewin, K. 68
Lewis, M. 68–69
Lidz, T. 109–10
linking 54, 57–60
Linnaeus, C. 28
Lyons-Ruth, K. 105–7

Madonna–child imagery 5*f*, 70
Malloch, S. 147
Marks, R. 107–9
marmosets 11–12, 150–51
Marvin, R. 111
Mead, M. 119, 123
mealtimes 76–91
meaning-making in infant groups 26–27, 30–31
measurement, *see* methods
mental illness 128
Mesman, J. 122, 123–24
methods
   case studies 28–30, 105
   coding 63, 113–15, 120, 148
   description 28–29, 30, 45, 46–47, 49–60
   ethnography 28–29, 30, 88, 119–20, 154
   ethology 118, 147
   hermeneutics 146
   laboratory-based 18, 19–20, 22, 113–15, 117–18
   measurement 117–18, 151–53
   natural history 27–31, 117–18, 124–25
   observation 24–27, 39–43, 77–80, 103, 114*f*, 117–18, 120, 121–22, 124–25, 141–43, 144, 146, 149, 154
   statistical analysis 60–64, 117
mind-reading 143–44
Minnesota study 152
Minuchin, S. 107
mirroring 34, 142–43
monotropy 29, 123
Moore, M.S. 105, 125
mother-blaming 96, 105–7, 112, 115, 132, 145, 154
Mozart, W.A. 69
multiple attachments 68–69, 154–55

multiplicity of infant worlds 2–3, 87–88, 119, 131, 133, 135–36; *see also* polyadic interaction
Munch, E. 51*f*
Murray, L. 143
music 19–20, 147
mutual gaze 25–26, 39–40, 54, 63–64; *see also* infants: means of communication; vision

Nadel, J. 17, 70
narcissism 21, 144–46
National Quality Framework, Australia 96
National Quality Standards (NQS) 76
natural history, *see* methods
neocortex 13–15
New Psychology 117
nuclear families, *see* families
Nursery Schools Association 136

object permanence 18
observation, *see* methods
Oedipus complex 67–68
Olds, D. 8–10
orangutans 10

Parnell, L. 126
Paul, C. 15–16, 105
peer review 120–21
peripheral vision, *see* vision
Perry, D. 71
perspective, attachment theory as, *see* attachment
perturbation experiments 143
phrenology 115–16
physics envy 117–18
Piaget, J. 18, 146
playgroups 137–38
policies, *see* Early Childhood Education and Care (ECEC) centres: policy in
polyadic interaction 29–30, 31, 135–36
Popper, K. 49
primal scene 102
primary narcissism 144–46
primary processes 145–46
primates 10–12, 103, 104*f*, 150–51
proximity 61–62
psychoanalysis 67, 70–71, 102–3, 113, 116, 130–31; *see also* Freud, A. and S.; Bion; Klein; Sinason
psychology 117–18

Reddy, V. 68–69, 143–44
replication crisis 27
rhesus monkeys 149, 150–51
rhythm 34–35
Riley, D. vii
routines in infant groups 53–60, 87–88
rude signs 39–43, 45–46

scaffolding 17, 20–21; *see also* infants: approaches to studying
schizophrenia 107–11, 154
science, *see* methods
 psychology of 115–25
secure attachment *see* attachment, categories of
Selby, J. 15–16
separation anxiety 44–45, 49, 113–14, 149; *see also* attachment
siblings 8, 50–51, 137
Siegel, D. 126
Sinason, V. 107–9, 121, 128–32
smiling 16, 35–36, 39–40, 41–43, 148, 150, 153
social brains 13–15
social development 65–69
socially directed behaviours 31–43
social support 11, 113, 137–38, 151–53, 154
sound-making 34, 147; *see also* vocalization
Spieker, S. 120–21
Spielman, E. 105–7
Spock, B. 3
Stapleton, M. 74–82, 97–98, 133
Stone Age 1–2, 150
stranger fear 49, 113–14, 123, 149; *see also* attachment
Strange Situation Procedure (SSP) 24–25, 113–14, 118, 120–21, 124, 148, 151–52
Strum, S. 151
subjectivity 113–15; *see also* intersubjectivity
Sudan 10
Sumsion, J. 74–75
supra-dyadic interaction 29–30, 61, 148, 153, 154–55; *see also* groupness; polyadic interaction
symbolic interactionism 47

tamarins 11–12, 11*f*, 150–51
taxonomy 28
teams 6–7, 140*f*

theory of mind 66, 146
therapies
    attachment-based therapy 125–28
    Circle of Security 111–13
    couples therapy 126–27
    Dialectical Behavioural Therapy (DBT) 125
    Eye Movement Desensitization and Reprocessing (EMDR) 126
    family therapy 127
    group therapy 15–16, 102–3, 111–13
    mother-blaming 105–7
    one-to-one 102–3
Thompson, R. 65–66, 115, 121–22
Thomson-Salo, F. 15–16
'time out' 57–60
Tinbergen, N. 117–18; see also methods, ethology
touch 37; see also infants: means of communication
transference-love 102
trauma 107–9, 126
Trevarthen, C. 16, 19–20, 141–42, 147
Trilogue Play procedure 17
Tuckman, B. 68

Vicedo, M. 121–22, 153
vision
    focal 31–33, 63
    peripheral 33, 63
vocalization 20, 34, 39–40, 42, 55–56, 86

Waugh, A. 4
Webb, E. 125
WEIRD (Western, Educated, Industrialized, Rich and Democratic) societies, see cross-cultural studies
wellbeing 95–96, 127
wet nurse 4
Willis, R. 4
Winnicott, D. 20, 111, 141, 143, 145–46
Wolff, P. 124–25
Woolf, V. 110
work, infants' capacity for 60, 71–72, 93–95
World War I 4, 117
World War II 3, 4–5, 8, 136, 138

Zeedyk, S. 121